COGNITIVE PSYCHOLOGY
Thinking and creating

The Dorsey Series in Psychology

Consulting Editor **Gerald C. Davison**
State University of New York at Stony Brook

COGNITIVE PSYCHOLOGY

Thinking and creating

John R. Hayes
Carnegie-Mellon University

1978

THE DORSEY PRESS Homewood, Illinois 60430
Irwin-Dorsey Limited Georgetown, Ontario L7G 4B3

ISBN 0-256-02065-5
Library of Congress Catalog Card No. 77–088317

Printed in the United States of America

1 2 3 4 5 6 7 8 9 0 MP 5 4 3 2 1 0 9 8

Dedicated to
GEORGE A. MILLER and HERBERT A. SIMON
whose pioneering work has shaped the field of cognitive psychology.

Preface

In writing this text, I was faced with an important choice, since there are many ways to introduce a student to cognitive psychology. I could have written a text that focused on the theoretical issues currently tantalizing researchers and on the experimental results bearing on these issues. I could have written a text focused on fundamental experimental techniques to provide the serious student with "the tools of the trade" and to acquaint other students with what cognitive psychologists "really do." I have chosen a different approach, however, because I believe that (1) the most important task of an introductory text is to give the reader a *general orientation* to the field, and (2) the approaches described above too often fail to do so.

The difficulty is this: If we present our science only in its modern form, students may have no idea that it has any intellectual roots. Further, unless we purposely present alternative views, they may fail to realize that cognitive psychology represents a special view about how to study the mind—a view importantly different, say, from the views of Behaviorism and Gestalt psychology. If we focus on experimental techniques, the students may recognize that the techniques can be used to solve some problems but fail to realize the sense in which cognitive psychology as a whole is an attempted solution of some broad problems in understanding thought and language. If students fail to realize these things, then they can't understand what cognitive psychology is really about.

This text, then, is designed to orient the reader to cognitive psychology. It is intended to answer such questions as, "Why is there cognitive psychology?" "What is different about its approach?" and "What problems does it solve?" These are questions that students should be able to answer if we are to expect them to take any further interest in the subject.

The text is divided into three sections: The first is about origins and alternatives. It discusses the scientific and philosophic background of cognitive psychology and describes some radically different alternatives including, as already mentioned, Behaviorism and Gestalt psychology. The second section is about some general problems in understanding language and mental structures that were troublesome for other psychologies and which led to the new approach embodied in cognitive psychology. The final section illustrates the application of cognitive psychology to the complex problems of language, problem solving, and creativity.

The text is intended primarily for students taking their first course in cognitive psychology. It provides an orienting framework within which instructors can vary emphasis to suit their own class needs through lecture and/or supplementary texts. The text could also be useful as a supplementary text in a general introductory psychology course or in a course on the history of psychology.

Acknowledgments

I wish especially to thank Sandra Bond who has put in an unreasonable number of extra hours to struggle with the editing, typing, reference searching, proofreading, and numerous other tasks required to turn my marginally legible handwriting into a reasonably orderly manuscript.

I am deeply indebted to Richard E. Mayer, James I. Chumbley, and Herbert A. Simon who have read and commented on the whole manuscript. Their advice resulted in major improvements in each of the chapters.

Lee Gregg, Linda Flower, Robert Neches, Barbara Hayes, and Susan Robinson have provided me with much valuable advice and comment in the course of preparing this text.

I wish to thank the Sloan Foundation for financial support during the writing of this text. In addition, I wish to thank those authors and publishers who have kindly granted permission to reproduce quotes and tables.

Finally, I wish to recognize the wisdom of my friend Herbert Rubinstein, who long ago discouraged me from undertaking this project.

January 1978   *John R. Hayes*

Contents

xi

SECTION I

ROOTS OF COGNITIVE PSYCHOLOGY

Introduction

This book is an introduction to cognitive psychology. Cognitive psychology is a modern approach to the study of the processes by which people come to understand the world, such processes as memory, learning, comprehending language, problem solving, and creativity. Cognitive psychology has been influenced by developments in linguistics, computer science, and, of course, by earlier work in philosophy and psychology.

The book is divided into three sections of four chapters each. The first section describes the roots of cognitive psychology in philosophy and in earlier schools of psychology. Chapter 1 describes early philosophical discussions of such topics as association and perception, which still have important influences in modern psychology. Chapter 2 describes the nearly forgotten Structuralists who first made psychology a science. Chapter 3 describes how the Behaviorists took the conditioned response as the key to understanding human behavior. Chapter 4 describes the Gestalt approach to psychology through the study of perception.

The second section describes developments in psychology, linguistics, and computer science which led psychologists to search for new ways to study human thought. Chapters 5 and 6 describe some of the investigations of Jean Piaget which revealed complex structures in the child's developing intelligence. Chapter 7 recounts some of the attempts and failures of earlier theorists to account for the comprehension of language. Chapter 8 discusses the computer revolution and its impact on psychological thinking.

The third and final section is a selective description of some of the very active research areas in cognitive psychology. Chapter 9 describes modern research on language comprehension. Chapters 10 and 11 explore human problem-solving processes, and Chapter 12 is a discussion of modern views of creativity.

1

Chapter 1

Origins of psychology:
The philosophers of the mind

THE HISTORICAL ROOTS OF PSYCHOLOGY

Interest in thought is very ancient, extending at least as far back as the Greeks of the sixth century before Christ (Brett, 1953). On this time scale, though, the scientific analysis of thought is quite a recent development. Not until the second half of the nineteenth century did scientists really begin to understand the possibilities of experimental research on the mind. Then psychology emerged as a special branch of natural science. Before 1850, most of those who studied thinking were philosophers, such as John Locke and Immanuel Kant, although others, including physicians and mathematicians, also made valuable contributions. The early investigations of thought were pursued in the armchair rather than in the laboratory. The investigator required no special equipment other than a mind with which to carry on the study, although it is claimed that some have attempted it with less.

While these early thinkers did not use laboratory methods to derive their results and were in this sense prescientific, they did originate many ideas of fundamental importance in present-day psychology. Certainly the most influential group among these prescientific workers were the Associationists, theorists who believed that thought could best be understood by examining the connections between ideas. Many of the Associationists were prominent British philosophers. Here is a list of some of the major Associationists to give you an idea of the brilliance of that company and also of the extended period during which Associationism was active:

John Locke	1632–1704
George Berkeley	1685–1735
David Hume	1711–1776
James Mill	1773–1836
John Stuart Mill	1806–1873

Clearly, the Associationists had to do something fairly impressive to remain influential for more than 200 years. What they did was to evolve a very broad-ranging psychology of thought. This psychology started small in modest attempts to account for certain types of recall but grew by the time of James Mill to include the whole of mental life. Associationist psychology was extremely influential in its time and that influence persists to the present day. Strong traces of Associationism may be found not only in our folk psychology but in many aspects of modern learning theory as well.

Associationist psychology is based on three ideas which are still important and controversial. These are:

1. *Atomism*—the belief that the mind consists of elementary parts such as ideas, sensations, images, or, in more modern theories, stimuli and responses.
2. *Connectionism*—the theory that these mental elements (ideas, images) become connected with each other by bonds called *associations* and that complex mental phenomena depend on combinations of these "atoms."
3. *Empiricism*—the doctrine that everything we know is learned through personal experience with the world.

In part the influence of Associationist theory may be explained by its strong appeal to common sense. Common sense tells us that there *are* ideas, that ideas *do* become connected to one another, and that experience *does* play an important role in thought. Does this mean that the Associationist position is correct? We will examine the ideas underlying Association theory more carefully now to decide which are still usable and which must be rejected as false.

Atomism

Locke (1690) considered ideas to be the sole object of thought. Ideas, he said, are of two kinds, the simple and the complex. "Whiteness," "hardness," and "sweetness" are examples of simple ideas. (Not everyone would agree, of course, but these are what Locke considered simple ideas.) Such ideas, Locke felt, cannot be analyzed into simpler elements nor can the mind create or destroy them. Simple ideas, then, are the elements, or atoms, of Locke's psychology.

Simple ideas may be combined to form complex ideas. The simple ideas *coldness* and *hardness*, together with other properties, can be combined in experience to form the complex idea *ice*. Similarly, the simple ideas *softness* and *warmth* can be combined to form the complex idea *wax*. Other examples of complex ideas are *man*, *elephant*, *army*, and *drunkenness*.

The complex ideas that we have mentioned come, according to Locke's theory, from experience. That is, complex ideas result from actually experiencing simple ideas in combination. For example, the complex idea *ice* would be formed when we experienced *coldness* and *hardness* together.

Locke's method of describing an idea as a combination of simpler ideas is an example of a very common tactic that is used again and again in psychology. The tactic is to try to find simple things which can be combined by simple rules to form the complex things we observe in human behavior. In Chapters 2, 3, and 4, we will see that this tactic is fundamental to Wilhelm Wundt's psychology and to Behaviorism, but that the Gestalt psychologists were acutely aware of its limitations. The tactic is used in modern psychology as well. For example, Gibson (1969) has analyzed children's perception of letters as the combined effect of their perceptions of elementary features of letters. Features are things such as horizontal and vertical line segments and intersections. The EPAM (Elementary Perceiver and Memorizer) model of memory discussed in Chapter 8 is also a feature model.

Locke held that there is another way to generate complex ideas. Some complex ideas are formed, he said, by reflection without the aid of experience. Thus, we may all form the complex ideas "green milk" or "80 year old woman in a bikini" even though most of us have been spared these experiences. This ability to form complex ideas by reflection was, for Locke, the basis of imagination.

Hume accepted Locke's doctrine of simple and complex ideas, but he held that thought has two objects rather than just one. He said, "All the perceptions of the human mind resolve themselves into two kinds, which I shall call *Impressions* and *Ideas*" (Hume, 1888, p. 51). Hume's impressions correspond to what we commonly call "sense impressions" or "sensations"—that is, to experiences such as seeing a mango or the horrible feeling of bumping a funny bone. Impressions are always directly initiated by events in the world.

Hume's category idea corresponds to common sense notions such as "remembrance" and "thought." Examples include the memory that we have seen a mango or the thought that we should avoid bumping our funny bone. While ideas depend on our having had appropriate sense impressions at some time in the past, we can have an idea even though the corresponding impressions aren't happening at present. Thus, we can have an idea of a mango even if we haven't seen one in a long time. Later Associationists, such as James Mill, adopted positions which closely resembled that of Hume.

Hume (1888, pp. 51–52) believed that we distinguish between impressions and ideas by the "force and liveliness with which they strike upon the mind." That is, he believed that ideas are similar to impressions but just not as strong. We will discuss some surprising support for this view in the next chapter.

We will postpone discussion of the various criticisms of the Atomist position until they are discussed in Chapter 4. Instead we will go on to discuss Empiricism.

Empiricism

In addition to his activities on behalf of Atomism, Locke was also a forthright spokesman for Empiricism. Locke held that the mind of the newborn child is perfectly blank until experience provides it with ideas to think about. Locke put it this way: "Let us then suppose the mind to be, as we say, white paper, void of all characters, without any ideas; how comes it to be furnished? Whence comes it by that vast store, which the busy and boundless fancy of man has painted on it with an almost endless variety? Whence has it all the materials of reason and knowledge? To this I answer, in one word, from Experience; in that all our knowledge is founded, and from that it ultimately derives itself" (Locke, 1924, p. 26).

If this position strikes you as trivial and obvious, you may not realize that there is much to be said in favor of an alternate position called Nativism. Nativists hold that people have some innate ideas, that is, some ideas which are not derived from experience. One well-known Nativist was the French philosopher and mathematician, René Descartes (1596–1650). He held that certain ideas are innate, for example, that everyone must believe in his or her own existence. A person who doubts his or her own existence may say, "I doubt; therefore I am!" Descartes identified a number of other ideas as innate because they presented themselves so naturally and forcibly to his mind that they seemed to require no evidence to establish their truth. Among the ideas which Descartes proposed as innate were the idea of personal existence, the idea of God, the geometrical axioms, and the concepts of space, time, and motion. Modern Nativists may consider Descartes' suggestions concerning God and the geometrical axioms to be charmingly out of date. They have seen, as Descartes could not, how easily atheistic and non-Euclidean ideas have been accepted. Some of Descartes' other suggestions are taken more seriously, however. In fact, there is a good deal of modern research concerning the extent to which the concept of space is innate (see Chapter 4). Further, Noam Chomsky believes that people have innate capacities for acquiring language.

Another important Nativist was the German philosopher Kant (1724–1804). Kant's Nativism differs from that of Descartes. Kant did not divide ideas into those that come from experience and those that are innate. Rather, he divided the forces which form *each* idea into two categories: on the one hand, there is experience; and on the other, the innate properties of the mind. In this respect, modern Nativists resemble Kant rather than Descartes.

Kant held that what we perceive depends not just on the way the physical world is, but also, and very importantly, on what we are. Much of what we perceive, he said, is the result of the innate categories we impose on the world. Among the attributes that Kant believed we impose on the world are unity, wholeness, cause and effect, space, and time. Thus, we see things in three dimensions, according to Kant, not because the world is intrinsically three-dimensional rather than, say, five-dimensional. Instead, we see three dimensions because that is what our perceptual mechanisms can see. Three-dimensional space, he claimed, is not a property of the world but rather of the people who perceive the world.

Locke's Empiricism was a reaction to Descartes' doctrine of innate ideas. Locke supported his argument with three kinds of evidence. First, he noted that the newborn infant is an incomparable dullard with negligible ability to think, little information, no small talk, and very few social graces. Fortunately, the infant improves in all of these departments as age and experience increase. (We all have our favorite exceptions, of course, but by and large the principle holds.) Thus, Locke believed that to be able to think at all, we must have experience of some kind. Second, Locke held that the particular kind of experience we have determines the particular way in which we think. He noted that people with different backgrounds and experiences have different ideas and make different judgments. Our surprise at each other's acquired tastes, for example, for sauerkraut or martinis, is a case in point. As his third argument for Empiricism, Locke pointed out that people can't imagine a sensation that they have not experienced. Those of you who have ever tried to invent a new color will be convinced that Locke's assertion is correct.

Critique of Empiricism

At this point, we must ask if Locke's arguments prove his point. His first two arguments can certainly be interpreted as evidence that experience influences thought. It is important to note, though, that the Nativists don't deny this. They simply insist that innate factors influence thought as well. Locke's third argument is a peculiar one in that it can be interpreted as evidence for either the Empiricist or the Nativist position. On the one hand, we might believe that the reason we cannot imagine a new color X is that nature has not yet presented us with the experience of X. On the other hand, we could argue for the Nativist side that the colors are innate categories of experience, and that the reason we have not seen the color X is not that it has not been presented, but rather than we couldn't see it even if it were. To illustrate their case, Nativists might point out that we often encounter ultraviolet stimuli in a color frequency range which bees see, but which we do not. Apparently, as humans, we have not inherited the appropriate perceptual mechanism to interpret the stimuli as a color.

Locke's inability to find a conclusive argument in support of Empiricism or a damning criticism of Nativism is not a real reflection of his skills as a debater but rather of the difficulty of the position that he was defending. The Nativist position is really a mild and conservative one which asserts very little. In comparison, the Empiricist position is radical. While the Empiricists insist that our ideas are derived *entirely* from experience, the Nativists insist only that our ideas are partly innate. To prove their position, the Empiricists would have to show that *every* factor involved in the formation of ideas is experiential. Nativists, on the other hand, need only show one innate factor in thought to prove their point. At present, it is generally recognized that there *are* some innate factors in thought. The radical Empiricism of Locke has been replaced by the relative Empiricism of modern learning theory. Present day psychologists do not ask whether or not innate factors are involved in thought. Rather they ask about the relative importance of experience and inheritance.

Psychologists and linguists are still very much concerned about the relative importance of these two factors. For example, Chomsky (see Chapter 7) has recently stirred up considerable controversy by suggesting that some of our knowledge of the grammar of language is inherited. He believes that children's language skills develop far too rapidly to be accounted for by learning alone.

Connectionism

We defined connectionism earlier as the theory that mental elements may become connected to one another by bonds called associations. It is now time for us to make clear what we mean by an association. An association is a special kind of mental connection between two ideas. It is used to explain the common observation that ideas tend to travel in company. For example, if we ask people to say the first word that occurs to them after we say "Boy," 75 percent will say "Girl." An association theory could account for this observation by assuming an association between the ideas "Boy" and "Girl."

An association is a special kind of connection because it is not necessarily symmetrical. If we connect a horse and a wagon, the horse is just as much connected to the wagon as the wagon is to the horse. This kind of connection is symmetrical and seems somehow the most natural or usual kind of connection. Associations, however, may be very unsymmetrical. For example, while the stimulus "Boy" produces the response "Girl" in 75 percent of cases, the stimulus "Girl" produces the response "Boy" in only 36 percent of cases. Thus, the association from "Boy" to "Girl" is much stronger than the association from "Girl" to "Boy."

If you find that explanations in terms of associations are obvious to the point of triviality, you should realize that association theory is a *theory*, and that it could be *wrong*.

An analogy may help to clarify this point. We can establish as an observational fact, for example, that sickness and hospitals are strongly connected. The simplest and most direct process explaining this relation would be to postulate that hospitals cause sickness. We know, however, that the relation between hospitals and sickness actually has a different and much more complicated explanation. In the same way, we believe that the relations between words observed in the free-association experiment result not from a simple link connecting a word with its associates, but rather through a complex process involving the intricate mechanisms for understanding language—mechanisms such as the scripts discussed in Chapter 9.

But my purpose at this point is not to dispute association theory. Rather, it is to explain it and to show how its proponents tried to use its properties to account for thought. The Associationists took on the problem of explaining the large differences which can be observed in the strengths of various associations. They attacked this problem with considerably more vigor than unanimity. Each major Associationist seemed to have his own version of the laws of association.

The laws of association

The first such laws came from John Locke. Unlike the later Associationists, Locke did not attribute all connections among ideas to association. Some connections, he thought, are logical in nature. For example, two ideas may go together because they are opposites or because they are related as premise and conclusion. Other ideas which are not related may become associated through custom. This happens because trains of thought, he said, ". . . once set agoing, continue in the same steps they have been used to, which, by often treading, are worn into a smooth path . . ." (Locke, 1924, p. 41). The effect is that associated ideas

". . . always keep in company, and the one no sooner at any time comes into the understanding, but its associate appears with it. . . ." (Locke, 1924, p. 41). Locke's law of association is essentially a law of practice or, as it is sometimes called, frequency. The more often two ideas are thought together, the stronger the association between them becomes.

Hume (1739), about 50 years later, suggested three laws of association, none of which resembled Locke's law of practice. Ideas, he said, may be associated because:

1. they resemble one another,
2. they are related by cause and effect, or
3. they have occurred contiguously in space or time.

James Mill, Hume's philosophical successor, could not accept the first two of Hume's laws. He felt that resemblance between ideas was important only when the ideas were contiguous and that cause and effect was important only because it produced contiguity. Thus, he replaced Hume's three laws with the single law of contiguity. He did, however, sneak in two "conditions" of association—frequency and vividness. By vividness Mill seemed to mean something like "impressiveness" rather than simply physical intensity.

James Mill's son, John Stuart Mill, proposed at different times two different sets of laws of association. In each of the sets, he reintroduced resemblance in his law of similarity.

In spite of the diversity, I feel that we can identify a central tendency in the Associationist position on the strength of associations. This central tendency is represented by the following four laws of association, arranged in decreasing order of importance:

1. Contiguity.
2. Frequency.
3. Vividness or impressiveness.
4. Similarity.

Using association to explain complex thought processes

In John Locke's psychology, association was just one explanatory principle among many. As Associationism developed, however, the role assigned to association became increasingly important until, by the time of the two Mills, association had become the one central explanatory concept. John Stuart Mill (1965, p. 379), for example, held that ". . . complex laws of thought and feeling not only may, but must, be generated . . ." from the simple laws of association.

The goal of the Associationists therefore was to understand even the

most complex of human thought processes through simple associations. The scientific excitement in this enterprise and its strength lay
in radical analyses—in the reduction of complex events to a very small
set of simple components. To see how this analysis was carried out, we
will examine James Mill's discussion of the processes by which humans
solve syllogisms.[1] Then we will explore early associative theories of
memory.

To solve a syllogism

Determine whether or not the syllogism shown below is correct
and then try to describe to yourself the processes you used to get your
answer.

> Joe is taller than Sam.
> Bill is taller than Joe.
> Therefore,   Bill is taller than Sam.

James Mill would give the following account of the solution process
(1878, pp. 424–427): In the first line Joe is compared to Sam. Comparison is a special case of association. In the second line, Bill is
compared to Joe. In the third line, Bill is compared to Sam through
Joe. That is, Bill is associated with Joe, Joe is associated with Sam,
and therefore Bill is associated with Sam by a complex but rapid and
almost imperceptible process.

For Mill, then, the solution of the syllogism is a rapid chaining together of association. This account, so far as it goes, does not seem
unreasonable. Typically, in solving such syllogisms, we do experience
something like a rapid chaining process. Let's examine Mill's account
more closely, though, to see if it will hold up under careful scrutiny.
Consider this (faulty) syllogism:

> Joe is taller than Sam.
> Bill is older than Joe.
> Therefore,   Bill is $\frac{(older)}{(taller)}$ than Sam?

Of course, we can't conclude that Bill is either older or taller than Sam.
What's the trouble? Things were going just as Mill said they should. In
the first line we associated (compared) Joe with Sam and in the second

---

[1] A syllogism is a logic argument such as the one shown below, which consists of two
premises and a conclusion. In a well-formed syllogism the conclusion must follow logi-
cally from the two premises.

> All men are animals.
> All kings are men.
> Therefore,   All kings are animals.

line we associated Bill with Joe. But these associations don't chain together. If the comparisons "taller than" and "older than" are to be thought of as special cases of association, then they must be *different* special cases, some of which chain together and some of which don't. In logic, these special cases are called "relations." An adequate model of how people solve syllogisms must include some control system that determines when relations can be chained together and when they cannot. Indeed, the control system may be required to do a great deal more than this, as my favorite faulty syllogism illustrates:

> Some dogs have fuzzy ears.
> My dog has fuzzy ears.
> Therefore,   My dog is some dog!!

I will leave it to the reader to sort out the logical atrocities which have been committed here.

Memory and association

We have all observed when we daydream that ideas seem to present themselves to us in a continuously flowing stream. Idea succeeds idea effortlessly and seemingly automatically. Often we feel that we are simply spectators, observing a sequence of ideas over which we have little control. It is this flow of ideas that William James has called "the stream of consciousness" and which James Joyce has used in his novel *Ulysses*. Many centuries earlier, Aristotle used this flow of ideas in an attempt to explain recollection.

Aristotle's theory of recollection is presented in the following passage.

> Oftentimes one is unable to recollect a thing, but after searching succeeds in finding it. This seeking and finding is what happens when one awakens a number of experiences and continues to do so until one sets that particular experience in motion upon which the desired thing is attendant. . . . One must, however, have a starting point. And so persons appear sometimes to recall things from local suggestions. The reason is that one passes rapidly from one thing to another, e.g., from milk to the suggested idea of white, from white to air, from air to the moist, and from this one recalls the late Autumn, which is the season one was trying to think of (Aristotle, 1902, p. 12).

Aristotle's associative theory of memory seems adequate to account for the loose flow of ideas found in daydreaming. Despite Aristotle's opinion, however, it really does not account for directed memory search, that is, for retrieval of specific desired information from memory.

To show what these weaknesses are, we will attempt to design the

"Aristotle Machine," a device built on Aristotelian principles to simulate human memory. Simulation is a very powerful tool for examining theories. If we really understand how some mental process, such as rote learning or anagram solution, operates, then we should be able to build a working model which imitates that process. If it turns out that we really don't understand the process, some of our omissions, vaguenesses, or faulty assumptions should become apparent to us as we attempt the simulation. We should emphasize that the purpose of computer simulation is *not* to make smart computer programs but rather to test theories about people. A computer simulation that remembers *more* than people do, or solves problems *better* than people do, is just as much a failure as one that remembers less or solves more poorly. A computer simulation is not an end in itself. It is an aid to understanding people. Now, on with the Aristotle Machine.

First, we must decide what sorts of tasks the machine must perform. It is clear from the passage we quoted that Aristotle wants to explain directed or active recall rather than passive recall. He is not trying to explain the recall of things which "just happen to occur" to us without any effort on our part. Rather, he is trying to account for the retrieval of memories that we are searching for actively, as, for example, in those last desperate moments before we have to introduce two old acquaintances whose names we have forgotten.

To explain passive recall in terms of associative chains is trivial. Associative chaining *is* passive recall. To explain active recall is another matter. The machine must be able to answer such questions as "What is the capital of Tasmania?" or, "Who was that machine I saw you with last night?" and to find the answers in some reasonably efficient way. By reasonably efficient, we mean that the machine should do something better than a random search of memory. It should use the information in the question to direct its search for the answer as well as to identify the answer when it is found.

The Aristotle Machine will need at least three parts: a memory structure, a procedure for entering the memory structure at a point determined by the question, and a procedure for leaving the memory structure when the answer has been found. Let us suppose that the Aristotle Machine has a very simple chain memory in which each element (or idea) appears just once and associates to just one other element. Figure 1–1 shows several possible configurations for such a memory. In A, all of the machine's information is organized into a single linear chain. In B, there are several separate chains. Notice that in configuration B, there is no way to use information in one chain to retrieve information from another chain. A loop is shown at C, as we shall see. Loops clearly create a special problem for chain memories. Given the cue *week*, the machine would cycle forever through *day, light, dark, night, day, light,*

Figure 1–1.   Memory configurations for the Aristotle machine

A	B			C
↓	↓	↓	↓	↓
milk	wine	women	song	week
↓	↓	↓	↓	↓
white	vine	girl	lullaby	day ←
↓	↓	↓	↓	↓
air	Wien	love	baby	light
↓	↓	↓	↓	↓
moist	Vienna	sex	Mother	dark
↓	↓	↓	↓	↓
late Autumn	etc.	friend	etc.	night ┘
↓		↓		
cold		Freud		
↓		↓		
snow		etc.		
↓				
etc.				

and so on. Thus, a loop in its chain memory would turn the Aristotle Machine into the worst sort of monomaniac. We will therefore assume that the memory has no such loops.

Given a memory structure, we now need a procedure for entering memory. A simple procedure would be to choose one or several words from the question as entry points. If the question were, "What is the capital of Tasmania?" the Aristotle Machine would use just *capital* or *Tasmania* to select its point of entry. This reduction of the question to a single element represents a great loss of efficiency in retrieving information. It is as if we had replaced the original question with questions like, "What do you know about Tasmania?" or, "Tell me all about capitals." With questions such as these, we would certainly expect to wait longer for the information we were after than with the original question.

Suppose that we had entered the memory structure at *Tasmania*, and the answer *Hobart* happened to be close to the entry point and downstream from it. In this case, the Aristotle Machine will find the answer quickly. If *Hobart* is downstream from *Tasmania*, however, the machine is going to have terrible trouble finding the answer to the question, "What island is Hobart the capital of?" We might try to solve this problem by putting *Hobart* in the chain twice, once upstream and once downstream from *Tasmania*. A little reflection, however, will show that this cannot be a general solution to the problem. If *Hobart* is to be reached from *every* associate in the chain, then it must be placed both first and last in the chain. Since only one word can be placed at both ends of the chain, this solution cannot work for the other words in the chain.

Another problem with the Aristotle Machine is that there is no obvious way for it to recognize an answer when it finds one. Let us assume that the Aristotle Machine has chosen an entry point at *milk* (see Figure 1–1) and has proceeded dutifully through a sequence of steps in the memory until it has arrived at the answer, *late Autumn*. What will it do next? Why it will do what it was built to do, of course. It will associate *late Autumn* to *cold* and sail busily on, associating to itself forever and ever. As yet, we have provided it neither with the ability to recognize an answer when it sees one nor with the capacity to do anything about it if it did.

If we ask people who the 13th President of the United States was, they may not get it right, but their answer will probably be a president, and will almost certainly be a person. If they were to answer, "Butte, Montana," or, "Rin Tin Tin," we could only hope that they hadn't heard us clearly. People do not act as if one associate is as good as another. Obviously, they take categories into account in choosing their answers.

If we ask people, "What is the capital of Tasmania?" we want the answer, "Hobart," not, "wombat," even if "wombat" is more strongly associated to Tasmania. The problem with Aristotle's theory is that it doesn't tell us how to use *both* "capital" *and* "Tasmania" to find the answer. To illustrate how both cues can be used in retrieval, we will describe a modern associative theory of memory proposed by Quillian (1968).

In Quillian's theory, each word in memory is associated with a set of definitions. For example, the word *plant* is associated with *plant 1*—a living structure with leaves, roots, etc.; *plant 2*—a place where people manufacture things; and *plant 3*—the activity of putting seeds in the earth. The words in the definitions such as *seed, leaf,* and *earth* are in turn associated with their own definition and so on. Thus, starting from the word *plant* and taking one step, we get to the three definitions. Taking two steps, we get to words in the definitions such as *root, seed, leaf.* By taking more steps, we would soon get to words such as *growth* and *tree.* Eventually, we would arrive at very distantly related words such as *democracy* and *licorice.*

We may think of the associative connections as spreading out in an ever expanding sphere from the original word. According to Quillian's theory, people find connections between two words by exploring the spheres of associations around each word. Points at which the two spheres intersect are connections between the words. Hopefully, the associates of *Tasmania* and *capital* intersect at *Hobart.*

Quillian tested his theory by simulating it on a computer. That is, he programmed a computer to act in just the way his theory held that people act.

The first step in the simulation for Quillian was to provide the computer with a vocabulary and the appropriate associations among the vocabulary items. When the computer had sufficient vocabulary, Quillian asked it to compare pairs of words. For example, he asked it to compare *cry* and *comfort*. To make the comparison, the computer searched the sphere of associates around each of these words. It did this by marking as active all of the associates one step from each cue word, then two steps, and so on. A word marked active twice was considered an intersection of the two spheres. In comparing *cry* and *comfort*, the computer discovered the intersection *sad* which it justified by typing out:

1. *Cry2* is among other things to make a sad sound.
2. To *comfort3* can be to *make2* something *less2 sad*.

Quillian's program is a very early memory simulation model. As we will see in Chapter 9, more sophisticated memory search programs have since been developed. However, the idea of "spreading activation" which Quillian's theory embodies is currently very influential in models making use of associations.

Because of its ability to take two things into account at the same time, Quillian's model is clearly an advance over the Aristotle Machine. Nonetheless, both models still have serious deficiencies, for they confuse 13th President of the United States, that is, Millard Fillmore, with 13th of the United States President, that is, about 15 pounds of meat. The confusion results from the fact that the machine cannot deal with the grammatical relations in the input question. Nevertheless, we must now abandon our attempts to perfect the Aristotle Machine, partly because grammatical problems are much too complex to deal with at this point (see Chapter 7), but mostly because we have accomplished with it all that we really intended. That is, we have looked into the idea of simulation, and we have explored the problems of building an associative memory in enough depth to give you a feeling of how association theory can be applied in a specific problem.

SUMMARY

Among the early theories of human thought, perhaps the most important was Associationism. The ideas underlying Associationism are:

1. *Atomism*—the belief that complex processes can be understood as combinations of simple elements. This belief will be contrasted (in Chapter 4) to Wholism.
2. *Connectionism*—the belief that mental processes may be understood as the operation of connections called associations among these simple mental elements.

3. *Empiricism*—the belief that all knowledge comes from experience. Empiricism is contrasted with Nativism, the belief that some aspects of knowledge are innate.

These ideas continue to influence present day theorists.

REFERENCES

ARISTOTLE. *Aristotle's psychology: A treatise on the principle of life.* Ed. and trans. W. A. Hammond. London: Swann Sonnenschein, 1902.

BILODEAU, E. A., and HOWELL, D. C. *Free association norms.* Washington, D.C.: U.S. Government Printing Office, 1965.

BRETT, G. S. *History of psychology.* London: G. Allen, 1953.

DESCARTES, R. "Discourse on the method of rightly conducting the reason," *The philosophical works of Descartes.* Trans. E. S. Haldane and G. R. T. Ross. Cambridge, England: Cambridge University Press, 1931.

GIBSON, E. *Principles of perceptual learning and development.* New York: Appleton, 1969.

HUME, D. *A treatise on human nature.* Ed. L. A. Selby-Biggs. Oxford: Clarendon Press, 1888, cited in J. M. and G. Mandler, eds. *Thinking: From association to Gestalt.* New York: John Wiley & Sons, Inc., 1964.

LOCKE, J. *Essay concerning human understanding* (1690). Ed. and abridged by A. S. Pringle-Pattison. Oxford: Clarendon Press, 1924, cited in J. M. and G. Mandler, eds. *Thinking: From association to Gestalt.* New York: John Wiley & Sons, Inc., 1964.

MILL, J. S. *Analysis of the phenomena of the human mind,* vol. 1, 2d ed. London: Longmans, Green, Reader, and Dyer, 1878, pp. 70–116. 1st ed.: London, 1829.

MILL, J. S. *A system of logic, ratiocinative and inductive, being a connected view of the principles of evidence, and the methods of scientific investiga-tion,* vol. 2, bk. 4, chap. 4. London: 1943, cited in R. J. Herrnstein and E. G. Boring, eds. *A source book in the history of psychology.* Cambridge, Mass.: Harvard University Press, 1965.

QUILLIAN, M. R. "Semantic memory," *Semantic information processing.* Ed. M. Minsky. Cambridge, Mass.: M.I.T. Press, 1968.

Chapter 2

The birth of the new science

FROM THE ARMCHAIR TO THE LABORATORY

Scientific psychology was finally born, in the second half of the 19th century, of two extremely domineering parents—Associationist philosophy and Wilhelm Wundt. The child resembled its philosophical parent in nearly every feature—it was empiricist, atomist, and associationist; and, as we shall see, for more than 30 years it was overwhelmed by the attentions of its human parent. Of course, many people contributed discoveries which prepared the way for the new science. Hermann Helmholtz had measured the speed of the nervous impulse, Frans Cornelis Donders had measured response times, and Gustav Theodor Fechner had devised means for measuring the sensations caused by light and sound. These developments and many others made it seem reasonable that a science of the mind was possible. It was the enormous energy of Wilhelm Wundt, however, that actually brought the infant into the world.

While others contributed individual facts and ideas, Wundt took the facts, combined them with Associationism, and built a system of psychology. He then publicized that system in the first psychology texts and in an almost incredible stream of other scientific papers. The system was the basis of the first school of psychology, Introspectionism, which had its heyday roughly from 1875 to 1910.

With Wundt as its leader, Introspectionism was off to a flying start. Wundt's stupendous productivity made it difficult for his colleagues to resist his influence. His impact may be understood in part by considering the minor tragedy of the English Introspectionist, Edward Bradford Titchener. Titchener had translated the entire third edition of Wundt's 2,000 page *Physiologiche Psychologie*. Before he could publish it, though, he learned that Wundt was about to publish the fourth edition.

18

Undaunted, Titchener abandoned the obsolete manuscript and translated the fourth edition, only to find that Wundt had done him in again with the fifth edition. If Titchener had any comment at this point, it has not been recorded. His stamina does seem to have been somewhat strained, though, for he never published more than the first part of the fifth edition.

Wundt's energy was a source of frustration to his critics and supporters alike. Consider William James' complaint (Boring, 1950, p. 346) "Whilst they make mincemeat of some of his views by their criticism, he is meanwhile writing a book on an entirely different subject. Cut him up like a worm and each fragment crawls; there is no *noeud vital* [vital center] in his mental medulla oblongata, so you can't kill him all at once."

In his spare time, Wundt established the first psychological laboratory (1879), conducted a program of research, founded a psychological journal, and trained many of the leading psychologists of the next generation. It is no wonder that Wundt dominated psychology's early childhood!

Introspectionism: The psychology of conscious experience

In promoting the new psychology, Wundt and the Introspectionists were urging some very definite positions on the world. Wundt held that the subject matter of psychology is immediate conscious experience. In this respect, he contrasted psychology with the other sciences such as chemistry and physics. The world of chemistry and physics is a very abstract world, far removed from immediate experience. We never see atoms and molecules. Rather, we infer their existence from objective measurements—that is, from pointer readings on such scientific instruments as chemical balances and voltmeters. Wundt wanted psychology to be very different from other sciences. He wanted it to be an entirely subjective science which drew its data not from pointer readings but rather from systematic introspection—that is, from the careful observation by trained individuals of their own immediate experience.

Reporting one's immediate experience accurately is no easy matter. In ordinary conversation we often confuse what we know (that the world is populated with objects) with what we see (patches of color arranged in space). For example, suppose I were to describe my immediate experience to an Introspectionist by saying, "Well, I see the typewriter and two tables and the lamp, and. . . ." The Introspectionist, with lips curling in a quick sneer, would say, "Oh, come now. At most, what you see is only one small portion of the surface of that lamp. A tiny bit of evidence from which you infer the whole lamp! How are we ever going to analyze immediate experience if people like you keep mucking it up with inferences? Why can't you face it? What you actually see is a semicircular patch of gray next to patches of brown, blue, and red. Calling it a lamp in front of a bookcase is pure inference on your part. Now, after this, watch it!"

The Introspectionist program

The Introspectionists planned a two-part program of research: one part analytic and one part synthetic. In the analytic part, conscious experience was to be broken down into its elements—sensations, images, feelings, and acts of will. The synthetic part was to be concerned with combining these elements, by the laws of perception and association, to yield the more complex things that we observe in conscious experience, things such as judgments, beliefs, and illusions.

The psychology which the Introspectionists planned was to be a self-contained science, one which did not draw on physics or physiology. Not that the Introspectionists thought the physical and the physiological views were wrong. Rather, they were other points of view, parallel to but independent of the psychological view. The physiologist could very appropriately be concerned with the firing of nerve cells but not the psychologist. The psychologist must deal only with immediate experience. Thus, the Introspectionists did not try to find laws relating immediate experience to the actions of nerves and hormones. They sought laws relating experience to experience.

Further, the Introspectionists restricted their science to *conscious* experience. Their concept of consciousness admitted of degrees. Something might either be at the focus of attention or on its periphery, but they saw no reason to consider things which were not conscious at all.

The primary research tool of the new psychology was, appropriately enough, experimental introspection. The introspective experiment was no casual matter of thinking about the properties of the mind from the armchair. Rather, it was a highly disciplined laboratory procedure in which trained observers reported the contents of their consciousness under carefully controlled conditions. The investigation of the process of association by A. Mayer and J. Orth (1901) is a good example of this type of experiment. They brought their observers (subjects were called observers) to a quiet room where they were instructed in the nature of a free-association task. They were asked to keep their eyes closed during the entire experiment to avoid visual disturbances. The experimenter then got the observer's attention with a ready signal, called out a stimulus word, and started the stopwatch. As soon as the subject began to say the response word, the experimenter stopped the watch. The observer then reported all the conscious processes which had taken place from the moment of the presentation of the stimulus word up to the end of the reaction. The data of the experiment consisted of the response words, the response times, and the introspective reports.

Successes of the Introspectionist program

How did the Introspectionist program work out? While the synthetic part never really got off the ground, the Introspectionists did launch into the analytic phase with great vigor. Hundreds of experiments were performed on sensation, imagery, feeling, attention, and association. Some of these were rather trivial by modern standards. Two studies showed that people really can't tell whether or not someone is staring at their backs. And at least one study was horrifying—Edwin Boring's (1915) study on the sensations of the alimentary canal. The subject (observer) in this experiment deserves the Psychology Hero Medal.

As one example of his extensive trials above and beyond the usual call of science, while he was having a balloon blown up in his esophagus, he reported: "Pressure first felt as below clavicle, 6 to 7 cm. . . . As pressure got more intense, it got more unpleasant. Suddenly I realized that this feeling was exactly the thing that gives warning when one is about to vomit" (sic) (Boring, 1915, p. 28).

As a kind of grand finale to a merciless series of pokings and proddings, the poor fellow was given an ice-water enema, which resulted in an incredible sequence of events, the last and least of which was the appearance of an "indefinite sensation" in the region of the umbilicus. The subject was able to describe it as "a faint sting, which was possibly cool. . . ." (Boring, 1915, p. 55). They don't make subjects like that anymore!

Some of the Introspectionist studies are still of interest. One of the most fascinating is a study done in Titchener's laboratory at Cornell by Cheves West Perky (1910). Hume, the British philosopher, had held that mental images are nothing but "faint copies" of sensations—that is, they are just like sensations only dimmer. Perky reasoned that if this were so, it should be possible to find conditions under which people would confuse them. This is just what she set out to do. First, she acquired a room with what appeared to be a plain white panel on one wall. Actually, it was a milk glass screen on which a concealed assistant could project images from the next room. Subjects were told that they were participating in an experiment on imagery. They were asked to imagine various colored images—a tomato, a banana, a leaf—while staring at a fixation mark in the center of the screen. Behind the screen, while the subjects were straining to picture a tomato in glorious technicolor, the assistant, signaled by a hidden foot switch, projected a very faint image of a tomato onto the screen and then turned the brightness up slowly until the subjects reported that they had a good image. The subjects were then distracted, the tomato was turned off, and the experiment proceeded in its underhanded way to the next image. All of Perky's 24 subjects, college students and graduate students, were fooled. They were sure that the images they saw proceeded from their own imaginations. Here are some of the subjects' comments (Perky, 1910, p. 432):

"I am imagining it all. . . ."

"It is just like seeing things in the dark; I had it in my mind."

"I get to thinking of it and it turns up."

"It is pure memory; with a little effort, I could move it to the wall."

"I can get the shading on it as I think of it. At first, I think of it as flat, as if painted." (All of the images were simply an outline filled in with uniform color.)

"I can see the veining of the leaf and all."

"The banana is up on end; I must have been thinking of it growing" (sic) (Perky, 1910, p. 432).

Many of the subjects volunteered the information that they could hold the image even after closing their eyes! Perky's results seem clear. People really do confuse mental images with faint visual images.

Difficulties

Not all of the Introspectionist experiments came out as well as Perky's. In fact, some of them were downright disastrous. The Mayer and Orth experiment on association, mentioned earlier, was one of the disastrous ones. Mayer and Orth had set out to conduct a perfectly straightforward Introspectionist experiment. The observers were expected to analyze the association process into the usual elements— sensations, images, feelings, and acts of will. Much to the shock of everyone concerned, the observers said that they could not do it. Some of what they had experienced, they said, simply could not be classified into those elements. These peculiar, unclassifiable experiences were soon observed by other investigators. "Imageless thoughts," as they came to be called, were found in succession by K. Marbe (1901), A. Messer (1906), N. Ach (1905), and K. Bühler (1907). Their existence, then, became established fact. "Fine," you may say, "But tell us what these imageless thoughts are." I'll do better than that. I will show you.

To experience an imageless thought, try to solve the following problem:

Given that:
Joe is richer than Bill, and
Joe is poorer than Ed,
Find the relation between Bill and Ed.

If you are like most people, you employed visual imagery in solving this problem. Perhaps you imagined a diagram in which three dots representing Ed, Joe, and Bill were arranged in that order, either vertically or horizontally. The relations among the three men are represented in the visual image and offer no problems for the Introspectionists. Imagery is an expected part of immediate experience for the Introspectionists.

Let's imagine, though, that we press the matter a little further as follows:

Experimenter: "You say the top dot represents Ed?"

Observer: "Yes."

Experimenter: "Does it look like Ed?"

Observer: "No, it's just a plain round dot like the other two."

Experimenter: "Does it have 'Ed' written on it?"

Observer: "No, it's just a plain dot."

Experimenter: "Then what is it about your image that tells you that one dot represents Ed and another Joe?"

Observer: "Nothing, I guess. I just know."

This knowledge about which dot corresponds to which name is not represented in the observer's imagery. It is an example of an imageless thought.

Was the discovery of imageless thought instrumental in the death of Introspectionism? If so, it was merely the last straw which finished an already hard-pressed camel. Behaviorism, as we will see, has also suffered severe reverses without expiring or even looking very much more swaybacked than usual. Had Introspectionism been otherwise healthy, psychologists would have shrugged their shoulders and said, "So, we counted the number of elements wrong. What else is new?" Introspectionism was not killed by a few experiments which gave negative results. It was killed by a host of experiments which gave no results. Psychologists were getting fed up with Introspectionism because the time and effort required to do an Introspection experiment simply did not yield a good return in interesting new facts about the mind.

T. Okabe's (1910) research on the formation of beliefs and disbeliefs give a good illustration of the kind of difficulties that the Introspectionists were having. Okabe showed his subjects a statement designed to produce either very strong agreement or very strong disagreement, e.g., "Wife beating is good exercise." He then asked them to introspect on the period between hearing the statement and deciding whether they agreed or not.

The results ranged from the trivial to the bizarre. On the trivial side, there were a great many reports that the observers were aware of saying the words *yes* or *no* to themselves or that they felt sensations of head noddings or head shakings. The appearance of these conventional signs of agreement and disagreement is understandable but not very illuminating.

On the bizarre side was the subject who always represented belief ". . . by a circle or a ball, of small size, two or three feet away from the eyes, which is very sharp in outline and seems very heavy. Doubt or hesitant belief may be represented by a larger, softer, vague, indefinite, and hazy ball" (Okabe, 1910, p. 576).

Somewhere in between was another subject who expressed a feeling of pressure "just below the ribs, a little to the left of center" when he believed something, and the woman who gave the following reports:

"A flash of belief came at this moment. Seems to take hold of me and envelope me. I felt light and airy, cool, rested, and relaxed. . . ."(Okabe, 1910, p. 579).

"Got at once clear, strong disbelief . . . felt disagreeable, cross and impatient."

"Strong and decided disbelief. Felt superior and rather cross. Felt like pounding the table."

"Intense belief—had tingling sensation all over me. Especially tingling sensations in the spine, which I am likely to have with intense belief" (Okabe, 1910, pp. 579–582).

These accounts are diverse. They differ not only from observer to observer, but also from one time to another in the same observer. The subject who felt the pressure under the ribs felt it only on occasion, and the subject with the tingly spine didn't tingle to every belief. But variability is not the really bad thing about these introspective reports. The bad thing is that somehow the most interesting information—information that would tell us about the process by which the subjects arrived at their belief states—was entirely missing from the reports. Apparently this process is largely unconscious.

Evidence of unconscious processes

Basically, the Introspectionists were just plain wrong when they thought they could build a psychology from conscious processes alone. By 1910, considerable evidence of unconscious influences in thought had been accumulated. The clinical evidence was the most spectacular. A case of Freud's illustrates the influence of unconscious determinants in the processes of association and forgetting.

While on a train trip, Freud fell into conversation with a young man who had the misfortune while trying to quote a line from Virgil to forget the word aliquis. From then on he was in trouble. Here is Freud's account (Freud, pp. 41–44):

"It was too stupid to forget such a word," he said. "By the way, I understand you claim that forgetting is not without its reasons; I should be very curious to find out how I came to forget this indefinite pronoun *aliquis*."

I gladly accepted the challenge, as I hoped to get an addition to my collection, and said, "We can easily do this, but I must ask you to tell me frankly and without any criticism everything that occurs to your mind after you focus your attention, without any particular intention, on the forgotten word."

"Very well, the ridiculous idea comes to me to divide the word in the following way: *a* and *liquis*."

"What does that mean?"

"I don't know."

"What else does that recall to you?"

"The thought goes on to *reliques—liquidation—liquidity—fluid*."

"Does that mean anything to you now?"

"No, not by a long shot."

"Just go ahead."

"I now think," he said, laughing sarcastically, "of Simon of Trent, whose relics I saw two years ago in a church in Trent. I think of the old accusation which has been brought against the Jews again, and of the work of Kleinpaul, who sees in these supposed sacrifices reincarnations or revivals, so to speak, of the Saviour."

"This stream of thoughts has some connection with the theme which we discussed before the Latin word escaped you."

"You are right. I now think of an article in an Italian journal which I have recently read. I believe it was entitled: 'What St. Augustine said Concerning Women.' What can you do with this?"

I waited.

"Now I think of something which surely has no connection with the theme."

"Oh, please abstain from all criticism, and—"

"Oh, I know! I recall a handsome old gentleman whom I met on my journey last week. He was really an *original* type. He looked like a big bird of prey. His name, if you care to know, is Benedict."

"Well, at least you give a grouping of saints and church fathers: St. Simon, St. Augustine and St. Benedict. I believe that there was a Church father named *Origines*. Three of these, moreover, are Christian names, like *Paul* in the name of *Kleinpaul*."

"Now I think of St. *Januarius* and his blood miracle—I find that the thoughts are running mechanically."

"Just stop a moment; both St. Januarius and St. Augustine have something to do with the calendar. Will you recall to me the blood miracle?"

"Don't you know about it? The blood of St. Januarius is preserved in a phial in a church in Naples, and on a certain holiday, a miracle takes place causing it to liquefy. The people think a great deal of this miracle, and become very excited if the liquefying process is retarded, as happened once during the French occupation. The General in command—or Garibaldi, if I am not mistaken—then took the priest aside, and with a very significant gesture pointed out to him the soldiers arrayed without, and expressed his hope that the miracle would soon take place. And it actually took place. . . ."

"Well, what else comes to your mind? Why do you hesitate?"

"Something really occurred to me . . . but it is too intimate a matter to impart . . . besides, I see no connection and no necessity for telling it."

"I will take care of the connection. Of course I cannot compel you to reveal what is disagreeable to you, but then you should not have demanded that I tell you why you forgot the word *aliquis*."

"Really? Do you think so? Well, I suddenly thought of a woman from whom I could easily get a message that would be very annoying to us both."

"That she missed her courses [menstrual periods]?"

"How could you guess such a thing?"

"That was not very difficult. You prepared me for it long enough. Just think of the *saints of the calendar, the liquefying of the blood on a certain day, the excitement if the event does not take place, and the distinct threat that the miracle must take place. . . .* Indeed, you have elaborated the miracle of St. Januarius into a clever allusion to the courses of the woman."

"It was surely without my knowledge. And do you really believe that my inability to reproduce the word *aliquis* was due to this anxious expectation?"

"That appears to me absolutely certain. Don't you recall dividing it into *a-liquis* and the associations: *reliques, liquidation, fluid?* Shall I also add to this connection the fact that St. Simon, to whom you got by way of *reliques,* was sacrificed as a child?"

"Please stop. I hope you do not take these thoughts—if I really entertained them—seriously. I will, however, confess to you that the lady is Italian, and that I visited Naples in her company. But may not all this be coincidental?"

"I must leave to your own judgment whether you can explain all these connections through the assumption of coincidence. I will tell you, however, that every similar case that you analyze will lead you to just such remarkable 'coincidences!' "

The coincidences are indeed remarkable. It seems plain that, without his being aware of it, the young man's problems were influencing his associations.

The idea of the unconscious is so strongly identified with Freud and with psychopathology that people tend to think that there is a family skeleton hidden behind each unconscious process. Actually, there are an enormous number of such processes and most of them are quite commonplace. People are continually making unconscious adjustments to social situations. For example, most people are not aware of the changes in themselves which cause them to laugh at a joke told at a party when that same joke would leave them quite cold if they read it in private. Marbe's (1901) observers were completely unable to find any conscious trace of the process by which they made simple judgments such as comparing two weights. Such processes as solving problems, keeping one's balance, generating sentences, and retrieving information from memory are all largely unconscious. The list could be extended, but the point is clear. Much of the mind is unconscious. To try to understand the whole mind just by examining the conscious part is like trying to understand the whole shark just by examining its fins. This is what the Introspectionists were trying to do, and this is why they failed.

What was it that Wundt and the Introspectionists accomplished? They added an astonishing new vigor to the investigation of the mind. They hauled psychology out of the study and pushed it into the laboratory. Under Introspectionist influence the tempo of events immediately quickened. New ideas born of fresh observations were being generated. Old ideas were being reexamined with careful scrutiny in the laboratory and being refined or rejected. That many of the ideas which were rejected were their own is a testimony to the power of the experimental spirit that the Introspectionists introduced.

SUMMARY

In the last half of the 19th century, psychology ceased to be a branch of philosophy and became instead a laboratory science. Most influential at this time were the Introspectionists, who believed that psychology should be concerned solely with conscious experience as observed through systematic introspection. The Introspectionist approach, however, ran into serious difficulties. Researchers were not able to reach agreement about the facts. For example, Wundt and Titchener could not agree with the Wurzburg psychologists about imageless thought. Further, many experiments yielded uninteresting results. A major weakness of the Introspectionist approach was that it could not take unconscious factors—factors which Freud showed were very important—into account.

FURTHER READING

A much more thorough and scholarly discussion of the topics covered in Chapters 1 and 2 may be found in George Humphrey's book and E. G. Boring's book, published in 1950, both listed in References following.

REFERENCES

BORING, E. G. "Sensations of the alimentary canal," *American Journal of Psychology, 26* (1915), pp. 1–57.

BORING, E. G. *A history of experimental psychology,* 2d ed. New York: Appleton-Century-Crofts, 1950.

FREUD, S. *The basic writings of Sigmund Freud.* Translated and edited by Dr. A. A. Brill. Copyright © 1938 by Random House, Inc. Copyright renewed by Giola B. Bernheim and Edward R. Brill. Reprinted by permission.

HUMPHREY, G. *Thinking: An introduction to its experimental psychology.* London: Methuen, 1951.

OKABE, T. "An experimental study of imagination," *American Journal of Psychology, 21* (1910), pp. 563–596.

PERKY, C. W. "An experimental study of imagination," *American Journal of Psychology, 21* (1910), pp. 422–452.

Chapter 3

Behaviorism

Psychologists were dissatisfied with the state of the psychological world. Hemmed in by the restrictions of the rigid Wundtian regime, they longed for the freedom to be more productive. Revolution was inevitable. The Behaviorist revolution in the United States and the Gestalt revolution in Germany broke out almost simultaneously. In this chapter we will discuss the Behaviorist revolution and the vast empire which the Behaviorists established in its aftermath. We will save the Gestalt revolution for Chapter 4.

THE SCIENCE OF BEHAVIOR

John Watson declared independence for the Behaviorists in 1913, when he published an article, "Psychology as the Behaviorist Views It." He stated the critical issue bluntly but firmly in his opening paragraph:

"Psychology as the Behaviorist views it is a purely objective experimental branch of natural science. Its theoretical goal is the prediction and control of behavior. Introspection forms no essential part of its methods, nor is the scientific value of its data dependent upon the readiness with which they lend themselves to interpretation in terms of consciousness (Watson, 1913, p. 158)."

With this declaration, the Behaviorists seized the freedom that they had been searching for. By redefining psychology as the study of behavior rather than the study of consciousness, they gave themselves the elbowroom they needed for creative work. By this stroke, they broadened their choice both of scientific method and of the subject matter which they could study.

29

Freedom of method

Psychologists had felt constrained to use the technique of introspection whenever possible. After all, it *was* the primary method for studying consciousness. This constraint was troublesome since the method was very time-consuming and it required extremely well-trained observers. And it was doubly troublesome since even the greatest care in training the observers did not guarantee that the results would be acceptable to other Introspectionists. If your theory was destroyed by Jones' introspective result, you needn't abandon it. You need only point out sympathetically how difficult it is for Jones to introspect clearly with all that fog swirling through his brain. Both Wundt and Titchener used this ploy in refusing to accept the Wurzburg School's discovery of imageless thought and in being totally unable to agree with each other as to the nature of feelings. Thus, psychologists were trapped in a situation where even the greatest care and effort could not guarantee a satisfactory yield of reliable knowledge.

By abandoning the study of consciousness, the Behaviorists were free to abandon Introspection and to substitute more objective and efficient behavioral techniques in its place. In studying learning, for example, they were quite happy to record objective facts such as the number and kinds of the students' errors, and the amount of time they required to learn, but to ignore completely the subjective processes which might accompany that learning.

Freedom of subject matter

Freedom of aim and method gave the Behaviorists a new freedom to select their subject matter. In using the technique of introspection, experimenters were forced to restrict themselves almost exclusively to studying well-trained human adults within the confines of the psychological laboratory. By switching to behavioral techniques, they could also experiment in the school or in the factory. They could even experiment on preverbal children or on animals. Thus, the Behaviorists were able to broaden their interests to include educational, industrial, social, and child psychology, and perhaps most important for them, animal psychology.

Completeness

The Behaviorists felt that even though they were abandoning the technique of introspection, they were actually leaving nothing out of psychology. After all, they said, everything we know about a person's consciousness we must infer from what people say or do, that is, from their behavior. The study of consciousness, then, is just one aspect of the more general study of behavior. The position is an important one and appears irrefutable. Whether we are Behaviorists or not, we must agree that we can only know the mind of another through that person's behavior. Whatever novels of young love may say, there is no direct contact between minds.

Associationist roots

Although they had rejected the subjectivity of the Introspectionists, the Behaviorists still shared the general Associationist framework in which the Introspectionists had worked. The Behaviorists were very clearly empiricist, atomist, and connectionist. Their empiricism is evident in the enormous emphasis which the Behaviorists have placed on learning, and their tendency to ignore heredity. The Behaviorist atoms are stimuli and responses (supposedly objectively measurable) and the connections are the S-R (stimulus-response) bonds between them.

B. F. Skinner and the radical Behaviorists have carried this point a big step further. They argue not only that we cannot study consciousness directly but that we should not talk about it at all [see, for example, Watson (1930) and Skinner (1953)]. They felt that discussing mental events which cannot be observed directly is potentially misleading. To be scientifically solid, they believed that psychology should discuss only observable behaviors and not the mental events inferred from them.

The objective psychology of the Behaviorists was well received in the United States. The idea of a science of behavior was enormously attractive, and it was taken up enthusiastically. American psychologists flocked to the Behaviorist banner. By 1920, Behaviorism was clearly the dominant force in American psychology and it has remained so, although much modified, to this day.

Behaviorism has played a Jekyll and Hyde role (or roles) in cognitive psychology. On the Jekyll side, it contributed many valuable facts and concepts. On the Hyde side, it created an atmosphere which has hampered the study of thought. We will look first at the Jekyll side.

BEHAVIORIST CONTRIBUTIONS TO PSYCHOLOGY

The Behaviorists have made two major contributions to the study of thought. First, they have provided enormous quantities of objective data about one of the most important of cognitive processes—learning. They have provided experimental analysis of such learning phenomena as classical and operant conditioning, generalization, extinction, discrimination, and a host of other phenomena. To do this required the invention of many ingenious experimental techniques, techniques which present-day experimental psychologists make use of every day. Second, by applying S-R theory to thought processes, they have made a bold attempt to explain cognition in terms of learning phenomena.

The experimental analysis of learning

In 1898, two researchers, thousands of miles apart, were conducting investigations which were to have enormous importance for the Behaviorists. In Russia, Ivan Petrovich Pavlov, working with dogs, Fidovitch and Spotovitch, had discovered the conditioned reflex. In the United States, Edward L. Thorndike was studying trial-and-error learning in cats. From these two investigations evolved the major lines of research in learning—classical conditioning and operant conditioning.

Classical conditioning

While carrying out investigations on the processes of digestion, Pavlov quite accidentally discovered the conditioned reflex. He was attempting to study the reflex salivation that dogs exhibit when food is placed in their mouths. His measurements of the reflex were being interfered with because after they had had some experience in the testing situation, the dogs began to salivate before the food was placed in their mouths. Any signal that they were about to be fed, such as showing them the food dish, would, after a few exposures, begin to cause salivation. He found that nearly any arbitrary stimulus such as a bell or a light which was presented with or just before food would act in the same way. Pavlov had happened on the conditioned reflex.

Fortunately, he saw that the phenomenon that was interfering with his experiment was more important than the one he had initially set out to investigate. He abandoned his research on digestion and turned to systematic study of the conditioned reflex.

A good example of a classical conditioning experiment was performed by G. V. Anrep (1920), a student of Pavlov's. In training his dogs, Anrep presented a tone for five seconds, and then, two to three seconds later, put food powder into the animal's mouth. Interspersed between these training trials were test trials in which he presented the tone by itself and then measured the number of drops of saliva secreted over the next 30 seconds. The time interval between trials was varied from 5 to 35 minutes to be sure that the animal was not just learning when it was "meal time." (Every tenth trial was a test trial in which he presented the tone without any food so he could measure how much salivation the tone produced by itself.) Table 3–1 shows the number of drops of saliva obtained on each test trial. In this case, the conditioned response was established in full strength in from 20 to 30 trials.

Table 3–1. Acquisition of a
conditioned reflex

Trial number	Number of drops in 30 seconds
1	0
10	6
20	20
30	60
40	62
50	59

Source: G. V. Anrep, "Pitch Discrimination in the Dog," *Journal of Physiology, 53*
(1920), p. 380.

In general, we can describe conditioning experiments in this way: The conditioning procedure starts with a well-established reflex, such as salivation to food in the mouth, and an initially neutral stimulus which does not trigger the reflex. The well-established reflex, called the unconditioned reflex, involves an unconditioned stimulus (UCS), for example, food in the mouth, which reliably produces the unconditioned response (UCR), for example, salivation. When the neutral stimulus (CS), (a tone or a bell), is paired repeatedly with the unconditioned stimulus (food), it begins to elicit the unconditioned response (salivation). These relationships are diagrammed in Figure 3–1.

Figure 3–1. Classical conditioning diagram

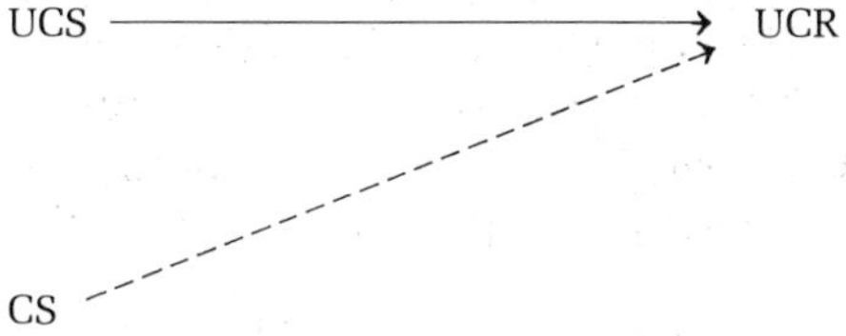

In many cases, the well-established reflex is an unconditioned reflex such as a knee jerk, or an eye blink to a puff of air. In some cases, though, the well-established reflex is itself a conditioned reflex. When the conditioned reflex is based on an unconditioned reflex, it is called a primary conditioned reflex. When the conditioned reflex is based on a primary conditioned reflex, it is called a secondary conditioned reflex, and so on. Conditioned reflexes of the third or higher order than the second have proved to be unstable and very difficult to establish.

A conditioned response is relatively easy to establish if the conditioned stimulus is simultaneous with or precedes the unconditioned stimulus. It appears to be impossible, however, to establish a backward conditioned response, that is, one in which the unconditioned stimulus precedes the conditioned stimulus.

While reviews of Pavlov's work were available in the United States as early as 1909 (Yerkes and Morgulis), the Behaviorists at first failed to pay it more than polite attention. Very likely, the reason for this initial coolness was that they thought of conditioning rather narrowly. They viewed it as a rather peculiar property of the glands and did not relate it to behavior generally. Not until 1915, when they learned that W. Bechterev had extended Pavlov's work to motor responses, was their enthusiasm really fired. Then they received the conditioned response as the long-lost heir of the associative bond. The reception was rather uncritical, however, as befits a long-lost heir. More than ten years passed before a clear distinction was made between classical conditioning and the importantly different instrumental conditioning (see below).

Rallied by Watson (1916), the Behaviorists began a long series of laboratory investigations of the conditioned reflex which have yielded valuable information concerning such topics as neurosis (Liddell, 1944), fear (Miller, 1948), and ulcer formation (Brady, 1958).

Instrumental conditioning

Figure 3–2 shows one of the puzzle boxes which Thorndike used in his experiments on trial-and-error learning. When the cat was put into the box, it would immediately begin its attempts to escape. It clawed and bit at the bars and pushed its paws through all available openings. This frantic activity might continue for eight or ten minutes until the cat accidentally pulled the string or struck the button that opened the door and it escaped. This was a trial-and-error process. To demonstrate that learning occurred during this process, Thorndike made the animal repeat the performance many times. As a result, the animal's perfor-

Figure 3–2. Puzzle box used by Thorndike in learning experiments with cats

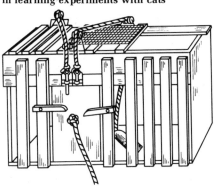

Source: H. E. Garrett, *Great Experiments in Psychology*. New York: Appleton-Century, 1930, p. 107.

Figure 3–3. Learning curve for a single cat escaping
from the puzzle box on a series of 24 trials.

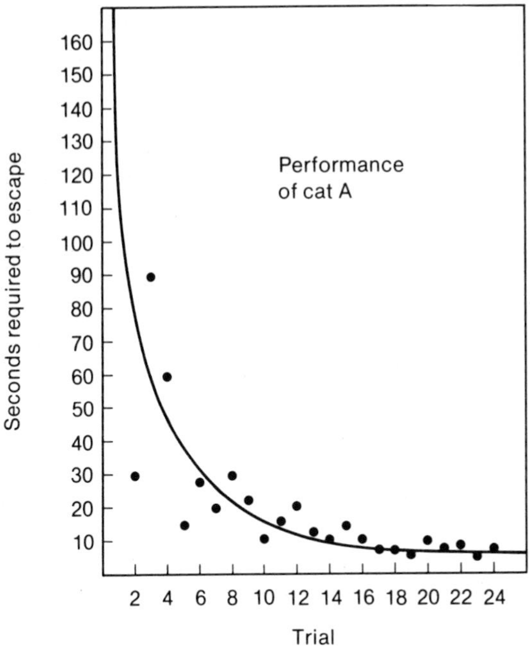

* Data are from Thorndike (1911).
Source: G. A. Kimble and N. Garmezy, *Principles of General Psychology*, 2d ed. New York: Ronald, 1963, p. 180.

mance gradually improved until it escaped in less than ten seconds (see Figure 3–3).

The law of effect. Thorndike (1898) extracted what he felt was the basic learning principle from the trial-and-error situation. His famous law of effect may be summarized as follows: If an animal does something in a situation and that something is followed by satisfaction, then the animal will be more likely to do it again when the situation recurs. Similarly, if the action leads to discomfort, the animal will be less likely to do it again when the situation recurs.

Early critics claimed that the law of effect was entirely circular. They said that the definitions of satisfaction and discomfort must rest ultimately on whether or not the animal learns to do the act in question. If this is so, the law of effect can be reduced to a statement such as, "The animal learns to do those things which he learns to do, but not other things." Statements of this sort arouse little or no interest in audiences who are much beyond five years of age.

Thorndike replied that the law was not circular since satisfaction and discomfort can be defined independently of the particular learning situation. We can imagine, for example, that we could put a rat through a series of tests in which it (1) chooses to move toward the food pellets rather than the rocks, (2) pulls hard against a harness in order to get to food pellets, (3) is willing to cross an electrified grid to get to food pellets, and (4) learns a T-maze to get to food pellets. At this point, we might reasonably be willing to say, "Gee, this rat seems to like food pellets," or even that food pellets seem to provide it with satisfaction.

Modern theorists agree with Thorndike that it is indeed meaningful to say that the learning of an act depends on the effect that the act has. They disagree, however, as to the nature of the mechanisms underlying the law. For example, modern Behaviorists would not agree that satisfaction and discomfort, or to use more modern terms, reinforcement and punishment, bear the complementary relation which Thorndike attributes to them. More modern theorists view reinforcers as providing data to a complex information-processing system—a process which may be considerably more involved than establishing a connection between temporally related events. Nevertheless, all psychologists accept the major point of the law of effect as one of the most important in psychology.

To understand the importance of the law of effect, consider what its absence would imply. Suppose we were to find a puppy in which the law was inoperative. Such an animal would frustrate us with its stupidity. It could not be housebroken, and it would never learn where to go for dinner. It might solve problems by trial and error, but its solutions would never improve. The 100th time it tried to open the screen door, it would have just as much trouble as the first. Thus, the law of effect is responsible for much of the intelligently adaptive behavior that living things show.

Perhaps the most striking aspect of the Behaviorists' work is the extent to which they have been able to exploit the law of effect. They have reformulated Thorndike's original law roughly as follows in the law of instrumental (or operant) conditioning: *If a response is followed by a reinforcer, then the response is strengthened.* Further, they have developed techniques which make it much easier to use the law in controlling behavior. Skinner has been a leader in the development of these techniques. Two of his most important contributions are the concepts of schedules of reinforcement and of shaping.

Schedules of reinforcement. Imagine a rat in a soundproof air-conditioned box. There are no disturbing sights, sounds, or smells from the outside world to distract it. This isolated environment, called a Skinner Box, is an important part of Skinner's experimental procedure. At the far end of the box is a horizontal, movable bar and below it a tray. When a red light over the bar is lit, the rat moves to the bar, rears up on its hind legs, and presses the bar at a rate of about ten presses per minute. After exactly 48 presses, an automatic mechanism clicks and delivers a food pellet into the tray. The rat picks it up in its paws, devours it, and is soon back at work pressing the bar at the rate of ten presses per minute. The rat continues in this way until the red light is turned off and a blue light is turned on. At this point, the rat suddenly slows its rate to about three presses per minute. Now the automatic mechanism feeds it at regular six-minute intervals. Finally, when the blue light is turned off, the rat stops pressing and moves to the far end of the box.

Skinner has been very successful in controlling the behavior of animals in isolated environments by manipulating their stimuli and reinforcements. He has shown that what the animal does depends very much on its *schedule of reinforcement*. In the example above, when the red light was lit, the rat was on a 48 to 1 *fixed-ratio* schedule. That is, after every 48 bar presses it received a pellet of food. Animals on fixed-ratio schedules produce very high rates of response. The highest ratios correspond to the highest rates of response. The slopes of the curves in Figure 3–4 indicate response rates for three fixed-ratio schedules.

Figure 3–4.   Response rates for three fixed-ratio schedules*

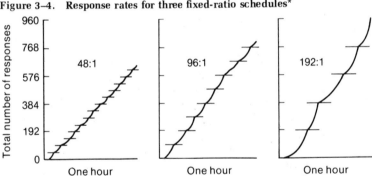

* Responses within ratio reinforcement. Responses from individual rats reinforced every 48, 96, and 192 responses, as indicated by the horizontal lines. Under these circumstances very high rates of responding develop, the highest rate being found with the lowest frequency of reinforcement.
Source: B. F. Skinner, *The Behavior of Organisms*. New York: Appleton-Century-Crofts, 1938. As reproduced by E. R. Hilgard and D. G. Marquis, *Conditioning and Learning*. New York: Appleton-Century-Crofts, 1940, p. 152.

In *variable-ratio* schedules, the reinforcements are presented after varying numbers of responses which have a fixed-average value. For example, on a six-to-one variable-ratio schedule, the animal may be reinforced after four responses, then after eight, nine, three, and six responses. On the average, the animal was reinforced every six responses, but the number required for any particular reinforcement varied. Variable-ratio schedules produce especially high rates of responding. A pigeon may respond as often as five times per second on a variable-ratio schedule and keep it up for hours. Further, the pigeon will persist in making responses after the reinforcements have been stopped for longer than if it had been reinforced on a fixed-ratio schedule. Skinner (1953) notes that many gambling situations involve variable-ratio schedules of reinforcement. He speculates that these schedules are an important factor in the gambler's legendary and often self-destructive persistence in the face of nonreinforcement.

Another major class of reinforcement schedules is based on a time interval rather than a number of responses. In a six-minute *fixed-interval* schedule, for example, the experimenter reinforces the first response which occurs six minutes or more after the last reinforced response. Shorter intervals lead to faster response rates, as Figure 3–5 shows.

Figure 3-5. Response rates for four fixed-interval schedules*

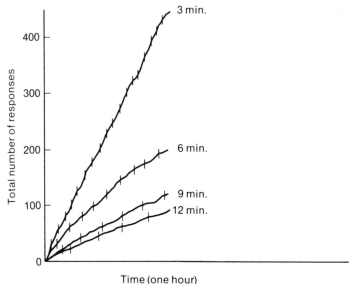

* Responses within one session of fixed-interval reinforcement. A pellet was delivered every 3, 6, 9, and 12 minutes, respectively. The more frequent the reinforcement, the more rapid the rate of responding, although each rate is relatively uniform.

Source: B. F. Skinner, *The Behavior of Organisms.* New York: Appleton-Century-Crofts, 1938. As reproduced by E. R. Hilgard and D. G. Marquis, *Conditioning and Learning.* New York: Appleton-Century-Crofts, 1940, p. 151.

With training, an animal can associate a schedule of reinforcement with a stimulus. In the example above, the rat was reinforced on the 48 to 1 fixed-ratio schedule only when the red light was on and on the six-minute fixed-interval schedule only when the blue light was on. When neither light was on, it was not reinforced at all. As training proceeded, the rat learned to discriminate among the stimulus condi-

tions and to respond with behavior appropriate to the current reinforcement schedule. The experimenter was able to control this animal's behavior, then, by manipulating stimuli and schedules of
reinforcement.

The behavior of the rat described above was that of a well-trained
animal. We would not expect an inexperienced rat placed in this situation to respond to the lights or to press the bar at all, let alone 50 times
in rapid succession. Typically, to attain such complex behaviors, naive
animals are subjected to a training procedure called shaping.

Shaping.   Shaping is training by successive approximation. Suppose, for example, that you want a dog to stretch up the wall and touch
a spot with its nose. Being a firm believer in the law of effect, you have
come prepared to reinforce the dog with delicious bite-sized cubes of
filet mignon. If you now sit back and wait for the dog to perform the
trick on its own, you will probably wait a very long time, so long, in
fact, that the reinforcers are likely to be in very poor shape (to say
nothing of the dog) by the time you get an opportunity to present the
first one. If your training procedure is to have a ghost of a chance, you
had better use a shaping procedure. Start by demanding only the gross-
est sort of approximations to the desired performance. For example,
reward the dog whenever it crosses into the half of the room that is near
the spot. Soon the animal will be spending most of its time in that half.
Now bisect the half and reward the animal only when it crosses into the
near quarter. By continuing these approximations, you will move the
animal closer to the position directly under the spot. Now reward the
animal successively for (a) facing the wall, (b) raising a foot, (c) placing
a foot on the wall, (d) stretching up the wall, and finally, (f) touching
the spot with its nose. If the dog is any reasonable sort of glutton, it
should be able to learn the trick in less than half an hour.

One of the most spectacular demonstrations of what can be accomplished by shaping is the performance of Barnabus, the Barnard rat.
Barnabus, in spite of his lowly origin (both of his parents were rats),
received the benefit of a Behaviorist education at one of our better
colleges (Lundin, 1961). The result is that when Barnabus wants his
dinner, he can (and must) perform the following routine. First, when
the dinner light announces that the meal is ready, he climbs a spiral
staircase to a platform. Then he pushes down a drawbridge and crosses
to a second platform. Here he finds a chain which he can pull in paw
over paw to bring the "Ratmobile" within reach. The Ratmobile is a
one-ratpower vehicle which Barnabus pedals along a track and through
a tunnel. And to what enticing terminus is he hastening? Why, to the
bottom of a 12-step staircase which he climbs so that he can then drag
himself through a tight fitting plastic tube. At the far end of the tube,
Barnabus enters a waiting elevator car. What is it waiting for? Why, it is

waiting for Barnabus to grab hold of a chain with his teeth and hoist aloft the Columbia University flag. This accomplished, the elevator whisks Barnabus to a lower level where he has merely to press a bar, and he is rewarded for his efforts by being allowed to eat food pellets for a whole minute. (See, education pays.)

While there are some limitations to the effectiveness of shaping which we will mention below, the example illustrates the great power of the method to teach nearly any behavior the experimenter might desire.

Behavior modification.   In behavior modification, the psychologist applies learning techniques such as shaping or classical conditioning in an attempt to alleviate troublesome behavior problems such as facial tics, smoking, inability to study, and even psychotic behavior. A good example of the successful treatment of psychotic symptoms was reported by Isaacs, Thomas, and Goldiamond (in Rachlin, 1976).

The patient, S, was a withdrawn schizophrenic who would neither move nor talk. He just stared. One day, when the therapist accidentally dropped a package of chewing gum, he noticed that S looked at it and then returned his eyes to their usual position. The therapist decided to try to modify S's behavior using gum as a reinforcer.

The therapist met with S three times each week. During the first two weeks, he held the gum before S's face and gave it to him as a reinforcement when he looked at it. By the end of two weeks, S looked at the gum as soon as it was held up. During the third and fourth weeks, S had to move his lips and, later, to make a sound as well, to be reinforced. By the end of the fourth week, S looked, moved his lips, and made a sort of croak whenever the gum was held up. During the fifth and sixth weeks, the therapist held up the gum and said, "Say gum, gum." Reinforcements were given for closer and closer approximations to the word *gum*. At the end of the sixth week, S suddenly said, "Gum, please," and answered questions about his name and age. Eventually, S was able to converse with the therapist and to speak to other members of the hospital staff as well.

Many similar examples could be cited. Behavior modification has become an important part of modern psychiatric therapy. It represents a major success of Behaviorist principles.

Superstition.   Many of Skinner's cleverly designed animal experiments suggested analogies to behaviors of humans. His observation of "superstition" in pigeons is a case in point. Skinner placed pigeons in Skinner Boxes, one to a box, and set the food-delivery mechanism to release some food every 15 seconds, no matter what the bird was doing. Now, the experimenter knew that the pigeons did not have to do anything to get the food, but the pigeons did not. In a few minutes, one of the pigeons was persistently doing pirouettes, another was hopping from left foot to right, a third was busily bowing, etc. Skinner suggests that humans may acquire their superstitions in much the same way that pigeons do.

Learning and heredity. Such cases as that of Barnabus served to bolster the already strong Behaviorist faith in empiricism. That faith is illustrated in the old Behaviorist motto: "If it moves, we can shape it," and in the following remarkable quotation from Watson (1930, p. 104): ". . . give me a dozen healthy infants, well formed, and my own specified world to bring them up in and I'll guarantee to take any one at random and train him to become any type of specialist I might select—doctor, lawyer, artist, merchant-chief and, yes, even beggar man, and thief, regardless of his talents, penchants, tendencies, abilities, vocations, and race of his ancestors." While most Behaviorists would consider Watson's boast extreme, it does reflect their empiricist faith. That faith can be summarized roughly as follows: Heredity has two primary functions. First, it provides the learning mechanism; and second, it sets the physical limits within which the learning mechanism can operate. Rats cannot learn to sing and apes cannot learn to fly. They have not inherited the necessary physical equipment. To this extent, heredity determines behavior. What the animal is able to do with the equipment it does have, according to the faith, is much more powerfully determined by learning than by heredity.

BEHAVIORIST THEORIES OF THOUGHT

One of the most intriguing aspects of the whole Behaviorist movement was the attempt to account for thought entirely in stimulus-response terms—a task which has distant similarities to building a skyscraper from damp Kleenex.

We will review two Behaviorist theories of thought. First, we will describe Watson's early—and relatively crude—theory that thought is implicit speech. Second, we will discuss the much more sophisticated work of Hull, work which has formed the basis for much of the later Behaviorist thinking in cognition.

Thought as implicit speech

In his characteristic style, Watson announced that ". . . what the psychologists have hitherto called thought is in short nothing but talking to ourselves" (1930, p. 238). More specifically, he identified thought with the minute muscle movements of subvocal speech. Watson believed that when children first learn to speak they say everything aloud. Soon, however, social pressures teach them that this is poor policy. For example, most children discover, at long last, that they should not announce their bathroom needs at dinner parties or public occasions. Responding to such social pressures, children learn the trick of speaking subvocally—that is, of thinking.

It occasioned Watson only momentary embarrassment when it was pointed out that patients who have had their larynxes removed are still able to think in words. Watson replied that speech involves not just the muscles of the larynx but also of the tongue, the throat, and the chest, and may include, as well, implicit gestures, such as infinitesimal shoulder shrugs. In Watson's view, we think with our whole bodies.

Even when vocal speech is entirely absent, Watson felt that other systems of muscle movements may substitute to serve the same function. He cited the fascinating observation that deaf-mutes sometimes talk to themselves in finger language when they are dreaming.

Attempts to find consistent patterns of muscle movements associated with thought have been discouraging. The drug curare made a definitive test of the muscular theory of thought possible. Curare is the poison used by the Jivaro Indians of Central America to tip the hunting darts they shoot from their blowguns. It is a quick-acting drug which causes a complete but temporary paralysis. It can kill by arresting breathing, but if the victim is kept alive by artificial respiration during the period of paralysis, the drug appears to cause no permanent ill effects.

Following Marquis' initial suggestion in 1933 that curare would be useful for studying the role of muscles in psychological processes, there was a great flurry of experiments. The basic idea of these experiments was to determine if an animal could learn something while it was completely paralyzed by curare. In a typical experiment, the paralyzed animal would be presented repeatedly with a light followed by an electric shock. If the animal could learn while paralyzed, then, when it recovered, it should respond to the light by trying to avoid the shock.

Alas! The results of the early experiments proved hard to interpret. The difficulty was that the animals appeared not only to be paralyzed under the influence of the drug, but, on the basis of evidence about their brain functions, seemed to be unconscious as well. Indeed, for a number of years, curare was used occasionally in human surgery both as a muscle relaxant and as an anesthetic.

About 1945, a new curare derivative was introduced, d-tubocurarine. Now, strangely, surgical patients began to complain that they had experienced severe pain during operations despite the fact that they had been completely unable to move. Apparently the new drug paralyzed but did not anesthetize. Smith, Brown, Toman, and Goodman (1947) tested the new drug on Smith (who, if he never raised another finger, earned his right to first authorship). After being given a large enough dose to paralyze him completely, Smith was kept alive by artificial respiration. The other authors entertained Smith by a variety of antics which included showing him things and jabbing him with pins while he was indisposed. When he recovered, he was able to give an accurate account of what had happened to him. He claimed that his senses had been extremely clear while he was under the drug. It appears, therefore, that cognitive functioning can proceed quite normally even though the peripheral musculature is paralyzed. Smith was able to sense, to learn, to think, and to know despite the fact that he was completely unable to respond. Evidence such as this indicates clearly that cognitive processes can proceed without the peripheral musculature.

Hullian theory of thought

During the 1920s, the crude but enthusiastic sort of Behaviorism which Watson represented began to draw increasingly sharp fire from critics who challenged the Behaviorists to explain such phenomena as foresight, insight, and goal directedness—phenomena which the Gestalt psychologists (see Chapter 4) had discussed in their theories and documented in their experiments. Some Behaviorists dismissed these challenges simply as renewed outbreaks of mentalistic mysticism. Hull, however, took them seriously. In the early 1930s, he published a remarkable series of papers dealing with these phenomena and in so doing greatly increased the sophistication of S-R theory.

While we cannot present a comprehensive account of Hullian theory here, we will present his model of foresight in some detail to illustrate something of the character of his theories.

Foresight. Imagine a novice table tennis player observing the following sequence of events:

S1. The opponent's paddle strikes the ball.
S2. The ball passes over the net.
S3. The ball strikes the near side of the table.
S4. The ball passes just over the novice's paddle. (Sigh!)

Eventually, the novice wants to be able to view the early elements of this sequence and to respond by moving the paddle into the appropriate position. That is, the novice wants to exhibit foresight about where the ball is going to be when it reaches his or her end of the table.

Hull's theory of foresight is, in essence, a detailed account of the stimulus-response chains which he believes underlie the process. Figure 3–6 shows the connections which Hull believed are present while the player is still naive. First, S1 is connected to S2, S2 to S3, and S3 to S4 because these are real-world events which are causally related. Second, each of these events acts as a stimulus to the player, who responds

Figure 3–6.   S–R connections for the naive player

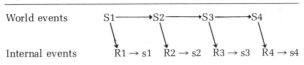

Source: C. L. Hull, "Knowledge and Purpose as Habit Mechanisms,"
Psychological Review, 37 (1930), p. 513.

with a characteristic response. For example, R1 (Reaction 1) might be an
orientation of the head to the sound of the paddle striking the ball, R2
might be an eye movement toward the net, and so on. Each of the Rs is
assumed, in turn, to produce a characteristic internal stimulation, s,
which is distinguished from world-event stimulus S. These s's would
be sensations of the muscles, balance mechanisms, etc., appropriate to
the response. At this point in the player's experience, these internal
stimuli are assumed not to be conditioned to any interesting responses.

When the player has seen the sequence a number of times, some
learning takes place. In particular, since s1 occurs close in time to S2,
and S2 elicits R2, s1 begins to elicit R2 by classical conditioning. In the
same way, s2 begins to elicit R3, and s3 to elicit R4 (see Figure 3-7).

Figure 3–7.   S–R connections for the experienced player

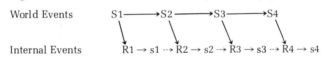

Source: C. L. Hull, "Knowledge and Purpose as Habit Mechanisms,"
Psychological Review, 37 (1930), p. 513.

The chain of internal events

$$R1 \rightarrow s1 \dashrightarrow R2 \rightarrow s2 \dashrightarrow R3 \rightarrow s3 \dashrightarrow R4$$

now corresponds to the sequence of external events,

$$S1 \rightarrow S2 \rightarrow S3 \rightarrow S4.$$

For Hull, the chain of internal events is in fact the player's knowledge of
the external sequence.

Now, if the internal chain ran at the same speed as the external
sequence, the player could never use that knowledge to behave with
foresight. The realization that the paddle should be lifted would always
occur just after the ball passed over the paddle. Hull argues, however,
that the internal chain can run faster than the external chain for two
reasons. One is the principle of *economy*, and the other is the process of
short-circuiting.

By the principle of economy, repeated acts tend to be reduced to the minimum amplitude necessary to accomplish their functions. Hull cited an experiment of Thorndike's in which a cat was rewarded for licking its fur. Within a few repetitions the lick was reduced to a mere nodding of the head. In the chains described above, the only function of the responses was to produce a characteristic stimulation. Hull calls these pure stimulus acts. He suggests that the principle of economy may cause especially marked reductions in the magnitudes of pure stimulus acts and that the resulting small magnitudes lead to high speeds of execution.

By short-circuiting, Hull meant a process by which some parts of the internal chain may be bypassed. Thus, if s1 were to be connected to R3, R2 and s2 could be bypassed and the chain could run faster.

Time has not been kind to Hull's model of foresight nor to his other S-R models of cognitive processes. We should note, however, that by constructing such models, Hull was departing from the tradition of radical Behaviorism. Radical Behaviorists, such as Watson and Skinner, regarded the construction of such models, or for that matter, any sort of theorizing about unobserved mental processes, as scientifically unsound. In this respect, time has been kinder to Hull than to the radical Behaviorists.

CRITIQUE OF BEHAVIORISM, OR:
FAR TOO MUCH OF A GOOD THING

So far, I have pictured Behaviorism as a heroic young Lochinvar rescuing fair Psychology from a life of Introspection or worse. I would like to say that they lived happily ever after, but I cannot. Unfortunately, Lochinvar had some character traits which proved to be quite wearing in the long run. Ironically, these peculiarities were simply exaggerations of some of his most solid and ingratiating virtues.

First, the strong empirical bent of Behaviorism which had led the Behaviorists to their very valuable explorations of learning also led them to see learning, and only learning, wherever they looked. Second, the Behaviorists' passion for objectivity, which had liberated them from their Introspectionist shackles, also gave rise to an extreme antimentalism which in the long run has hampered the study of thought.

Too much Empiricism

By all odds, the favorite topic of the Behaviorists was learning. Their emphasis on learning, however, led to an underemphasis on such other topics as perception, language, and reasoning. Heredity is a good example of a topic the Behaviorists underemphasized. In their view, heredity determined the limits of the animal's physical capability. Within those limits, however, they believed that the animal could be trained by appropriate procedures and without regard to heredity to do almost anything. Spectacular successes in the laboratory, such as that illustrated by Barnabus, seemed to confirm that belief. Evidence has now come to light that this simple view is wrong.

An enterprising husband and wife team, K. Breland and M. Breland, set out to apply the "If it moves, we can shape it" doctrine in developing a practical technology for animal training. They applied Behaviorist principles to projects for zoo displays, television shows, and tourist attractions, and trained a wide variety of animals including reindeer, raccoons, and whales. Many of the Brelands' projects were successful, but the failures they report (1961) were also "disconcertingly frequent."

These failures are well illustrated in the following examples (Breland and Breland, 1961, p. 682), of ill-fated attempts to condition a raccoon and some pigs.

> Raccoons condition readily, have good appetites, and this one was quite tame and an eager subject. We anticipated no trouble. Conditioning him to pick up the first coin was simple. We started out by reinforcing him for picking up a single coin. Then the metal container was introduced, with the requirement that he drop the coin into the container. Here we ran into the first bit of difficulty: he seemed to have a great deal of trouble letting go of the coin. He would rub it up against the inside of the container, pull it back out, and clutch it firmly for several seconds. However, he would finally turn it loose and receive his food reinforcement. Then the final contingency: . . . that he pick up both coins and put them in the container.
>
> Now the racoon really had problems (and so did we). Not only could he not let go of the coins, but he spent seconds, even minutes, rubbing them together (in a most miserly fashion), and dipping them into the container. He carried on this behavior to such an extent that the practical application we had in mind—a display featuring a raccoon putting money in a piggy bank—simply was not feasible. The rubbing behavior became worse and worse as time went on, in spite of nonreinforcement."

And also (Breland and Breland, 1961, p. 683):

> Here a pig was conditioned to pick up large wooden coins and deposit them in a large piggy bank. The coins were placed several feet from the bank and the pig required to carry them to the bank and deposit them, usually four or five coins for one reinforcement. (Of course, we started out with one coin, near the bank.)
>
> Pigs condition very rapidly, they have no trouble taking ratios, they have ravenous appetites (naturally), and in many ways are among the most tractable animals we have worked with. However, this particular problem behavior developed in pig after pig, usually after a period of weeks or months, getting worse every day. At first the pig would eagerly pick up one dollar, carry it to the bank, run back, get another, carry it

rapidly and neatly, and so on, until the ratio was complete. Thereafter, over a period of weeks the behavior would become slower and slower. He might run over eagerly for each dollar, but on the way back, instead of carrying the dollar and depositing it simply and cleanly, he would repeatedly drop it, root it, drop it again, root it along the way, pick it up, toss it up in the air, drop it, root it some more, and so on.

We thought this behavior might simply be the dillydallying of an animal on a low drive. However, the behavior persisted and gained in strength in spite of a severely increased drive—he finally went through the ratios so slowly that he did not get enough to eat in the course of a day. Finally it would take the pig about ten minutes to transport four coins a distance of about six feet. This problem behavior developed repeatedly in successive pigs."

While the troubles of the raccoon appear quite different in detail from those of the pigs, they have closely related causes. The raccoon's performance was being interfered with by an innate food-washing pattern, and the pigs' performance by rooting, another innate pattern related to eating. The Brelands attribute the difficulties in these two cases, and in many similar cases, to what they call instinctive drift.

They conclude: "The general principle seems to be that wherever an animal has strong instinctive behaviors in the area of the conditioned response, after continued running the organism will drift toward the instinctive behavior and even to the delay or preclusion of the reinforcement. In a very boiled-down, simplified form, it might be stated as 'Learned behavior drifts toward instinctive behavior' " (Breland and Breland, 1961, p. 684).

While it is important in attempting to understand the Behaviorists to note that they overemphasize learning and underemphasize heredity, these faults are really not very serious ones. The Behaviorist faults which stem from overzealous objectivity really are serious, however.

Too much objectivity

Criticizing anyone for an excess of objectivity may seem strange to you. It is a bit like cursing a bishop for too much holiness. But, alas! the Behaviorists have proved once and for all that objectivity is one of those virtues which can be overdone.

The Behaviorists' reaction against the subjectivity of their predecessors were understandable but excessive. Not only did they reject the technique of introspection, for which they had considerable justification, but they went on, with much less justification, to try to purge psychology of all concepts which they felt were tainted with any hint of mentalism. Watson sounded the hue and cry in statements such as the following:

"Behaviorism claims that consciousness is neither a definite nor a useable concept. The Behaviorist, who has been trained always as an experimentalist, holds, further, that belief in the existence of consciousness goes back to the ancient days of superstition and magic (Watson, 1930, p. 2)." And again, ". . . the Behaviorist began his own formulation of the problem of psychology by sweeping aside all medieval conceptions. He dropped from his scientific vocabulary all subjective terms such as sensation, perception, image, desire, purpose, and even thinking and emotion as they were subjectively defined" (Watson, 1930, p. 5).

While the purge was quite successful in the sense that it influenced the thinking of many psychologists for many years, it had two very unfortunate effects. First, it frightened people away from the study of the higher mental processes. A psychologist might observe in the privacy of his office that he solved problems by manipulating imagined figures. He would have been ill-advised to try to study such phenomena scientifically, though, for surely his "hardheaded" colleagues would have branded him as an unscientific thinker or perhaps a mystic. The result was that very little research on higher mental processes was done where Behaviorism was dominant, as in the United States. For example, Perky's interesting findings were not followed up until 1968 (Segal, 1968), when Behaviorist influence had waned. Psychologists were encouraged instead to study simpler processes (learning was so regarded) in lower animals, where there was less danger of being led into mentalistic interpretations. It is not surprising that behavioristic psychology was sometimes criticized for triviality and lack of relevance to human problems.

All of this was especially unfortunate because the attitude which inspired the purge was quite ill-founded. Briefly stated, the attitude was that explanations in terms of mental states and processes were at best confusing and at worst caused brain rot. Mental states such as attitudes, intelligence, images, and memory are inferred from observations of behavior. They are not in themselves directly observable. If a person calls you horrible names, stomps on your foot, and sets fire to your tie, you may infer that he has a negative attitude toward you. You never, however, observe the attitude directly.

Behaviorists objected to the use of such mentalistic concepts on a number of grounds:

1. If the concepts are carefully defined in terms of observations, then they can be of no real use because they add no new information. They may be harmful, however, either by misleading us into thinking that we have explained a phenomenon when in fact we have only named it, or by making us believe that the patterns we observe are things which have their own existence separate from the data.

2. If the concepts are not carefully defined, then the dangers are

greatly multiplied. Such concepts can smuggle in hidden assumptions to confuse and limit our thinking. They can conceal ambiguities which allow our would-be honest minds to play fast and loose with theory, interpreting it one way here and another there, never realizing its self-deception.

3. In either case, these concepts take our attention away from what is really important—the behavioral observations to which the concepts refer. It would be far better, the radical Behaviorists feel, to abandon such abstract concepts altogether, and deal directly with the observations themselves.

I agree with the Behaviorists that there are risks involved in using mentalistic concepts. I strongly disagree, though, that there are no corresponding advantages to be gained which could make the risks worth taking. In evaluating these advantages, I should make it clear that I disagree quite fundamentally with the radical Behaviorists' approach to psychology. For me (and for many others), the purpose of psychology is to infer the mental mechanisms which underlie behavior.

Behaviorists and nonBehaviorists alike agree that simply cataloging the facts of behavior is not an adequate approach to a science of psychology. The number of facts we could observe is huge and most of them are not worth knowing, by psychologists or anyone else. To understand the way in which people and animals behave, scientists need laws which summarize masses of complex facts. Where I differ (and where most cognitive psychologists differ) from the radical Behaviorists is that I believe these laws are best stated in terms of internal mental concepts and processes such as attitudes, memory structures, language-comprehending processes, and problem-solving strategies.

SUMMARY

The Behaviorists held that psychology was best viewed as the science of behavior. They rejected the method of introspection and de-emphasized or banished interpretations in terms of internal mental states or processes. The Behaviorists' primary interest was in the study of learning. They invented many useful research techniques and discovered a great deal about this topic. An important application of Behaviorist discoveries is the use of behavior modification in the treatment of mental patients. A negative effect of the Behaviorist program was that it tended to discourage the study of complex processes such as problem solving and language comprehension.

FURTHER READINGS

Howard Rachlen's very readable book, *Modern Behaviorism* (2d ed. San Francisco: Freeman, 1976) provides more information about the background of

Behaviorism and much more information about the Behaviorist program of research than is contained in this chapter.

More examples of applications of behavior modification may be found in L. Krasner and L. P. Ullman's *Research in Behavior Modification* (New York: Holt, Rinehart, and Winston, 1965). A thorough review of this important topic is provided in W. E. Craighead, A. E. Kazdin, and M. J. Mahoney's *Behavior Modification: Principles, Issues, and Applications* (Boston: Houghton-Mifflin, 1976).

In *Science and Human Behavior* (see References following), B. F. Skinner speculates about the application of Behaviorist principles to a wide variety of human concerns. In *Walden II* (New York: Macmillan, 1948), he presents his Behaviorist Utopia. Some claim that his Utopian dream is really a nightmare. In any case, it is intriguing.

REFERENCES

ANREP, G. V. "Pitch discrimination in the dog," *Journal of Physiology, 53* (1920), 367–385.

BRADY, J. V. "Ulcers in 'executive monkeys,' " *Scientific American, 199* (1958), 95–103.

BRELAND, K., and BRELAND, M. "The misbehavior of organisms," *American Psychologist, 16* (1961), 681–684.

GARRETT, H. E. *Great experiments in psychology*. New York: Appleton-Century, 1930.

HILGARD, E. R., and MARQUIS, D. G. *Conditioning and learning*. New York: Appleton-Century-Crofts, 1940.

HULL, C. L. "Knowledge and purpose as habit mechanisms," *Psychological Review, 37* (1930), 511–525.

ISAACS, W.; THOMAS, J.; and GOLDIAMOND, I. A case history, reported in *Introduction to modern behaviorism*, 2d ed. Ed. H. Rachlin. San Francisco: W. H. Freeman & Co., 1976. Pp. 182–184.

KIMBLE, G. A.; GARMEZY, N.; and ZIGLER, E. *Principles of general psychology*, 4th ed. Copyright © 1974, The Ronald Press Company, New York.

LIDDELL, H. A. "Conditioned reflex method and experimental neurosis," *Personality and the behavior disorders*. Ed. J. McV. Hunt. New York: Ronald, 1944.

LUNDIN, R. W. *Personality: An experimental approach*. New York: Macmillan, 1961. Pp. 178–183.

MILLER, N. E. "Studies of fear as an acquirable drive: I. Fear as motivation and fear reduction as reinforcement in the learning of new responses," *Journal of Experimental Psychology, 38* (1948), 89–101.

SEGAL, S. J. "The Perky effect: Changes in reality judgments with changing methods of inquiry," *Psychonomic Science, 12* (1968), 393–394.

SKINNER, B. F. *The behavior of organisms*. New York: Appleton-Century-Crofts, 1938.

SKINNER, B. F. *Science and human behavior*. New York: Macmillan, 1953.

SMITH, S. M.; BROWN, H. O.; TOMAN, J. E. P.; and GOODMAN, L. S. "The lack of cerebral effects of d-Tubocurarine," *Anesthesiology, 8* (1947), 1–14.

SOLOMON, R. L., and TURNER, L. H. "Discriminative classical conditioning in dogs paralyzed by curare can later control discriminative avoidance responses in the normal state," *Psychological Review, 69* (1962), 202–219.

THORNDIKE, E. L. "Animal intelligence: An experimental study of the associative processes in animals," *Psychological Review Monograph*, Suppl. II, No. 4 (1898).

WATSON, J. B. "Psychology as the Behaviorist views it," *Psychological Review, 20* (1913), 158–177.

WATSON, J. B. "The place of the conditioned reflex in psychology," *Psychological Review, 23* (1916), 89–117.

WATSON, J. B. *Behaviorism*. Chicago: University of Chicago Press, 1930.

YERKES, R. M., and MORGULIS, S. "The Method of Pavlov in animal psychology," *Psychological Bulletin, 6* (1909), 257–273.

Chapter 4

Gestalt psychology

The Gestalt revolution against Introspectionism was based on theoretical grounds entirely different from the Behaviorist revolution. The Behaviorists rebelled against the subjectivity of Introspectionism, but they accepted its Atomism. That is, they accepted the notion that psychological phenomena must be analyzed into elementary parts to be understood. In contrast, the Gestalt psychologists had no objection to subjectivity, but they objected very strenuously to the Introspectionists' insistence on analyzing phenomena into parts. They argued (convincingly, as we shall see) that psychological phenomena are organized wholes, which are likely to be destroyed by the kind of analysis the Introspectionists practiced. This emphasis on psychological phenomena as *organized wholes* is the central idea which shaped Gestalt theory and research.

FORM-QUALITIES

The primary breeding ground for the Gestalt rebellion lay in the field of perception. In 1890, C. von Ehrenfels, the most important predecessor of the Gestalt school, identified what he called form-qualities. These may best be understood through examples. Look at Figure 4–1A. What we see is a spiral formed of dots. If we examine each dot separately—for example, by looking at it through a narrow tube—we no longer perceive the spiral quality. This quality clearly does not come from the dots viewed separately. One must look at the dots in relation to one another to perceive it. Further, Figure 4–1B, which consists of entirely different elements, has the same spiral quality as Figure 4–1A. The spiral quality is an example of a form-quality.

Consider a simple tune such as "Yankee Doodle" played on the piano. If you were to tape-record it and play the notes back with long time-intervals between each, you would no longer perceive the tune.

Figure 4–1. Examples of form-qualities

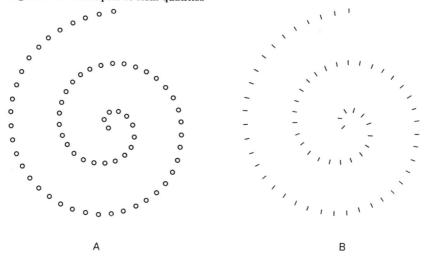

A   B

Hearing the tune depends not just on hearing the notes but on hearing them in relation to each other. Further, perceiving the tune does not depend on hearing one particular set of sounds. You can recognize the tune played in various different keys on the piano, or played on a bassoon, or hummed by a moderately tone-deaf drunk. The tune is another example of a form-quality.

These examples have two properties in common which make them both form-qualities:

1.   Perceiving them depends on perceiving parts in relation to each other—that is, in perceiving the parts as an organized whole. When we are dealing with form-qualities, the whole is more than the sum of its parts. The form-quality comes into existence only as a result of perceiving the relationship of the parts.

2.   The qualities are *transposable*. The same quality may be perceived in entirely different collections of parts as long as the critical relationships are present among the parts. For example, a tune is a form-quality that can be recognized whether it is sung in low registers or high.

For the Gestalt psychologists, form-qualities illustrated just what was futile about the Introspectionist program. Analysis into elements is the wrong way to study form-qualities since such analysis destroys what one would study, the organized whole. These qualities simply are not contained in the individual parts so that it is useless to search for them there. Rather, the appropriate way to study form-qualities is to identify the relationships on which they depend.

Organized wholes

An organized whole has some distinctive properties that depend on the relationships of its parts—that is, it has some form-qualities. Figures 4–1A and B are each organized wholes which share a form-quality. In addition to form-qualities, organized wholes typically have properties which are derived from the parts without considering their relationships. For example, if all of the dots in Figure 4–1a were red, the whole would have that property too.

Organized wholes are to be contrasted with mere collections of parts which are not perceived as having form-qualities. A chair is an organized whole. If we separate it into its parts, it becomes a mere collection of sticks. If we view Figure 4–1A through a tube which allows us to see only one dot at a time, we will perceive it as a mere collection of dots. If we view a painting through such a tube, we will perceive it as a disjoint collection of colored patches.

Analysis into parts destroys form-qualities and reduces organized wholes to mere collections. Clearly Introspectionist analysis is the wrong way to study organized wholes.

We should note that just as our perception of a whole depends on the relationships of the parts, our perception of the parts may be influenced by their relationship to the whole. For example, the horizontal lines in Figures 4–2A and B are in fact straight, though we perceive them as curved either up or down, depending on the whole in which they are embedded. Similarly, a radiantly happy smile which would look appropriate at a wedding would take on a distinctly sinister character if seen at a hanging.

For the Gestalt psychologists, the most interesting problem in psychology concerned the properties of organized wholes. Further, the Gestalt school was very productive in identifying such problems in the most diverse areas of psychology—in visual perception, brain physiology, memory, learning, problem solving, interpersonal relations, and so on and on. Perceiving the color of an object depends not just on the properties of that object but on its relation to the visual field taken as a whole. A piece of coal in sunlight looks black even though it reflects more light to the eye than a white piece of paper in the shade. It looks black because our perception of brightness depends not on the amount of light coming from the object but on the relation of that amount to the amount coming from other objects in the visual field. How we remember an item of information depends on its relation to the story in which it was embedded. Solving a detour problem depends on seeing relations between paths and goals. Understanding a comment depends upon knowing the person who said it and hearing the conversation of which it was a part.

Figure 4–2. The Hering figure, or fan illusion

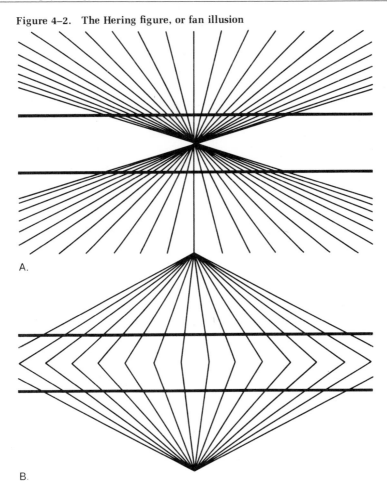

A.

B.

Since the interesting problems in psychology concerned the properties of organized wholes, and since these properties could not be
studied by Introspectionist analysis, it was clear to the Gestalt psychologists that they would have to introduce new methods if psychology
were to prosper. The first Gestalt study, which marked the beginning of
the rebellion, will illustrate these new methods and introduce the psychologists who championed them.

The Phi phenomenon

Throughout its period of prominence, Gestalt psychology was dominated by three major figures: Max Wertheimer (1880–1943), Kurt

Koffka (1886–1941), and Wolfgang Köhler (1887–1967). All contributed in important ways to Gestalt theory and experiment. The originating genius of the group, though, was clearly Wertheimer. It was he who in 1910 conceived and conducted the study of illusory movement which launched the school. As it happened, Köhler, Koffka, and Koffka's wife, Elisabeth, were the subjects of the experiment, but they were not collaborators. Because of the need to avoid subject bias, they were not even told the purpose of the study until it was completed. Clearly, Wertheimer was in charge.

The physical arrangements for the experiment were simple. The subjects were shown a pair of stimulus pictures, each presented very briefly in rapid succession by means of a tachistoscope. The time interval between the pictures was varied. Typical stimuli, shown in Figure 4–3, consisted of a white bar on a black background. While there was

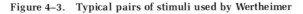

Figure 4–3. Typical pairs of stimuli used by Wertheimer

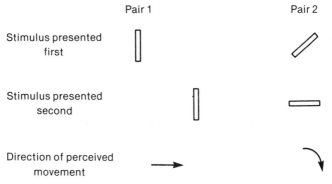

nothing unusual about the physical arrangements, the way the experiment was carried out was radically different from studies in Wundt's or Titchener's laboratories. This was true both in the way the subjects were trained and in the purposes for which the data were collected. First, Wertheimer's subjects were not trained to analyze their experience into elements. Failure to do so would have been unthinkable in an Introspectionist laboratory. Rather, the subjects were asked to report their experience freely, naively, in common sense terms, and utterly without analysis. If there were form-qualities in the subjects' perceptions, Wertheimer did not want them destroyed by analysis. This free and unbiased reporting of immediate experience is called the phenomenological method. It probably deserves a simpler name since it is just the familiar way we describe everyday experience in conversation. A subject in Wertheimer's experiment might say, for example, "I see a very clear smooth movement from the first place to the second," or, "I see the vertical line lay itself down."

The second innovation in experimental technique was that rather than trying to analyze the perceptions into elements, the experiment focused on identifying the conditions under which the perceptions occurred. Since the perception of motion depends on the relations of the stimulus elements, for example, the distances and time-intervals separating them, the sensible thing to do was to vary those relations to see how the perceived motion changed. This is just what Wertheimer did.

What the subject experienced depended on the time-interval between the stimulus pair. When the interval between the two exposures was small—less than 30 milliseconds—the subject saw the two lines as being simultaneously present with no motion at all. When the time-interval between exposures was increased, the subject reported seeing a single bar which moved (or rotated) from the first position to the second position. The best time-interval for seeing this movement was about 60 milliseconds. (Motion picture film typically runs at 18 to 24 frames per second or 42 to 55 milliseconds per picture.) When the time-interval was increased beyond 200 milliseconds, the two bars were seen as appearing successively but without any movement between them.

In the interval between 60 and 200 milliseconds, subjects reported two phenomena. The first was "partial" movement in which two separate bars were seen and one or both of them appeared to move. The second was the odd phenomenon of "pure movement." Here, the subjects saw two stationary bars and saw movement occurring in the region between the two. The movement, however, was not attached to any object. This pure movement is what Wertheimer called the Phi phenomenon.

Wertheimer's experiment was a clear and important success which helped to get the Gestalt school off to a running start. The experimental innovations—that is, the use of phenomenological observation tied to systematic variations of the experimental conditions—followed directly from the Gestalt view of what experimental psychology should be. Further, the major result, the discovery of the Phi phenomenon, provided an especially clear example of a form-quality which would be hard or impossible to deal with in Introspectionist terms. The experiment itself constituted an empirical breakthrough. Wertheimer showed that interesting results could be obtained by applying a new method to an old problem. The attention of the psychological community was captured. In the next 30 years, more than one hundred papers exploring and expanding Wertheimer's initial discovery tumbled from the scientific presses. A very auspicious start!

Principles of organization

It was natural that the Gestalt psychologists would give special attention to finding laws by which wholes are organized. They did this by borrowing from the work of others those principles they found useful and by conducting a great deal of research. Much of this work was in the field of visual perception. Combining new work with old, they were able to identify more than a hundred separate Gestalt laws of organization, and then generalize them to apply to such other mental functions as memory, learning, and problem solving. In much of their work, the Gestalt psychologists used visual perception as their primary model for the mind.

Below, I will describe five organizational principles which have been applied to a wide variety of psychological phenomena.

1. *The perceptual field is structured into figure and ground.* In general, when we look, we direct our attention to some thing in the visual field. That thing becomes the figure in our perception, and the rest of the visual field becomes the ground. Typically, we see the figure in greater detail than the ground and perceive it as being in front of the ground. The contour that separates the two is seen as bounding the figure but not the ground. This phenomenon is illustrated in Figure 4–4A. The drawing shown in Figure 4–4A is a reversible figure. It may be seen either as a white figure on a black ground or as a black figure on a white ground, depending on how we attend to it. Experiment with seeing it both ways and notice how the spatial relations between the white and black areas change and how the contour bounds either the white area or the black, depending on which area is seen as the figure.

Notice also that the ground is perceived as continuing behind the figure even though, of course, one cannot see it there. This perceived continuation of the ground behind the figure applies very widely in everyday perception. Think how surprised you would be if you picked up your knife and fork at dinner and found that they just neatly covered knife and fork shaped gaps in the table. Or worse, if a friend took off his hat and . . . but that's too horrible to consider. We really do assume that the ground continues behind the figure.

Another important aspect of the figure-ground relation is that it can be reorganized very rapidly. In Figure 4–4A, when you see the white area as figure first and then change to seeing the black area as figure, the shift is not gradual. It is sudden, like a light bulb turning on.

Perception of other relations is also subject to sudden reorganization. The cube shown in Figure 4–4B may be seen either with Corner A forward or with Corner B forward. When we switch from seeing the one to seeing the other, again the transition is extremely rapid. Sudden reorganization of perceptions such as these plays an important role in

Figure 4–4.   A reversible figure (A) and the necker cube

A. A reversible figure

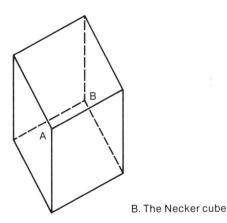

B. The Necker cube

Gestalt interpretations of phenomena such as humor and problem solving, as we will see.

Why are our perceptions subject to sudden reorganizations? The Gestalt psychologists suggested a physical analogy. Suppose that you have placed a loop of thread on a soap film, as shown in Figure 4–5A. The thread will lie in some irregular shape on the film with no particular tendency to change. If you now take the point of a pencil and break the soap film inside the loop of thread, a sudden reorganization will

Figure 4–5.   Action of a loop of thread on a soap film

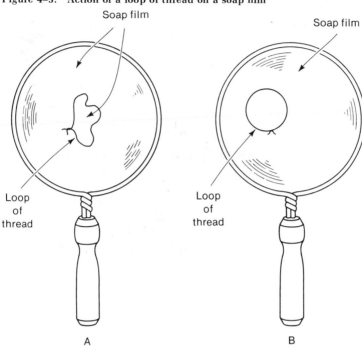

take place. Because of the forces inside the soap film which tend to contract it, the thread will now take on a circular shape. This new organization will be relatively stable. That is, if you try to change its shape by pushing on its edge with a pencil, it will change right back to its circular shape when you stop pushing.

The forces within the soap film established a stable equilibrium which was maintained until something disturbed it. Then, suddenly, the forces established a new equilibrium. According to the Gestalt psychologists, the figures in our visual field are like parts of the soap film exerting forces on each other. These forces establish an equilibrium. When the equilibrium is disturbed by some change in the visual field, these forces will suddenly establish a new equilibrium.

The Gestalt psychologists took this analogy between perceptual and physical situations very seriously. They believed that when we perceive a shape in the world, say, a square or a triangle, a corresponding shape is represented in nerve action somewhere in the brain. The internal square may be distorted in shape, but it will have four corners and four sides, just as the external square does. This matching of perceived forms to forms in the brain is the Gestalt principle of *isomorphism*. The internal representations are physiological and interact with each other in the brain through chemical or electrical effects. It is for this reason that figures in the perceptual field seem to interact as physical systems do. Gestalt psychology viewed mental phenomena as *isomorphic* to underlying physical phenomena. Thus, Gestalt psychologists often employed physiological theories to explain psychological events. One such theory is developed very elegantly by Köhler and Wallach (1944).

Figure-ground organization also characterizes our perception when we are listening to music or reading a story. When we listen to a song, typically we attend to the singer's voice, which becomes the figure, while the orchestral accompaniment becomes the ground. In a story, the main theme is the figure, and the peripheral details, the ground.

2. *The grouping of elements into wholes depends on the properties of the elements and their arrangement.*

a. Grouping depends on proximity. In Figure 4–6A, we see vertical rather than horizontal rows because the vertical distances between adjacent elements are smaller than the corresponding horizontal distances. In the same way, rhythmic groupings in music depend on closeness in time.

b. Grouping depends on similarity. In Figure 4–6B, although horizontal and vertical distances between elements are equal, we see horizontal rows because the elements are similar in the horizontal but not in the vertical direction.

The principle of grouping by similarity also applies to memory. W. A. Bousfield's (1953) experiment on free recall of word lists illustrates the point well. In this experiment, the subjects heard lists of words drawn from various categories such as names of trees, fish, places, and so forth. Within each list, the categories were thoroughly intermixed. For example, a subject might have heard the list *pine, flounder, carrot, Toronto, perch, zucchini, oak, Miami, maple, shark,* etc. When asked to recall the items in any way the subject pleased, the subject tended strongly to group them into their categories, recalling first a group of items in one category, then a group of items in another category, and so on.

c. Grouping depends on good continuation. In Figure 4–6C, we see the elements grouped into two strings, A–E–C and B–E–D, rather than, say, A–E–D and B–E–C, or into four strings. According to the principle, this grouping occurs because the string E–C is a good continuation of string A–E, whereas the string E–D, which makes a sharp corner with A–E, does not. This principle of good continuation has been used in a computer program for identifying objects from line drawings (Guzman, 1968).

Figure 4–6. Various groupings of elements

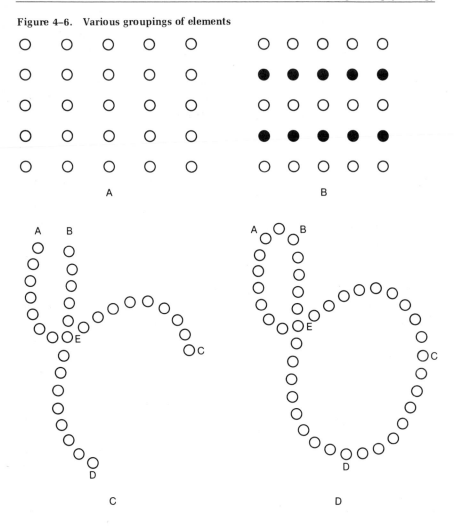

d. Grouping depends on closure. In Figure 4–6D, the strings
A–B–E–A and C–D–E–C are seen as grouped together because each
forms a closed whole. In this case, the principle of closure clearly dom-
inates the principle of good continuation which, as we saw in Figure
4–6C, would have given a very different grouping. These four principles of grouping—proximity, similarity, good continuation, and closure—are very important ones for Gestalt psychology.

3. *Organized wholes tend toward closure, simplicity, symmetry,
and regularity.* When visual forms are seen under bad viewing conditions, that is, conditions of great distance or poor illumination, the
forms will be perceived as more closed, simple, symmetric, and regular

than they actually are. Similarly, when we recall a story or a picture, we tend to remember it as more closed (or complete), simple, symmetric, and regular than it actually was. We repeated an experiment on memory for pictures by Bartlett (1932) to dramatize this point.

The experiment involved the subjects in a kind of team effort to remember a picture. For ten seconds the first subject was shown the picture marked "Original" in Figure 4–7. When the picture was taken away, the subject was asked to draw it from memory as well as possible. Reproduction 1 is the drawing which the first subject produced. Reproduction 1 was then shown to the second subject for ten seconds, who drew Reproduction 2 when asked to recall. The sequence of drawings in Figure 4–7 was produced by asking each of the subjects in sequence to recall the reproduction of the previous subject. Notice that three of the four marks inside the original figure are gradually transformed into a symmetric and regular whole (see especially Reproductions 5 through 7), while the fourth mark disappeared. This whole was then broken up (starting with Reproduction 8) to become the eyes and mouth of a still larger whole, the face, seen clearly from Reproduction 11 on.

Try this experiment yourself. As long as you start with a fairly complex irregular figure such as the original in Figure 4–7, you should be able to obtain similar results. That is, you should find that, step by step, the figure becomes simpler, more closed, more symmetrical, and more regular. If you start with a figure that is simple, closed, symmetrical, and regular to begin with, however, you can expect relatively little change. Such a figure is called a "good Gestalt." The circle is perhaps the best example of a good Gestalt. More generally, a good Gestalt is a whole whose organization resists change despite conditions which tend to distort other poorer figures. The best forms are simple, closed, symmetric, and regular.

4. *Organized wholes tend to be perceived as objects.* With an effort, we can view Figure 4–8A as a single group of lines arranged on a flat page. From one point of view, that is just what it is. What we interpret as a pyramid is actually the set of lines shown in Figure 4–8B. It is much easier and more natural, though, to see it as a set of geometric forms arranged in space. Rather than seeing the line groups in Figure 4–8A as flat shapes adjacent to each other on a flat page, we see a pyramid partly hidden by a cube and a sphere. The forms that we see are thing-like. They appear solid and permanent. We can imagine walking around them to see their other side. We can imagine picking them up and rotating them or painting them green. In short, we perceive them as *objects.*

This point is extremely important. For the Gestalt psychologists, our perception of the world is a perception of objects arranged in space. It is not a perception of colored patches from which we infer objects in

Figure 4–7.   Step-by-step results of an experiment on memory for pictures

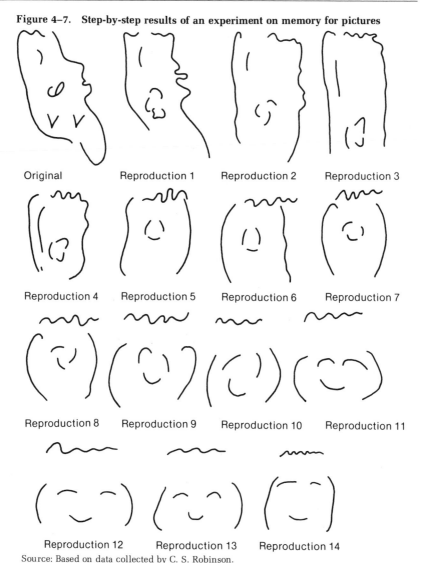

Source: Based on data collected by C. S. Robinson.

space. The objects are given immediately in perception without an extra-inference process.

5.   *Objects are perceived as having constant properties.* As we mentioned earlier, we see a lump of coal as black and a piece of paper as white despite very large changes in the amount of light coming to our eyes from these objects. Under most viewing conditions objects are perceived as having constant color.

Figure 4–8. Tendency to be perceived as objects of organized wholes

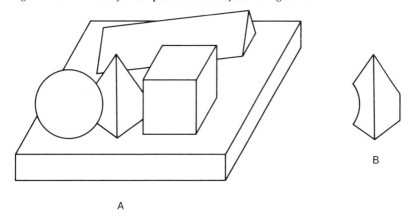

A

B

Objects are also perceived as having constant shape and size. We see all of the dinner plates on the table as circular disks of the same size although the images they project on our retina are elipses of various sizes and eccentricities.

You can perform a simple demonstration that illustrates very dramatically how important shape-constancy is in determining the appearance of objects. Construct a one to one-and-a-half inch cube from thin wire, leaving an extra piece of wire projecting from one corner to hold it by. Look at the cube with one eye (to remove the binocular cues to depth), and rotate it slowly. The outline which the cube projects on the retina is constantly changing, of course, but usually you will perceive a cube of fixed shape rotating in space. Sometimes, though, as you watch the cube, you are fooled about the direction in which it is rotating. When this happens, the cube seems to suffer a strange series of distortions. As it rotates, some of its parts seem to shrink while others expand in a most repellant way. When shape-constancy is not operating in the usual way, the world looks very strange indeed!

Objects also show constancy in size. When a friend walks away from us, our retinal image of the person shrinks in proportion to the distance. We do not, however, see the person as shrinking, but rather as being of a constant size located successively at greater distances. Size-constancy works over a very wide range of horizontal distances. An object the size of a person will keep its apparent size for distances up to a half mile (Gibson, 1950), or about as far as it can be distinguished. Size-constancy does not work very well, however, for vertical distances. This is why people look strangely ant-like when we look down at them from the top of a building at a vertical distance of well under 100 feet.

Clearly, the Gestalt principles of organization are powerful and pervasive. In the next section, we will discuss their origins in learning and inheritance.

Nativism

Gestalt psychology has often been associated with the Nativist position in the Nativist-Empiricist controversy. Actually, it was not so much that the Gestalt psychologists were *for* Nativism. Gestalt theory was quite neutral on this issue. Rather, they were not *against* Nativism as the Behaviorists (and other Associationists) vehemently were.

The Gestalt psychologists recognized the influence of experience in perception. They recognized that familiarity could be an important factor in determining how wholes were organized and remembered. They knew that one could learn to take an analytic attitude in perception (as the Introspectionists trained their subjects to do) and that this attitude could influence the subject's perceptions.

In addition, however, they felt that there were very important innate factors in perception. In particular, they felt that such fundamental processes as segregation into figure and ground and depth perception were primarily innate.

M. V. Senden (1960) amassed a fascinating collection of observations on people who first achieved sight when they were old enough to talk about it. These people were cataract victims from birth who had their vision restored by operation somewhere between the ages of 3 and 40. Up until the time of the operation, their visual world was an amorphous blur which would be brighter by day and darker by night. Some could distinguish changes in the color of the blur, but none could see form.

What the patients were able to see in their first look at the world was both surprising and disappointing. When an object was presented to the patients shortly after the operation, they saw it as a whole—as a figure against a ground. If two objects of different shape were presented, say a circle and a triangle, the patients could often, but not always, tell that they were different. However, if they were asked to say which one was the triangle, a shape they knew by touch, even the most cooperative and intelligent patients had to search painstakingly for corners.

These observations suggest that figure-ground organization and the ability to discriminate form are innate. However, visual form recognition—that is, connecting an object's visual form with its tactual form or its name—requires training. Recognizing even such simple forms as squares and triangles may require weeks of training.

Koffka (1924) noted that coordinated eye movements occur as early as the first day of life. This suggested to him that depth perception was present at birth. Since that time, considerable evidence has been amassed on the perceptual capabilities of human infants to indicate that Koffka was right. This evidence will be reviewed in Chapter 5.

The Gestalt psychologists, then, believed that perception depends in important ways *both* on learned and on innate factors.

Goals

In addition to the Gestalt laws of perceptual organization, there is another organizing principle concerned with actions which was extremely important in the work of the Gestalt school. This is the principle of *purposiveness.* Kurt Lewin, who extended Gestalt ideas to social psychology, illustrated the principle with a simple example contrasting the Gestalt and stimulus-response points of view (Lewin, 1926). The example below is paraphrased from Lewin.

Suppose that you are going for a walk and you have decided to take a letter along to mail on the way. You put the letter in your pocket and remind yourself that when you see a mailbox, you should mail the letter. Interpreted in stimulus-response terms, you are setting up a bond between the mailbox as stimulus and mailing the letter as a response. On the walk, you see a mailbox and you mail the letter.

So far, the incident fits the stimulus-response view reasonably well. But, according to the S-R psychologists, the bond should have been strengthened by practice. When you come to a second mailbox, your letter mailing response should be even stronger. You should feel a powerful urge to mail your wallet, old ticket stubs, lint, or anything else that you find in that same pocket. Actually, of course, your letter-mailing response is much weaker. It is as if by putting the letter in the box and saying, "Well, that's done," you have wiped the bond out entirely.

A better way to describe the situation, according to Lewin, is to forget all about S-R bonds. Instead, we should say that when you put the letter in your pocket with the intention of mailing it, a *tension* was set up. When you put the letter in the box, you relieved that tension and so it no longer influenced your behavior. If you had given the letter to a mail carrier on the way to the first box, that action or any action which would have gotten the letter safely on its way would have dispelled the tension. The tension, then, is to accomplish a goal, not to perform a specific response.

Action may be described as purposive, or goal-directed. We perform actions in order to accomplish goals. Anything that separates us from the goal is a gap which must be closed by action. The tension which motivates the action is analogous to the forces which tend to close perceptual gaps. The principle of purposiveness may be viewed as an extension of the law of closure to actions.

In the next section, we will see how Köhler used the principle of purposiveness in describing problem solving in chimpanzees. It will again be extremely useful to us in the chapter on computer simulation when we discuss the organization of computer programs designed to simulate thought processes.

Köhler's apes

In 1913, after three years of working in close association with Wertheimer, Köhler went to the primate station on the island of Tenerife in the Canary Islands to study the behavior of apes. Trapped there during World War I by a British blockade, he did the work which resulted in his most famous book, *The Mentality of Apes*. While the work was done early in the history of the Gestalt movement, it illustrates very nicely how the Gestalt laws of perceptual organization and the principle of purposiveness could be applied in the analysis of problem solving and understanding.

To study problem solving, Köhler took quite a different approach from that of Thorndike. As we saw in the last chapter, Thorndike had decided, on the basis of his experiment, that problem solving was a gradual process. Köhler felt that Thorndike's experimental method determined the results that he obtained. In the puzzle-box experiments, the cats were given no opportunity to behave intelligently. They had no way of seeing or understanding the latch mechanism in the puzzle box. Hence, the only procedure available to them was blind trial and error. It would be wrong to conclude from such an experiment that trial and error was all that the animals were capable of.

In contrast to Thorndike's procedures, Köhler always made sure that his subjects could see (or know about) all of the problem elements and their relationships. Under these circumstances, Köhler found that *sudden* problem solutions are not uncommon.

A typical experiment was arranged as follows. The ape Sultan was brought alone into a large outdoor enclosure. A basket of fruit was hung from the wire ceiling too high for the ape to reach without help of some sort. A number of objects was available in full view inside the cage, including two boxes and some sticks of various lengths. At first Sultan paid no attention to the boxes. Rather, he tried to knock down the fruit with the sticks. First, he used a stick that was far too short. Then he abandoned the short stick for one that was the right length but was too heavy for him to use effectively. Exercising great restraint, he kicked and hammered on the walls, threw the sticks across the cage, and slumped down in a heap to pout. After he had recovered a little, he gazed at the boxes momentarily and then suddenly leaped up, grabbed the nearest one, dragged it under the fruit, climbed up and got his snack.

In this case, there was a clear search of the visual field before the sudden appearance of the solution. In the case described below, however, no such visual search is observed. The solution occurs to the animal suddenly while he is very intently doing something else.

In this study, the experimenter made sure that Sultan had seen a box in a corridor leading to the main cage. Again a basket of fruit was hung out of reach from the ceiling of the cage. Sultan searched for a tool to aid him in knocking down the fruit and settled on the long bolt attached to the door of the corridor. Hanging on the door, he pulled at the bolt with all his strength, trying to get it loose. Suddenly and without apparent cause, Sultan stopped what he was doing and remained motionless for a moment. Then he jumped down, ran into the corridor, and returned with the box to solve the problem. At the moment when his behavior took a new direction, he could not see the box because the door hid it from his view. It would appear that he suddenly remembered the box and perceived its relation to the problem he was trying to solve.

Both of these cases may be interpreted as sudden reorganizations of Sultan's perception of the situation. In one case, the reorganization was triggered by seeing a box and in the other by remembering a box. The reorganization involved not just becoming aware of the box but understanding its relation to the goal and how it could be used in the problem solution. Such sudden reorganization of the perception of a situation and seeing the important relationships is called *insight*. For the Gestalt psychologists, insight characterizes intelligent problem solving.

The animal's behavior just after the moment of insight also reveals important properties of the problem-solving process. Suppose that one of the apes is slumped down in a corner thinking ravenous thoughts about the fruit hanging from the ceiling. Suddenly, he has the insight that he can use the stick about ten feet away on his right to knock down the basket. In an instant, he is up and running toward the stick. As he approaches it, his hand is already extended to grab it, and he has started to lean into the left-hand turn he will have to make toward the fruit once he has the stick. The whole performance is smooth and continuous. It is an organized whole in which the properties of the parts are modified to fit well into the whole. This smooth-running action sequence convinces us that the animal knew what he was doing when he started—that he had a preformed plan.

The process of insightful problem solving may be described in Gestalt terms as follows. A tension to achieve a goal is established and the problem solver searches for a way to achieve it. Until a way is found, there is a gap in the plan for solution which demands closure. An insight allows the problem solver to perceive new relations in the situation and to construct a plan for solution. The plan is then carried out, barring mishaps, in a smooth-flowing sequence of actions. The goal is achieved and the tension dissipated.

The Gestalt psychologists characterized insightful problem solving as intelligent and contrasted it with noninsightful trial-and-error behavior such as Thorndike's cats displayed. Now, the behavior of Köhler's apes was by no means uniformly intelligent or insightful. In many problem situations, even though all of the elements needed for solution were visible, an ape simply failed to see the appropriate relations. In other cases, the apes would attempt solutions that were really stupid. In one case, when food was placed on the ground outside the cage, Sultan built a tower of boxes to reach it! In the same situation, Grande dragged heavy stones around in her cage. In these and many similar examples of apparent ape idiocy, the attempted solution procedure was one that had been appropriate in previous problems. Sultan, for example, had just been involved in box-building experiments continuously for four weeks, and Grande had been through a series using stones. Köhler attributes such errors to *mechanization*—that is, to the tendency for a solution technique to be used less and less intelligently when it is repeated many times. In the next section we will discuss mechanization and related phenomena in human thinking.

Set and functional fixity

"Set" may be defined as a readiness to perceive or act in particular ways in a situation. For example, in a baseball game if you expect a fast pitch, you set yourself to swing early. If you hear that people like you, you may be set to perceive good qualities in them when you meet, for example, excellent judgment, intelligence, and so on. If you expect to be presented with a problem of a particular type, you may be set to use a particular solution procedure.

A. S. Luchins (1942) studied set in a sequence of water-measuring puzzles. In each problem, the subject's task was to measure out a specified quantity of water using several imaginary jugs. The capacities of the jugs varied from problem to problem. For example, in Problem 1 shown in Figure 4–9, the solution is to fill the 29-quart jug (A) and then to fill the 3-quart jug (B) from it three times. This leaves the desired quantity—20 quarts—in the large jug. Problem 2 and all the remaining problems except Problem 9 can be solved by the formula B minus A minus 2C—that is, by filling the large jug and then using it to fill the A jug once and the C jug twice. The critical fact about Luchins' experiment is that Problems 7 through 11 can also be solved by a simpler procedure which does not involve the big jug at all. Thus, Problems

Figure 4–9. Luchins' water jug problems

Problem	Jug A	Jug B	Jug C	Quantity desired
1. Practice	29	3		20
2. Difficult method only	21	127	3	100
3. Difficult method only	14	163	25	99
4. Difficult method only	18	43	10	5
5. Difficult method only	9	42	6	21
6. Difficult method only	20	59	4	31
7. Either method	23	49	3	20
8. Either method	15	39	3	18
9. Easy method only	28	76	3	25
10. Either method	18	48	4	22
11. Either method	14	36	8	6

Source: Adapted from A. S. Luchins, "Mechanization in Problem Solving," *Psychological Monographs,* 54 (6) (1942), Whole No. 248, p. 1.

2 through 6 may be viewed as set-inducing problems, Problems 7 and 8 and 10 and 11 are set-measuring problems, and Problem 9, since it can not be solved by the formula B minus A minus 2C, is a set-breaking problem. Using college students as subjects, Luchins found that 81 percent used the more difficult method in Problems 7 and 8, and 79 percent used the more difficult method in Problems 10 and 11. Apparently, the set-breaking problem did not have its intended effect of reducing the subjects' set for using the more difficult procedure.

Functional fixity may be defined as an inability to perceive that an object which is known to have one use may be used for an entirely different purpose. For example, we may search through our desk drawers for a straight edge, fail to find one, and draw the line freehand. It never occurs to us that the drawer itself could have been used as a straight edge.

An experiment performed by R. E. Adamson (1952) illustrates how functional fixity can interfere with problem solving. The subjects' task was to mount three candles in burning position on a wall within a 20-minute time limit. To do this, the subjects could use any of a number of objects which were spread on a table. These included three candles, three cardboard boxes, some matches, some thumbtacks, and a number of irrelevant objects which served to confuse and distract. In the experimental condition, one of the boxes contained the candles; a second, the matches; and a third, the tacks. In the control condition, the boxes were empty. Twenty-four of the 28 subjects in the control condition solved the problem whereas only 12 of the 29 subjects in the experimental group did so. The difference between the two groups was statistically reliable. Clearly, using the boxes as containers made it more difficult for the subjects to see their possible use as candle holders.

A surprising example of functional fixity turned up in Köhler's experiment with apes. What was surprising was that it was the experimenter rather than the ape who showed functional fixity. The experimenter had hung a basket of fruit from the ceiling for the usual climbing experiment and stood off to the side to observe. The ape, making a variety of begging noises, tugged at the experimenter's hand and led him over to the goal. Then, instead of pointing and indicating, "Help, help," the ape climbed up on him, planted his furry feet on his head, and grabbed the fruit. The ape was able to see a person as an ambulatory stepladder, but the person, perhaps because of human dignity, could not. After this, the experimenter always resisted the apes' entreaties to come and stand under the goal.

Clearly, both set and functional fixity can interfere with problem solving. In recent years, considerable money and effort have been devoted, especially in business settings, to reducing these negative effects. A. Osborn's (1952) brainstorming technique and W. J. Gordon's (1961) Synectics are two examples of a large number of schemes which have been marketed to help business people and engineers improve their problem-solving skills by reducing the effect of set and functional fixity. These techniques will be discussed in Chapter 12.

SUMMARY

We have seen that Gestalt psychology differs from other psychologies in a number of important ways. The Gestalt psychologists were concerned with the properties of organized wholes rather than analysis of consciousness into its elements. They were much more interested in perception than in learning, and they believed that the mind was influenced in important ways by heredity as well as by experience. They explained mental phenomena through the laws of perceptual organization rather than the laws of association or the laws of conditioning. Finally, they emphasized a number of phenomena such as closure, goal directedness, insight, and set which other schools had difficulty explaining.

FURTHER READING

For the reader who would like to investigate Gestalt psychology in greater detail, there are several good sources, listed in References following. Köhler's Gestalt Psychology (1947) and his Dynamics in Psychology (1940) are easy introductions to Gestalt psychology and make very pleasant reading. In Productive Thinking (1959), Wertheimer applies Gestalt ideas to education and problem solving. His writing style is excellent, and the book is fun to read.

REFERENCES

ADAMSON, R. E. "Functional fixedness as related to problem solving: A repetition of three experiments," *Journal of Experimental Psychology, 44* (1952), pp. 288–291.

BARTLETT, F. C. *Remembering.* Cambridge, England: Cambridge University Press, 1932.

BOUSFIELD, W. A. "The occurrence of clustering in recall of randomly arranged associates," *Journal of General Psychology, 49* (1953), pp. 229–273.

GIBSON, J. J. *The perception of the visual world.* Boston: Houghton Mifflin, 1950.

GORDON, W. J. *Synectics: The development of creative power.* New York: Harper & Row, 1961.

GREGORY, R. L. *Eye and brain.* New York: McGraw-Hill Book Company, © 1966. Used with permission of McGraw-Hill Book Company.

GUZMAN, A. "Decomposition of a visual scene into three-dimensional bodies," *Automatic interpretation and classification of images,* ed. A. Grasselli. New York: Academic Press, 1968.

KOFFKA, K. *The growth of the mind.* New York: Harcourt, Brace, 1924.

KÖHLER, W. *Dynamics in psychology.* New York: Liveright, 1940.

KÖHLER, W. *Gestalt psychology.* New York: Liveright, 1947.

KÖHLER, W. *The mentality of apes.* London: Routledge & Kegan Paul, 1925.

KÖHLER, W., and WALLACH, H. "Figural aftereffects: An investigation of visual processes," *Proceedings of the American Philosophical Society, 88* (1944), pp. 269–357.

LEWIN, K. "Vorsatz, Wille und Bedurfnis," *Psychologische Forschung, 7* (1926), p. 335.

LUCHINS, A. S. "Mechanization in problem solving," *Psychological Monographs, 54* (6) (1942), Whole No. 248.

OSBORN, A. *Your creative power.* New York: Scribner, 1952.

SENDEN, M. V. *Space and sight.* Glencoe, Illinois: Free Press, 1960.

WERTHEIMER, M. "Experimentelle Studien uber das Sehen von Bewegung," *Zeitscrift fur Psychologie, 61* (1912), pp. 161–265.

WERTHEIMER, M. *Productive thinking.* New York: Harper & Row, 1959.

SECTION II

DEVELOPMENTS IN PSYCHOLOGY

Introduction

We have seen that the Structuralists tried to account for psychological phenomena through the laws of association, the Behaviorists through the laws of conditioning, and the Gestalt psychologists through the laws of perceptual organization.

These groups contributed greatly to our knowledge of association, learning, perception, memory, and problem solving. Further, many of their ideas are still influential. We saw that there are modern association theories of memory. Behaviorist and Gestalt principles such as the law of effect and the laws of perceptual organization are still recognized as valid.

In the next section we will discuss developments in the fields of psychology, computer science, and linguistics which forced psychologists to look beyond these early psychologies for new ways to study human thought.

Chapter 5

Child development I: The infant looks at the world

In this chapter and the next one, we shall leave Behaviorism and Gestalt temporarily and consider the problem of thought from another point of view—that of developmental psychology. The dominant figure in the psychology of children's thought for the last 40 years has been the Swiss psychologist, Jean Piaget. Consequently, much of what is said here will be drawn from his observations and his theories.

In this chapter, we will introduce Piaget's approach to psychology by describing a small but revealing segment of his work, his research on the infant's perception of objects. In Chapter 6, we will discuss the whole range of Piaget's work on development from birth through adolescence.

Piaget

American psychology has been slow to assimilate the work of Piaget. Part of the trouble has been that Piaget is not an easy author to read. His subject matter is difficult, his style is often unclear, and many of his original French works have not been translated into English. He has been enormously prolific, turning out 30 books and more than 150 articles.

The real barrier to Piaget's acceptance, however, has not been his literary style but rather his scientific style. Among American psychologists, tradition favors rigidly controlled experimental procedures, careful statistical analysis of data, extreme caution in drawing conclusions, and an all-pervading interest in the process of learning. It would be difficult to find a psychologist who fits this tradition more poorly than Piaget. Piaget uses what he calls a clinical method in which the experimenter may vary the procedure from trial to trial in ways that he feels appropriate to the individual child. Piaget does almost no statistical analysis of his data. He rarely goes so far as to compute an average value, and he often fails even to mention how many subjects he observed. If he is interested in the study of learning, that interest certainly is not reflected very strongly in his work. Rather than being cautious in drawing conclusions, Piaget is daring. He is interested in generating a broad-ranging theory of human cognitive development, and to do this he proposes bold hypotheses which may have little factual support. He does not stop to establish each point firmly before going on to the next. Indeed, it would have cramped his very creative scientific style to do so.

In this section, we will present observations by Piaget and others about the way the world appears to the infant. In the next chapter we will discuss Piaget's ideas about how the child moves from motor skills to intelligent thought.

What the infant sees

How does the world look to infants when they first open their eyes? Almost certainly the answer is "Terrible." Our best evidence is that during the first few hours of life, infants cannot bring the world into clear focus. They can neither converge their eyes on an object nor can they accommodate the lenses of their eyes to the distance of the object. The resulting image of the world must be a very blurry and confusing one indeed. For these first few hours at least, we can believe William James (1890, p. 496) when he says that the world of the infant is "probably one unanalyzed bloom of confusion."

Fortunately, this initial period of confusion does not last forever. After the first few hours of life, infants begin to show rudimentary accommodation (the ability to adjust the lens of the eye to focus on far or near objects) and convergence (the ability to turn both eyes toward the same object). As early as the first day, they will track moving lights with their eyes (Mussen, Conger, and Kagan, 1969). By eight weeks of age, children are thoroughly adept at convergence (Mussen et al., 1969).

As children get better at convergence and the other visual motor skills, they see the world more and more clearly. R. L. Fantz (1961) demonstrated this increasing ability in an extremely clever series of experiments. He placed an infant on its back in a well-lighted observation box so that (1) the child could observe a pair of patterns displayed about ten inches above on the ceiling of the box, and (2) the experimenter could observe the child's eyes by looking through a peephole in the top of the box. By noting which way the child's eyes were turned, the experimenter could determine what proportion of time the child spent in looking at each pattern. Fantz reasoned, quite sensibly, that if children showed a preference for one pattern over another, then they must at least be able to distinguish between them. Fantz then attempted to use evidence of preference to test visual acuity in the following way. He presented children with a choice between a uniform gray card and a card with a set of black and white stripes of the same average brightness as the gray. Children less than one month old prefer the striped card to the gray one only if the stripes are at least an eighth of an inch across. The fact that they show no such preference for narrower stripes means, presumably, that the narrower blur together into a uniform gray. By six months of age, children show a preference for stripes as narrow as 1/64th of an inch in width. Thus, visual acuity improves radically over the first six months of life. Starting from almost nothing in the first hour of life, the one-month-old child can see well enough to distinguish the lines of print in a book at ordinary reading distance, and by six months of age can see well enough to distinguish the individual letters.

Fantz extended his experiment to determine if the child could respond to pattern as well as to detail. Children between 15 days and five and a half months of age chose between two faces: one with normal features and one with scrambled features. The children showed a preference for the real face even at the youngest ages tested.

In similar tests, children between one and six weeks of age displayed a clear preference for a striped pattern instead of a bull's-eye. These results show that the very young child responds not just to the presence or absence of details in the visual field but also, and more importantly, to the arrangement of these details. Within the first six months, then, children are able to discriminate patterns.

Pattern recognition, that is, identifying a pattern as one that was seen before, must be differentiated clearly from pattern discrimination. While discrimination is certainly essential for recognition, it is not sufficient in itself to guarantee recognition. The fact that these two processes are distinct is made dramatically clear in cases of individuals who can discriminate patterns but not recognize them. One such case is that of a boy who first acquired vision at nine years of age as the result of a cataract operation. A few days after his operation, he was shown a sphere and a cube together. While he had never seen either before, he could tell immediately that there was a difference between the two forms. This easy discrimination, however, was not accompanied by correspondingly easy recognition. In fact, he acquired the ability to name them correctly only after many days of intensive practice (Senden, 1960).

Two experiments definitely establish that the infant can recognize visual patterns by the age of six months. The first experiment was performed by Bing-Chung Ling (1946). Ling presented infants with two different solid, wooden shapes which they could see and touch. One of the two shapes, say, a circle, was always attached firmly to the table so that it could not be moved. The other, say, a triangle, was free to be picked up. Children being what they are, the triangles went directly into their mouths. At this point, the children discovered that wily old Ling had coated the triangles with syrup (presumably in partial compensation for the fact that he was feeding them old pine board already well-chewed by hundreds of other infants). Under these circumstances, even the six-month-olds (the youngest subjects tested by Ling) learned to reach consistently for the triangle rather than the circle.

The second experiment, performed by Harriet Rheingold (1956), concerned the recognition of a human by an infant. For her subjects, Rheingold selected 16 six-month-old infants who were being raised in an institution. By institutional practice, each of the infants received care from many different people. Eight of the infants were continued on the usual institutional care. The other eight were mothered by Rheingold herself eight hours a day, five days a week, for eight weeks. (If you wonder why only five days a week, try your own hand at raising octuplets!) During this time, Rheingold attempted to be as good a substitute mother as possible, caring for all the children's needs and playing with them. Each week the infants were tested for social responsiveness to the experimenter and to the examiner, a person who was exposed equally to the experimental and the control infants. The test of social responsiveness consisted of several items. First, the adult would stand near the child's crib and smile without speaking. Then the adult would lean over the crib and say, "Hello, baby, how are you?" and so on. The child's social responsiveness was gauged by such measures as quickness and duration with which the child looked at the adult, smiling, screams, and so on. By the second week, children who had been raised by the experimenter were considerably more responsive to her than they were to the examiner. The control children showed no such difference in responsiveness between experimenter and examiner. This responsiveness continued throughout the experiment and for at least a month beyond—that is, for as long as the measurements were continued. Clearly, the experimental children had learned to recognize Dr. Rheingold.

Together, the Ling and Rheingold studies demonstrate that the infant can recognize visual patterns, either simple or complex, as early as the sixth month of life.

In another very ingenious experiment, Gibson and Walk (1960) showed that young children have depth perception, which they demonstrate in a very dramatic way by perceiving depth well enough to avoid crawling over a cliff. To do this safely, Gibson and Walk designed the "visual cliff" (see Figure 5–1). Basically, the apparatus is a thick

Figure 5–1.   The visual "cliff"

Source: E. J. Gibson and R. R. Walk. *Scientific American, 202,*
1961, p. 65. Photographer: William Vandivert. By permission.

sheet of glass suspended about chest high above the floor. The glass is
divided in half by a plank which serves as a starting platform for the
infant. On one side of the plank, the shallow side, a checkerboard surface is placed directly under the glass. On the other side, the deep side,
the checkerboard surface is placed several feet below the glass. In an
experimental trial, an infant between 6 and 14 months of age is placed
on the starting platform. The mother then calls the infant to come to
her, first from the deep side, and then from the shallow side. The question, of course, was, "Will the child crawl out onto the deep side or
avoid it?" The answer was quite clear-cut—the babies refused to crawl
out on the deep side. E. J. Gibson and R. R. Walk, (1960, p. 64) put their
result this way: "The experiment thus demonstrated that most human
infants can discriminate depth as soon as they can crawl."

Do not take this evidence as license to leave a child on the edge of the
stairs, however. Some of the children, when trying to reach their
mothers on the shallow side, accidentally shifted into reverse, and
ZAP!—right over the cliff! (unhurt, of course). A six-month-old may be
able to perceive depth and still be clumsy.

Now what does all this add up to? We have seen that by six months
of age the child has the ability to see detail, to discriminate and
recognize patterns, and to perceive depth. Can we now conclude that
the child sees the world in much the same way we do? In the common-

sense view, the answer is clearly "Yes." In fact, it is difficult for most of us to imagine that the world could appear different to others. We can handle a few variations from the standard because we have experienced them. We can imagine a blurry world because we have all seen blur. We already know, though, that the child sees more than blur. We also know that the appearance of things depends on familiarity with them. Turkish script looks strange and unintelligible to us compared to English, and a new neighborhood may look quite forbidding until we are used to it. We can conceive that the child's world, then, may look strange because it is so new. When it comes to really fundamental matters, however, common sense demands that children must see things much as we do. Uncle Charlie may appear strange and out of focus to the child, but he is still an entity separable from his cigar and the wallpaper. He is solid, located in space, with a back as well as a front. Furthermore, he will persist and continue to occupy space, even if we do not look at him. In short, Uncle Charlie is what we adults call "an object."

These points seem terribly trivial, but they are just the kinds of properties which Piaget, in *The Construction of Reality in the Child* (1954), says do not apply to the infant's view of the world. Piaget claims that infants younger than eight or nine months of age do not have the object concept. He claims that the child's world is populated instead with images, that is, with evanescent visions which arise from nothing, which have a front but no back, and which, when they are out of sight, are nowhere.

In this view, the child treats the world much as we would treat a three-dimensional movie. When the heroine looks out at us from the screen, we do not expect the back of her image to stick out the back of the screen. Nor do we expect the images of the characters from the last episode to be waiting beside the screen, or anywhere, until their next appearance. We do not assign them a location in space the way we do for a real object. When they are not visible on the screen, they are simply gone. They are still capable of being recreated, of course, but for the moment, they have no spatial location at all.

Why does Piaget take this wild position? Why does he reject the simple natural commonsense position that the world looks essentially the same to child and adult? For two reasons. First, he believes that the adult conceptions of space and objects are complex—so complex that he does not believe an infant can handle them. Second, in his observations of children, Piaget has noticed certain difficulties which children have dealing with objects. For example, children younger than eight or nine months behave differently from older children toward a vanished object. When an object vanishes behind a screen, younger children simply give up the search instead of trying to remove the screen. In the following example, Piaget reports the behavior of his daughter, Jacqueline:

At 0;8 (16) [that is, at zero years, eight months and 16 days] . . . while she watches, I place her little bells under the coverlet . . . . I shake the whole thing to make the bells ring. No reaction. As long as she hears the noise she laughs but then her eyes follow my fingers instead of searching under the coverlet.

Then I pull the string attached to the bells, which has remained visible. She imitates the sound and listens to it but still does not look under the coverlet. I then raise it in order to reveal the object; Jacqueline quickly stretches out her hand, but just when she is about to get it, I cover it up again and Jacqueline withdraws her hand. I repeat the experiment but this time hide the bells behind a fold in the sheet; same negative reaction, despite the sound (Piaget, 1954, p. 40).

According to Piaget, the reason that children fail to look for the object behind the screen is not that they are physically incapable of doing so. Indeed, by six or seven months children are able to do a great deal of grasping and removing of such objects as eyeglasses and noses. Piaget claims that children fail to look behind the screen because they can not represent a space that they can not see. When the bells disappear under the coverlet, in effect they fall off the end of the world.

But surely, you may say, the scientific evidence must show that Piaget is mistaken. Doesn't the fact that even day-old infants track images mean that they attribute some permanence to them? Indeed, Piaget believes that the skills which infants use to prolong an image, such as the ability to track, are precursors of the object concept. But clearly these skills are not in themselves sufficient to guarantee that infants have the object concept. A sophisticated radar can do as good a job of tracking images as an infant, perhaps better. It can lose sight of its airplane for brief periods of time, predict where it ought next to be seen, and be looking there expectantly when the plane reappears. The radar acts as if it believes in its airplane, at least for a little while, even while it can not see it. Even so, we do not attribute an object concept to the radar. We know that there are no mechanisms in its innards to represent other planes it has seen in the past. It would be thoroughly out of character if our radar set were to say to us, "Say, isn't that the same DC–3 that came by last Thursday? I'd recognize its reflectance pattern anywhere."

If the ability to track is not sufficient evidence that the child has the object concept, perhaps the ability to recognize is. After all, an image that the child has recognized must have some sort of lasting representation in the child's mind. Piaget grants this permanence but feels that recognition is not necessarily a recognition of objects. He can imagine that the child could recognize the image of Mother and yet not have the cognitive equipment which would be required to assign her a location in space when she is out of sight. For Piaget, recognition is a necessary step toward the object concept but it is not in itself sufficient.

THE SENSORIMOTOR PERIOD

If the child does not have the object concept to start with, then where does it come from? The object concept develops, according to Piaget, during the first year and a half of life—that is, during the part of the child's life that Piaget calls the *sensorimotor period*.

Piaget divides the sensorimotor period into six stages. The child's schedule for passing through these stages is shown very roughly in Table 5–1.

Table 5–1. Progression in the sensorimotor period

Stage	Months
1	0– 1 month
2	1– 4 months
3	4– 8 months
4	8–12 months
5	12–18 months
6	18–24 months

Piaget intends these boundaries to be taken as approximations. They are meant only as estimates of extremely variable quantities. The boundaries between stages may vary not only from child to child but also from culture to culture, depending on the child's experiences. Piaget believes that the age limits of the various stages are flexible, but that the sequence in which children go through them is not. The accomplishments of each stage are built on the accomplishments of the previous stage. Thus the order of the stages is immutable in the developmental process.

While the object concept makes its first official appearance in Stage 4 of the sensorimotor period, its development is continuous from Stage 1 through Stage 6. According to Piaget, the object concept and the child's conception of space develop out of the child's activity in trying to adjust to the world. Piaget sees human development as a continuous interaction of the adaptive processes by which children *assimilate* the world to themselves—that is, change the world to suit themselves—and those processes by which they *accommodate* themselves to the world—that is, change themselves to suit the world. Two such interrelated processes which are important in the development of the object concept are *intersensory coordination* and *sensorimotor accommodation*.

Intersensory coordination

Piaget holds that the very young child has many spaces—a visual space, a buccal (mouth) space, a tactile space, an auditory space, and so on, but that these various spaces are not well coordinated in the infant. A major development during the first two years is that these spaces are unified into a single space. The process by which this unification occurs is called intersensory coordination.

Intersensory coordination promotes the object concept in two ways. First, it leads to expectations. When children begin to look in the direction of a ringing bell, they are coordinating auditory and visual space. At the same time, they develop the expectation of seeing a bell where they look. Thus the image of the bell achieves a bit more permanence (because children believe in it before they see it) and a bit more solidity (because it is an image supported by a sound).

Second, and perhaps more important, intersensory coordination often makes use of one sense to understand another sense. Here is a particularly dramatic example of a man whose vision was grossly disturbed when he lost his vestibular sense, the sense having to do with balance and head position.

John Crawford, a physician and later a professor at Harvard Medical School, suffered the loss of his vestibular sense as a side effect of intensive antibiotic therapy. His first indication of trouble occurred one morning while washing his face. When he covered his eyes with the washcloth, he fell down as if pushed. He reports the progress of his disease first hand:

Through that first day symptoms increased rapidly. Every movement in bed now gave rise to vertigo and nausea, even when I kept my eyes open. If I shut my eyes, the symptoms were intensified. At first I found that by lying on my back and steadying myself by gripping the bars at the head of the bed, I could be reasonably comfortable. Later, even in this position the pulse beat in my head became a noticeable motion disturbing my equilibrium.

Making an analogy to a motion picture, Crawford says:

Imagine the result of a sequence taken by pointing the camera straight ahead, holding it against the chest and walking at a normal pace down a city street . . . . the street seems to career crazily in all directions, faces of approaching persons become blurred and unrecognizable, and the viewer may even experience a feeling of dizziness or nausea as he watches. Our vestibular apparatus normally acts like the tripod and smoothly moving carriage on which the camera of the professional motion picture taker is mounted. Without these steadying influences, the motion picture is joggled and blurred (Crawford, 1952, p. 57).

Crawford never did recover the use of his vestibular sense. He did find, however, that he could compensate greatly for the effects of his sensory loss. Concerning reading, for example, he says:

By bracing my head between two of the metal bars at the head of the bed I found I could minimize the effect of the pulse beat that made the letters on the page jump and blur. By using a finger or a pencil on the page I gradually learned to keep my place.

Concerning movement, he says:

> Already I had discovered as I lay in bed that turning my head from side to side while looking forward produced the sensation that the room was turning around me, rather than that I was turning around in the room (Crawford, 1952, p. 58).

Concerning walking, he says:

> There was too much motion in my visual picture of the surroundings to permit recognition of fine details. I learned that I must stop and stand still in order to read the lettering on a sign (Crawford, 1952, p. 60).

Crawford's case makes two things very clear. First, maintaining an understandable schema for space in an adult, and presumably developing such a schema in the child, depends critically on coordination of the senses. Piaget believes that these coordinations develop as a result of the child's activity in the early stages of the sensorimotor period. Thumb-sucking allows contact between buccal and tactile space, for example. Second, the maintenance of a unified spatial schema is not just a convenience. It is essential to normal adult functioning. Until he built new coordinations to replace the old, Crawford was effectively crippled.

Sensorimotor accommodations

For Piaget, sensorimotor accommodations are extremely important in the genesis of the object concept. Sensorimotor accommodations are the activities which children engage in to adapt their senses to the world—activities such as following a moving object with the eyes or groping to find an object which has escaped the hand. Sensorimotor accommodations are important in preparing the way for the object concept because they act to increase the permanence of our images. Suppose that we could not track rapidly moving objects. Every time we dropped something from our hand, it would simply disappear. This condition could hardly strengthen our belief in the permanence of the things in the world around us.

If we are to believe Piaget, sensorimotor accommodations bring with them a surprising property of the children's world, the tendency of children to view the world as being at the disposal of their actions. This conception of the world at the children's disposal is a pure inference on Piaget's part, but it is a very interesting inference. Piaget reasons as follows: Adults believe that when they turn their heads, they are simply seeing a new section of an all-enveloping space, and that the things they see in that section of space were located there even when they were not looking at it. To keep oneself located in this space requires (1) very complex coordination of vision with the senses which designate body position, and (2) the ability to represent things not presently visible. Young children have not mastered the coordination of space as the adult has. Piaget believes that these functions are beyond children and that, as a result, their interpretation of what they see is much less sophisticated. When children turn their heads, somehow images leap into view. They do not think of them as coming from anywhere—they can not conceive of the space from which the images might have come because they can not see it. The images are simply created out of nothing by the children's act of turning their heads. Such a belief would be quite in line with the children's other experiences. After all, it is no more remarkable to be able to create images by turning your head than it is to create sound by moving your hand against the side of the crib or to create milk by sucking. Images created out of nothing by the children's act also disappear into nothing. This does not mean that they can never appear again. As Piaget put it: ". . . the vanished image remains, so to speak, 'at disposal' without being found anywhere from a spatial point of view. It remains what an occult spirit is to a magician; ready to return if one catches it successfully . . . ." (Piaget, 1954, p. 12).

The idea that things cease to exist when they are out of sight applies not only to whole things but also to parts of things. Thus, Piaget claims that when we bring a child's bottle out from concealment, the child believes it is being recreated right there on the spot. When the child is looking at one side of an object, the concealed side does not exist for the child. Piaget illustrates his position with an observation of his son Laurent:

> . . . Laurent recognizes his bottle no matter what part of it is visible. If he sees the nipple, his reaction is natural, but even when he sees the wrong end his desire is the same; hence he admits at least the virtual entireness of the bottle. . . . But . . . this wholeness is considered by the child as only virtual. Everything occurs as though the child believed that the object is alternately made and unmade; if . . . the bottle is presented to Laurent upside down, he will consider it incomplete and lacking a nipple, at the same time expecting the nipple to appear sooner or later in one way or another. When the child sees a part of the object emerge from behind the screen . . . [he believes] it is in the process of being formed at the moment of leaving the screen (Piaget, 1954, p. 33).

> From 0 ; 7 (0) until 0 ; 9 (4) Laurent is subjected to a series of tests . . . to see if he can turn the bottle over and find the nipple when he does not see it. The experiment yields absolutely constant results; if Laurent sees the nipple he brings it to his mouth, but if he does not see it, he makes no attempt to turn the bottle over [although he is clearly capable of doing so]. The object, therefore, has no reverse side or, to put it differently, it is not three dimensional (Piaget, 1954, pp. 33–34).

Thus, during the first three sensorimotor stages, that is, during the first eight months or so of life, children are developing skills which extend the permanence of the images they see. As yet, however, they have no concept of the object. As Piaget puts it, "The child's world is still only a totality of pictures emerging from nothingness at the moment of action, to return to nothingness at the moment when the action is finished" (Piaget, 1954, pp. 46–47).

The object concept finally emerges in Stage 4. Children can now represent things spatially with sufficient facility so that they can imagine something being hidden behind a screen. Piaget describes an early instance in his daughter Jacqueline:

> At 0 ; 9 (8) . . . Jacqueline is seated on a sofa and tries to get hold of my watch. I place it under the edge of the coverlet on which the child is seated; Jacqueline immediately pulls the edge of the coverlet, spies the watch, and takes possession of it. I again hide the object, she finds it, and so on eight times in succession (Piaget, 1954, p. 51).

While the child may be said to have a true object concept, that does not mean that the concept is fully developed in the adult sense. Piaget provides several rather startling observations which make this point quite clear. First, Piaget hides an object at a location A and the child finds it at A. Then Piaget takes the object and, while the child watches, hides it at B. What does the child do?

> At 0 ; 10 (18) Jacqueline is seated on a mattress without anything to disturb or distract her (no coverlets, etc.). I take her parrot from her hands and hide it twice in succession under the mattress, on her left, in A. Both times Jacqueline looks for the object immediately and grabs it. Then I take it from her hands and move it very slowly before her eyes to the corresponding place on her right, under the mattress, in B. Jacqueline watches this movement very attentively, but at the moment when the parrot disappears in B she turns to her left and looks where it was before in A (Piaget, 1954, p. 56).

> At 0 ; 10 (9) Lucienne [Piaget's other daughter] is seated on a sofa and plays with a plush duck. I put it on her lap and place a small red cushion on top of the duck (this is position A); Lucienne immediately raises the cushion and takes hold of the duck. I then place the duck next to her on the sofa, in B, and cover it with another cushion, a yellow one. Lucienne has watched all my moves, but as soon as the duck is hidden, she returns to the little cushion A on her lap, raises it and searches. An expression of disappointment; she turns it over in every direction and gives up.

> Same reaction three times in succession (Piaget, 1954, p. 57).

An adult might do this sort of thing once in a while when distracted or on an especially bad morning. On just such a morning recently, while I was flogging my night table for concealing my watch, I discovered it on my wrist where I had strapped it only moments before.

The behavior of Stage 4 children really is not like that of adults, though. When the Stage 4 children search in the wrong place, it is not an inadvertance that they feel stupid about for the rest of the day. It is a systematic aspect of children's search which is the rule rather than the exception. Stage 4 children will make this same "mistake" several times in a row.

Progressing from Stage 4 to Stage 5, children gradually become more adult in their methods of searching for hidden objects. Late in Stage 4, the child searches first at B, but still shows traces of a tendency to search at A. Piaget gives the following example:

> At 0 ; 11 (7) Jacqueline is seated between two cushions, A and B. I hide a brush under A. Jacqueline raises the cushion, finds the brush and grasps it. I take it from her and hide it under B, but quite far down. Jacqueline searches for it in B, but indolently, and then returns to A where she pursues her investigations with much more energy (Piaget, 1954, p. 61).

By Stage 5, the child responds appropriately to visual cues about where things are hidden. Again Jacqueline demonstrates:

> At 1 ; 0 (20) Jacqueline watches me hide my watch under cushion A on her left, then under cushion B on her right. In the latter case she immediately searches in the right place. If I bury the object deep she searches for a long time, then gives up, but does not return to A (Piaget, 1954, p. 74).

At this point you might think that children have achieved the full object concept, but not so! By Stage 5, children can deal with transformations of objects that they can see, but cannot as yet deal as an adult would with transformations that they cannot see. Piaget did the following experiment to demonstrate this Stage 5 characteristic. He placed a potato in a box without a top. Then he hid the box behind the screen and removed the potato. Here is an example, again starring Jacqueline at age 1 ; 6 (8):

> I then take the potato and put it under the box while Jacqueline watches. Then I place the box under the rug and turn it upside down, thus leaving the object hidden by the rug without letting the child see my maneuver, and I bring out the empty box. I say to Jacqueline, who has not stopped looking at the rug . . . : "Give Papa the potato." She searches for the object in the box, looks at me, again looks at the box minutely, looks at the rug, etc., but it does not occur to her to raise the rug in order to find the potato underneath.
>
> During the five subsequent attempts the reaction is uniformly negative. I begin again, however, each time putting the object in the box as the child watches, putting the box under the rug, and bringing it out empty. Each

time Jacqueline looks in the box, then looks at everything around her including the rug, but does not search under it (Piaget, 1954, pp. 75–76).

At Stage 5, the defect in Jacqueline's object concept was that she could not imagine transformations of the object which she could not see. By Stage 6, this defect disappeared. Another Piaget example illustrates what he feels is, at last, the mature form of the object concept.

At 1 ; 7 (20) Jacqueline watches me when I put a coin in my hand, then put my hand under a coverlet. I withdraw my hand closed; Jacqueline opens it, then searches under the coverlet until she finds the object. I take the coin back at once, put it in my hand and then slip my closed hand under a cushion situated on the other side (on her left . . .); Jacqueline immediately searches for the object under the cushion. I repeat the experiment by hiding the coin under a jacket; Jacqueline finds it without hesitation (Piaget, 1954, p. 88).

Thus, Piaget feels that far from being born fully equipped with an object concept, children have to develop it over the course of more than a year and a half.

SUMMARY

Piaget holds that the infant does not have an object concept similar to that of the adult. The adult object concept is a complex mental structure which enables us to represent objects as having a location in space or as undergoing changes even when they are not in view. This structure develops in a series of stages over the first two years. Important in its development are processes of intersensory coordination (for example, visually guided reaching) and sensorimotor accommodation (for example, visual tracking).

FURTHER READING

More detailed information about the development of the object concept is presented in Piaget's *The Construction of Reality in the Child,* see References following.

REFERENCES

CRAWFORD, J. "Living without a balancing mechanism," *When doctors are patients.* Eds. M. Pinner and B. F. Miller. New York: Norton, 1952.

FANTZ, R. L. "The origin of form perception," *Scientific American, 204* (1961), pp. 66–72.

GIBSON, E. J., and WALK, R. R. "The 'visual cliff,' " *Scientific American, April* (1960), pp. 64–71.

JAMES, W.   *The principles of psychology.* New York: Holt, 1890.

LING, BING-CHUNG.   "The solving of problem situations by the preschool child," *The Journal of Genetic Psychology,* 68 (1946), pp. 3–28.

MUSSEN, P. H.; CONGER, J. J.; and KAGAN, J.   *Child development and personality,* 3d ed. New York: Harper & Row, 1969.

PIAGET, J.   *The construction of reality in the child.* Trans. M. Cook. © 1954 by Basic Books, Inc., Publishers, New York.

RHEINGOLD, H. L.   "The modification of social responsiveness in institutional babies," *Monographs of the Society for Research in Child Development,* 1956.

SENDEN, M. V.   *Space and sight.* Glencoe, Illinois: Free Press, 1960.

Chapter 6

Child development II: From reflexes to scientific thought

In the last chapter, we treated a very narrow segment of Piaget's work, his research on the infant's perception of the world. Piaget is concerned with more than how the world looks to an infant. He is interested in the whole range of intellectual development from birth to adolescence. His theories cover such diverse accomplishments as how infants learn to suck their thumbs and how teen-agers achieve scientific thought (if, by good fortune, they achieve thought at all). In fact, as we shall see, Piaget believes that these two accomplishments, thumb-sucking and scientific thought, are distantly related to each other.

Piaget's task is to explain how the enormous complexity of adult intelligence develops from the simple reflexes which the child possesses at birth. The transition from the infant's mind to that of the adult involves many complex changes. Observing development is something like watching clouds on the horizon. At first you may see very little that is recognizable, but soon you discover some definite structures—a buffalo, a long thin face, and so forth. As you continue to watch, these initial structures slowly change. They are distorted, divided, and/or combined to form new structures. The changes, of course, continue and the new structures are soon transformed into still newer ones by the same processes.

The developmental changes which Piaget describes in mental structures are like the changes in cloud structures. In development, the initial structures are reflex activities such as sucking and grasping. These structures change with experience. They are modified, elaborated, differentiated, and combined to form new and more complex structures. As development continues, these new structures are

92

transformed into still newer ones and so on into adult life. (Yes, despite rumors to the contrary, development does not end at 16 or 21.)

Adapting and organizing

Piaget attributes developmental change to two important tendencies in the child (and indeed in any living thing)—a tendency to adapt and a tendency to organize. The tendency to adapt is a tendency to increase the fit between one's self and the world. This can be done by changing the world to fit ourselves—a process called assimilation—or by changing ourselves to fit the world—a process called accommodation—or by both. Assimilation and accommodation, then, are complementary aspects of adaptation. The more we can change the world, the less we have to change ourselves, and vice versa. Most adaptive acts involve *both* assimilation and accommodation. When eating, people both assimilate and accommodate. They assimilate the food first by chewing it and thus changing it into a form suitable for swallowing, and then by digesting it to change its chemical structure into one the body can use. People accommodate by driving to the hamburger stand (and thus changing their position) in order to get the food to assimilate. Assimilation and accommodation occur in intellectual activities as well. Thus, if a lecturer speaks very quietly, we may accommodate by being quiet and listening attentively. If the lecturer inserts unfamiliar foreign phrases in the lecture, we may assimilate them to more familiar English words. For example, when my young daughter first heard the name of the French composer, Jacques Ibert, she assimilated it to the more familiar and friendly name, Jacky Bear.

Actually, in Piaget's theory, it is not people or at least not whole people who do the assimilating and accommodating. It is schemas. A schema is an organized process for taking some action or for handling some information. My daughter, and the rest of us, may be said to have a word-recognition schema which can assimilate unfamiliar sounds to familiar words. The young infant has a sucking schema. While the primary object of this schema is the nipple, it will assimilate other objects such as the infant's fingers and toes and visiting aunts' noses. When the schema assimilates a new object, it may have to accommodate to the object as well. For example, if the infant gets the pacifier turned around backwards, the plastic ring may be assimilated to the sucking schema. In doing so, the infant may have to accommodate the sucking schema to the ring, as we may readily judge by the odd expression the effort gives to the infant's face.

The tendency to organize is responsible for combining originally separate schemas to serve a joint goal. At about three months, Piaget finds that vision and prehension (grasping) are essentially independent schemas. For example, when Lucienne was three months and 13 days old, Piaget (1963) observed that she spent considerable time watching her hands. If the hand moved, she would follow it with her eyes, but vision seemed to exercise no control over the movement. If her hand was grasped, she tried to free it but did not look. If her rattle was placed next to her hand, she would watch both but would not bring her hand closer. If the rattle touched her hand, however, she grasped it immediately. Piaget makes similar observations with Jacqueline and Laurent, his other children. If the hand or an object in the hand happens to come into the field of view, the child will look at it.

By six months or before, the child does coordinate vision and grasping much to the consternation of those in charge. Anything that comes into sight—eyeglasses, noses, tonsils—will be seized promptly in the child's steely grip, to be released only when some more interesting event, such as a piercing scream of agony, distracts the child's attention.

How is this skill developed? Piaget tells us that it is not through any external reinforcement of correct responses such as Behaviorists might suggest. Nor is it a simple matter of maturation as Gestalt psychologists might propose. Rather, it is the result of the unreinforced experience of watching the hands move about and manipulate the world. This experience provides the opportunity for the schema of vision and the schema of prehension to be coordinated with each other.

The evidence which Piaget presents for his conclusions is characteristically scanty. We might be tempted to dismiss them if it were not for the startling support they receive in a brilliant experiment by Held and Bauer (1967).

Monkeys raised in the usual way are very skillful before they are a month old in reaching for things they see. To find out what role the experience of seeing their hands might play in the development of this skill, Held and Bauer raised two macaques so that the monkeys were completely deprived of the sight of their hands for their first 35 days. The monkeys were confined to a chair, and their necks were surrounded by a wide collar which hid the rest of their bodies from sight. From Day 16 to Day 34, the monkeys were conditioned to extend their hands whenever their bottle was presented. At first the presentation of the bottle resulted in flailing responses, but soon the animals settled down to making a stereotyped extension unrelated to the position in which the bottle was presented.

On Day 35, the experimental monkeys were first allowed to view their hands. The collar was removed, one arm was restrained, and the bottle was presented. The stereotyped arm extension was started but was soon interrupted when the animals caught sight of their own hands for the first time. The monkeys now forgot everything else and simply watched fascinated at the strange new objects which moved about now in a manner quite unlike the stereotyped conditioned extension. Visual following of their own hands was much more prolonged than the following of other visual objects such as the hand of another baby monkey. In fact, at first the monkeys' fascination with their own hands made it quite difficult to get a good estimate of the accuracy of their visually guided reaching. They just were not interested in looking at anything else. After a few days, when the initial fascination began to wear off, it became clear that the monkeys were very clumsy at reaching. Not until the animals had had 20 days of practice (one hour a day) did they become skillful.

Now that one hand had been trained, the procedure was repeated with the other hand for each monkey. Again, as soon as the unexposed hands came into view, the monkeys went into an orgy of hand watching. On several occasions, the newly exposed hands were grabbed by the old familiar hands and moved around as if they were foreign objects. The second limbs improved rapidly, however, and after about ten days they seemed nearly as good as the first ones for grasping.

Held and Bauer came to essentially the same conclusion that Piaget did:

1.   That visually guided reaching is not innate. Rather its development requires the specific experience of watching the moving hand.
2.   That the function of this experience is in Held and Bauer's terms to integrate the control system for head-and-eye movements with the control system for hand movements. Translated into the equivalent Piagetian language, the experience coordinated the schemas of vision and prehension.

Periods of development

While development is really continuous, progress seems more rapid at some times than at others. Perhaps we judge progress for a child as we do for an inventor. The inventor may work hard every day perfecting a device a bit at a time. When it finally works, though, we see the inventor as having made sudden enormous progress and mark the day as the day of "the invention." In the same way, the child makes progress each day by accumulating experience in diverse areas. When over a relatively short period of time this experience is organized into a principle, for example, that thought can substitute for action, that a name is not a part of a thing, that pouring never changes the volume of a liquid, and so forth, we see the child as having made sudden progress. Piaget uses such apparently sudden discoveries by the child—sudden changes in the child's way of dealing with the world—to mark the boundaries between four major periods of development:

1. The sensorimotor period from birth to two years.
2. The preoperational period from two to seven years.
3. The period of concrete operations from seven to eleven years.
4. The period of formal operations after eleven years.

In the previous chapter, we were concerned entirely with the six stages of the sensorimotor period. During this period the child's intelligence seems to be primarily motor in character. That is, problems are solved not by manipulating internal images and symbols but rather by direct physical attack. The child does not represent the world; instead, the child acts on it.

At the end of the sensorimotor period, the nature of the child's thought changes radically. The motor acts which had previously served the functions of thought now give way to a more flexible method. The child can now solve problems by manipulating internal representations of the world. When this development has occurred, the child has entered the second or preoperational period.

The thought processes of preoperational children differ from those of children in later periods in a number of ways:

1. The logical processes of preoperational children are relatively loosely organized. For example, preoperational children frequently contradict themselves and seem to feel no need to resolve the contradiction.
2. Preoperational children have difficulty in recognizing points of view other than their own. They are egocentric in their thinking.
3. Preoperational children have difficulty in dealing with more than one aspect of a situation at a time. For example, in comparing areas, their judgments may depend on length or width, but not on both together.

Concrete operational children differ from preoperational children in the following ways:

1. Their logical processes are much more tightly structured. Self-contradiction is no longer acceptable.
2. They can recognize points of view other than their own; and
3. They can take several aspects of a situation into account simultaneously. For example, they can use height, width, and depth in making judgments of volume.

The characteristic of concrete operational children which distinguishes them from formal operational children is that while they can reason very well about concrete situations—that is, about things they can see and touch—they have difficulty in dealing with imaginary and hypothetical situations.

Finally, when the child reaches the stage of formal operations, thought is essentially adult. The child can now deal comfortably not only with concrete but also with hypothetical or imaginary situations and is now capable of the hypothetical-deductive reasoning characteristic of scientific thought. While Piaget suggests ages for each of these periods, they are intended only as rough approximations and are in no way essential to the theory. He freely recognizes that the boundaries of the stages occur at different ages for different children. The thing that is essential to Piaget's theory is the order of the stages, not the specific times at which the stages occur. Since each stage builds on the previous one, it is inconceivable in this theory that the period of formal operations, for example, should come before the period of concrete operations.

From the sensorimotor period to the preoperational period

Newborns do none of the things that are typically described as intelligent. They solve no problems. They have neither language nor social graces. What *can* they do? They can sneeze and hiccough. They can suck and grasp reflexively. They can cry and they can look at things. All of these activities are very useful to the infant, but they are very primitive. Nevertheless, Piaget holds that human intelligence has its origins in these elementary actions. He believes that these unpromising raw materials—these reflexive motor schemas—are modified to form new and intelligent action patterns by the tendencies to organize and adapt.

The connection of thought and motor activity may suggest Behaviorism to our suspicious minds, but in fact Piaget is no Behaviorist. While he agrees with the Behaviorists on some points, he disagrees with them on many others:

1.   He agrees with the Behaviorists (and the Associationists) that experience is essential for the development of intelligence. For example, he believes that a child is able to coordinate vision and grasping from about three to six months of age, depending on the child's experience.

2.   More dramatically, he differs from the Behaviorists because he believes that the child's thought soon outgrows the motor level. By two years of age, the child has developed the ability to make internal representations of the world. Internal representation turns out to be a very powerful problem-solving tool indeed. With the advent of this new tool, some problems become solvable for the first time and others are solved more quickly than before.

In the sections below, we will describe the properties of each of Piaget's developmental periods in more detail and will then discuss the implications of Piaget's theory for cognitive psychology.

Symbolic thought.   In the sensorimotor period, children make many fundamental advances. They learn to guide their hands with their eyes, to recognize familiar faces, to walk and explore, and they are well on their way to acquiring speech and symbolic thought. The child's intelligence during this period, however, is still severely limited. It is still largely motor in character.

In the previous chapter, we saw a typical example of sensorimotor problem solving. The child saw a rattle and reached for it. When vision was blocked, however, effort ceased. Out of sight *was* out of mind. The child showed no persistent plans—no symbolic representations of things not currently in view—just a chain of actions and perceptions which was easily broken when sensory contact failed.

The advent of symbolic thought marks one of the most important transitions in the child's intellectual development. It is the most important outcome of the sensorimotor period. As we saw in the previous chapter, by about 18 months children have acquired a fully operational object concept. They can persist in trying to find an object which is out of sight and they can imagine things happening to that object while it is out of sight.

The ability to represent unseen objects and to manipulate the representations provides the child with powerful new problem-solving procedures. Piaget presents some examples to illustrate the effectiveness of these new procedures. When his daughter Jacqueline was 15 months old and in the fifth stage of the sensorimotor period, Piaget posed a problem which she found surprisingly difficult (Piaget, 1963, pp. 305–306). While Jacqueline was sitting in her playpen, Piaget placed a stick on the outside parallel to the side of the pen. Jacqueline's problem was to get this interesting stick inside the playpen. Her first approach was the very direct one of grabbing the stick by its middle and pulling. The result was that the horizontal stick jammed itself against the bars and obstinately refused to come through. On her second attempt, she accidentally tilted the stick. Seizing her opportunity, she turned the stick vertically and pulled it through. On her third through 16th trials, she pulled the stick up to the bars in the horizontal position, and when it jammed she turned it to the vertical position. Finally, on Trial 17, she tilted the stick into the vertical position before it touched the bars, and pulled it without difficulty into the pen. On Trials 18 and 19, she tried to bring the stick through horizontally again. Then when it jammed she quickly recognized her mistake and brought it through vertically. Finally, from Trial 20 on, she systematically turned the stick before it hit the bars.

Let us compare this rather pedestrian performance of Jacqueline's with that of her sister Lucienne (Piaget, 1963, p. 336). At 13 months, Lucienne was already in Stage six of the sensorimotor period. Given the same problem as Jacqueline, Lucienne reached through the bars of her crib, grabbed the stick, and tried to bring it through horizontally. When it jammed on this first trial, she tilted it vertically and brought it into the crib. On all subsequent trials, Lucienne tilted the stick before it touched the bars and brought it into the crib easily.

According to Piaget, the crucial difference between these two children was that Jacqueline, in Stage five, still dealt with the world through actions. To solve the problem, she learned a motor response by trial and error. Lucienne, however, in Stage six, solved the problem by manipulating internal representations.

Before Stage six, children can solve problems only by active experimentation, that is, by trial and error. In Stage six, however, they switch over to a new mode of operation. Now they can discover things by mental rather than physical experiment.

Piaget believes that the internal representations develop out of motor acts. He has observed many instances in which the child, before developing the ability to represent the world internally, represents things and events through motor acts. An example is provided in the phenomenon he calls motor recognition. Piaget's children played with familiar toys in very characteristic ways (Piaget, 1963, pp. 337–338). Lucienne made her celluloid parrots move by shaking them with her foot and played with her doll by swinging it in her hand. Laurent typically played with his rattle by striking it. Often when the children noticed a familiar object at a distance, they would very briefly execute the characteristic action appropriate to the object. Piaget believes that the action substitutes for internal representation in the recognition process.

A more dramatic example of representation occurred when Lucienne was in Stage five (Piaget, 1963, pp. 337–338). Piaget had hidden a watch chain inside a match box and then closed it so that only a narrow opening remained. Lucienne did not know how to open the box, but she did know how to turn the box over so as to dump the chain out and how to poke her finger inside the box to fish the chain out. She tried this last strategy, but failed because the box was too nearly closed. Now Lucienne had a problem and here is how she solved it.

She looked very attentively at the slit. Then, again and again she opened and shut her mouth—just a bit at first, but then wider and wider. Then, without hesitating, Lucienne put her finger into the slit, pulled to enlarge the opening, and finally grasped the chain.

Piaget believes that Lucienne used the motor representation to help her solve the problem. The motor act, he feels, served the same function that a mental image might for an adult.

The preoperational period

During the sensorimotor period, the child forges fundamental concepts and dimensions on which later development in thought will be built. Space, time, objects, causality, symbols—all are examples. In this section, we will be concerned with the next period of development, which Piaget calls the preoperational period. This period extends from about two years of age to approximately seven. The differences between adult and child are much less radical during this period than during the sensorimotor period. At the beginning of the preoperational period, when children are about two years old, they seem surprisingly human to adults who knew them as infants. They can speak whole sentences such as "Allgone dogfood," which means that they have again beaten Spot to the dog's dish, and "Bye-bye tick-tock," said as mother's wristwatch disappears into the toilet.

By three-and-a-half, children have many accomplishments. They can carve their own mashed potatoes unassisted, they can apply the question "Why?" in any situation whatsoever, and they have acquired an awesome command of language. They use about a thousand words in their own conversation and can understand many more in the conversation of others (Miller, 1951). In spite of these accomplishments, the child's thought is still unmistakably childish. It is the nature of this childishness that we will explore here.

While four-year-olds have a firm grasp of the object concept, they still do not understand the physical world in the same way the adult does. For example, they do not understand that the quantity of a substance remains the same when it is poured from one container to another. Further, young children do not understand the thinking of those around them in the same way that adults do. We will explore this topic by describing the child's progression from egocentric to socialized thought.

Egocentrism

One of the most important properties which Piaget attributes to the thought of preoperational children is the property of egocentrism. As the name implies, egocentrism is a kind of self-centeredness, but it is not the kind that we call selfishness. Rather it refers to the surprising inability of young children to realize that there are points of view other than their own.

Egocentrism must be clearly distinguished from selfishness. A child can be egocentric without being selfish or can behave selfishly without being egocentric. For example, an older child may say to a younger one, "If you give me that little penny [a dime], I will give you this great big penny [a nickel]." Here, the older child is being selfishly acquisitive but also very nonegocentric. The behavior is nonegocentric exactly because it requires the older child to take the younger child's point of view concerning value and size of coin into account. It is selfish because the child's own values are put first, not because the child fails to realize that other values exist.

On the other hand, a child may be egocentric and yet unselfish. One child, for example, is reported to have offered a work-sodden father the use of a good left sucking thumb to help Daddy recover from the effects of the day. Such an offer is clearly unselfish above and beyond the call of filial devotion. It is egocentric in that the child assumes that what comforts the child would comfort anyone.

Piaget diagnoses egocentrism in childish thought on the basis of three kinds of symptoms. First, in observing children's play groups, he noted that many of the remarks that children make do not appear to be directed to anyone. They are soliloquies in which the child pays little attention to the audience and appears not to expect a reply.

Imagine a nursery school in which children are sitting around a low table drawing.

First child (who is drawing a house): "I'm putting in the big tree that's in front of my house." (No one answers—the child doesn't notice.)

First child: "I'm making it green."

Second child (who is drawing people): "You can't make them green. They'll look sick."

Third child: "I have my own crayons at home."

First child: "I'm putting in my dog."

Etc.

Piaget finds that between 50 and 60 percent of the remarks of three-year-olds fall in this egocentric category, but only about 30 percent of the remarks of seven-year-olds.

The second symptom Piaget finds in the nature of childish argument. It is not until seven or eight years of age that the child gets beyond the "It is, it isn't" variety of argument. According to Piaget, young arguers are unable to take into account their opponents' point of view or even to realize that their opponents have a point of view distinct from their own. Young children, therefore, are unable to take the kind of action that would be required to change their opponents' view. They rarely say why "it isn't," because they assume that this is as apparent to the opponent as it is to them.

The third symptom Piaget found in his experiment on children's explanations. The experiment was performed as follows: The subjects of the experiment were 30 children between the ages of six and seven years. Each experiment involved two children of the same age, one chosen arbitrarily to be the "explainer" and the other to be the "reproducer." Piaget set the situation up as a kind of game or contest. He told the explainer,

Are you good at telling stories? Very well then, we'll send your little friend out of the room, and while he is standing outside the door, we will tell you a story. You must listen very carefully. When you have listened to it all, we'll make your friend come back, and then you will tell him the same story. We will see which of you is best at telling stories. You understand? You must listen well, and then tell the same thing. . . . (Piaget, 1974, pp. 96–97).

Piaget answered the child's questions and repeated the instructions as often as necessary.

Once the children had understood the instructions, the reproducer was sent away. The experimenter told the explainer a simple story or explained a simple device such as the tap shown in Figure 6–1. In

Figure 6–1.   Two diagrams of a tap

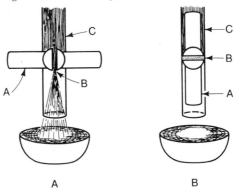

A   B

Source: J. Piaget, *The Language and Thought of the Child*. Trans. M. Gabain (New American Library, 1974), p. 100.

giving the explanation, the experimenter was careful to cover a sequence of specific points as follows:

1.   Look, these two pictures are drawings of a tap.
2.   This here (a) is the handle of the tap.
3.   To turn it off, look, you have to do this with your fingers (moves the fingers on the diagram), and so forth.

There were nine points altogether in this explanation.

When the points had been covered, the reproducer was called back and the explainer attempted to tell "the same thing." Immediately afterwards, explainer and reproducer were questioned separately to determine how many of the points each had understood.

Some results of the study are shown in Table 6–1.

In this experiment, children understood adults better than they did other children. Average scores for adult to child communication were considerably higher than for child to child communication. Piaget attributed this difference to the egocentrism of children's thought.

Table 6–1.   Child's success in understanding adults and other children

	Age	
Measure of understanding	6–7	7–8
Adult to child		
Number points understood by the explainer divided by total number points to be understood	0.80	0.93
Child to child		
Number points understood by the reproducer divided by number points understood by the explainer	0.56	0.68

Source: Data from J. Piaget, *The Language and Thought of the Child*, trans., M. Gabain (New American Library, 1974); table by author.

Egocentrism influences communication between children in two ways: It influences the way children explain and it influences the way children listen. Because egocentric children do not realize that there are points of view other than their own, they may fail to realize what they need to communicate. Indeed explainers left out nearly 25 percent of the points they understood when making their explanations. Further, points that are mentioned may be explained in a way that is very difficult to understand. Here is an explanation by one of Piaget's seven-year-old explainers, named Pour.

> Pour (7 ; 6) explains the tap to Pel (7 ; 0): "*The water can go through there* [points to the large pipe in Fig. 6–1 without designating the exact spot, the opening] *because the door* [which door?] *is above and below* [the movable canal b which he does not show] *and then to turn it* [turn what?] *you must do so* [makes the movement of turning fingers but without pointing to the handles a]. *There, it* [what?] *can't turn round* [= the water can't get through,] *because, the door is on the right and on the left. There, because the water stays there, the pipes can't get there* [the pipe is lying down. Note the inversion of the relation indicated by the word 'because.' What ought to have been said was: "The water stays there because the pipes can't . . . etc."] *and then the water can't run through*" (Piaget, 1974, pp. 117–118).

Pour has failed to give a clear explanation of the working of the tap in spite of the fact that he himself understands it. His explanation abounds in pronouns whose reference may be clear to the speaker but which must certainly be unclear to the listener. At this point, the reader may say, "Hell, that's not surprising. I do that myself." All Piaget would claim, I think, is that the child does more of it than the adult. Children are less critical of their explanations than the adult would be because children are less able than the adult to put themselves in the position of the listener. What is more surprising, perhaps, is the behavior of the childish listener. We can put ourselves in the position of the child who is so carried away being eloquent as to forget intelligibility. It is harder to put ourselves in the position of the reproducers who listen happily to this rot, ask never a question, and think they understand it. Egocentric children, then, are not only terrible explainers; they are also terrible listeners. When they hear something they interpret it, and they assume that their interpretations are the ones that the speaker intended. It never occurs to them to question if what they understand is what the speaker intended.

Piaget draws a number of conclusions from such cases. While children believe that they are speaking intelligibly, in fact they speak in a way that is very hard for others to understand. Their speech abounds in elliptical statements and pronouns without clear reference. Further, children listening to such speech believe, quite incorrectly, that they understand what it was that the speaker was trying to convey to them. Hence they rarely ask for any sort of clarification, feeling that it is unnecessary. Each child then is locked into a personal point of view; speakers are unaware that listeners could misinterpret their words, and listeners are unaware that they have done so.

Because egocentric children cannot distinguish the subjective (what is known or felt by them alone) from the objective (what is known or agreed to by all), they have trouble constructing a logical argument designed to convince another person. Indeed, Piaget believes that the appearance of true logical thought awaits the disappearance of egocentric thought. Egocentric thought disappears when the child enters the concrete operational period.

Most of us would not have formulated a clear concept of egocentrism if Piaget had not pointed it out. The symptoms of egocentrism, however, are apparent, and they likely contribute heavily to our sense that the preoperational child's thought is immature. There are, however, other important respects in which preoperational thought is immature which most people never suspect. A good example is the preoperational child's lack of conservation.

Conservation. Imagine a four or five year old child sitting comfortably across the table from the experimenter. On the table is a jug of orange juice and three smaller glass containers. Two are identical—short, broad-based tumblers, T1 and T2—and the third is a tall, thin cylinder. The experimenter fills T1 and T2 to the same depth with orange juice and asks the child, "Is there more here [pointing to T1] or here [pointing to T2]?" The experimenter adjusts the levels until the child says that they are the same. Now, as the child watches, the experimenter takes the juice in T2 and pours it into the cylinder. The liquid level, of course, is now much higher than before. The experimenter asks, "Is there more juice here [indicating T1] or here [indicating the cylinder]?" The child points to the cylinder. When the experimenter asks, "Why?" the child answers, "Because it's higher here" [pointing to the fluid level in the cylinder]. Some children answer that there is less juice in the cylinder and justify their answer by pointing out the narrowness of the cylinder.

These results are typical of those obtained with children younger than above five and a half years old. They fail to realize that the quantity of juice *must be* the same before and after pouring. Such children are said to lack conservation of quantity. (Try this experiment with a young relative or acquaintance. The results are easy to reproduce.)

By the age of seven, most children have acquired conservation. They may have given the wrong answers as little as six months ago, but now they regard the correct answers as perfectly obvious. They may even consider the experimenter a trifle slow for asking questions about it. Piaget notes that most children who have achieved conservation of quantity act as if it were a very simple and obvious principle. Unlike children who have not yet achieved conservation, conservers seem to make their judgments either with very little examination of the perceptual evidence or actually in spite of it ("This one seems bigger but it's really not").

In the orange juice example above, we were concerned specifically with conservation of the quantity of a liquid. The idea of conservation, however, applies to many types of substances and many physical measurements. It applies to solids in continuous form, such as clay, or in discontinuous form, such as beads, and it applies to measurements such as length, area, volume, weight, and number. In conservation experiments using clay, the experimenter will ask the child to make two balls (or other shapes) which have exactly the same amount of clay. When the child is satisfied that the two are equal, the experimenter takes one of the balls and changes its shape—for example, makes a snake out of it. Then the experimenter asks the child if there is still the same amount of material in the two shapes. The results parallel closely those for liquids. That is, the young child fails to realize that a change in shape does not cause a change in quantity.

When a discontinuous material such as beads is used, the results are even more striking. It is not that the shift from nonconservation to conservation is any more marked. It is the fact that nonconservative children fail to conserve even when they have counted out the two quantities of beads and matched them one for one to start with.

A typical experiment will involve a quantity of beads and, as before, three glasses—two identical and one tall and thin. The dialogue between the child (C) and the experimenter (E) proceeds as follows:

E: "Let's count out the beads. I'll put one in my glass then you put one in yours. OK?"

C: "OK."

E: "One for me [clink] and one for you" [clink].

C: "One for me."

E: "And another for me [clink] and another for you" [clink], etc. [They count out nine beads in this way.]

E: "Do you have more beads or do I have more beads?"

C: "We have the same!"

E: "How do you know?"

C: "We counted them."

E: "OK. Now I'm going to pour your beads in here. [pours child's beads into tall, thin glass] Now who has more beads, you or me?"

C: "I do."

E: "How do you know?"

C: "Mine are higher."

E: "If we made necklaces with these beads, whose necklace would be longer?"

C: "Mine."

Clearly, there are many kinds of conservation. As we saw above, there is conservation of the quantity of liquids, and of continuous and discontinuous substance. There is also conservation of weight, area, length, and number (see Piaget, 1952). These forms of conservation do not all appear at the same instant. For example, a child may understand that discontinuous quantity is conserved weeks or months before recognizing that continuous quantities are conserved.

Given this sample of the phenomenon called conservation, you may find yourself asking, "So, what's the big deal about conservation? Lots of grown-ups make mistakes about quantity, too. The packaging business depends on it." True enough! A tall, thin quart bottle may appear to hold more than a short, squat quart bottle to adults as well as to children. Such illusions are very real in the sense that they are used in the marketplace to encourage us to buy more of Brand A than Brand B. However, the point about conservation which you mustn't miss is this: If you pour the contents of Bottle B into bottle A *while the person watches*, the adult will realize that the quantity is the same, but the nonconservative child will believe that it has increased. Despite size illusions, the adult realizes that a substance does not change its quantity when it changes its shape, and the child does not.

Adults who did not have conservation of quantity would run into many practical difficulties. They might buy only a pint of milk because the container matched the height of their glasses or buy five legs of lamb because five people were coming for dinner. These examples seem silly in an adult context, but they do parallel errors which nonconservative children make in judging quantity.

A theory of conservation of quantity

In Piaget's view, an important difference between children who conserve and those who do not is:

a. Nonconserving children can attend to only one dimension (such as height or width) at a time, while
b. Conserving children can attend to several dimensions at once and can understand that an increase in height can compensate for a decrease in width and vice versa. That is, conserving children can trade off one dimension against another.

In the orange juice example above, we saw that very young children make their judgments of quantity by focusing either on the height or on the width of the column of juice. They never try to use height and width simultaneously in making their judgments. Shortly before they acheive conservation, however, some children pass through a stage in which they attempt to use both height and width, but fail. The following imaginary interview illustrates the dilemma which such children face.

The child and the experimenter sit at a table on which there are two glasses—a wide one, W, and a narrow one, N. The experimenter fills W about one-fifth full of juice and asks the child to put the same quantity of juice in the narrow glass, N.

C: [fills N to a level a little bit higher than the level in W and says] "No, it's too much." [Child then makes the levels equal.]

E: "Are they the same now?"

C: [examines the glasses and says] "No, this one [pointing to W] has more because it's wider. [Child adds a little to N, compares the glasses, and then says] No, it's too much." [Child then starts over.]

This process can go on for some time. In some cases the child never reaches a satisfactory conclusion. The child appears to know that both height and width should be taken into account at the same time but cannot quite manage to consider more than one dimension at a time.

Children who have achieved conservation often seem to make their judgments quickly and with very little consideration of the dimensions of the particular glasses. Piaget believes that these children are actually trading off height and width, but that their skill at this task allows them to do it very quickly and easily. As evidence, Piaget cites cases involving children who have recently achieved conservation in which the process of trade-off is evident. In one instance, a child watched as the contents of a tall, thin glass was poured into a short, fat one (Piaget, 1965, p. 17). The experimenter asked, "Is there as much orange juice as before?" The child said, "There is less. No—it's the same. It just looks like less because this glass is wider, but it's really the same."

Piaget, then, believes that to conserve quantity, children require the ability to trade off. Further, he believes that the ability to trade off depends on the completion of a complex mental structure—a structure which also underlies the child's ability to use the concept of number. This structure encompasses three interrelated skills. The child must:

1. take more than one dimension of the situation into account at a time;
2. develop an "atomic" theory of matter (that is, the child must think of the material being dealt with as made up of small parts which simply change their positions when the shape of the material is changed);
3. be able to *imagine* a change followed by its inverse, e.g., pouring liquid from A to B and then from B to A, will restore the original situation.

The interested reader should consult Ginsburg and Opper (1969) and Piaget (1952) for a more complete discussion of Piaget's theory of conservation. We have said enough here to indicate that for Piaget the development of conservation and the number concept depends on the completion of a complex mental structure. Consistent with Piaget's view of development in general, this mental structure is a schema which has been constructed under the influence of experience by modifying and combining earlier schemas.

Piaget's emphasis on mental structures is in sharp contrast with the Behaviorist doctrines which played down (or in some cases forbade) consideration of mental structures. This theoretical difference led to different expectations about the effects of experience on development. When word of the phenomenon of conservation reached America, it seemed natural, in the hotbed of Behaviorism, to teach conservation through the direct reinforcement of "conservative responses." Piaget would not expect such a simple approach to work. Direct reinforcement of conservative responses would not build the structures which underlie conservation.

Consider a crude mechanical analogy to Piaget's view of the development of mental structures. An engine is manufactured first by fabricating parts and then assembling these parts a few at a time into a complex structure. The engine typically will not run at all until it is complete. Pressing the starter button early neither starts the engine nor hastens the manufacturing process. In Piaget's view, the Behaviorists' attempts to hasten the appearance of conservation by direct reinforcement is like pressing the starter button before the engine is complete. It neither makes the mental structure operate nor hastens its development.

Smedslund, a Norwegian psychologist, has explored this issue in detail (1961). He has attempted to teach conservation of weight to young children by direct reinforcement. In the training procedure, five to seven year old children were given clay in the form of a ball which they were allowed to weigh. After weighing the ball, they were asked to predict the effects on its weight of flattening it into a pancake or of rolling it out into a hot dog. At first, of course, nonconservative children predicted that these changes in shape would result in changes in weight. After they had made their predictions, the children checked them by weighing the clay again. In each experimental session the children made 16 such predictions and checks. After two training sessions, Smedslund was able to identify 11 children who showed no conservation beforehand and perfect conservation afterwards.

Now comes the dirty part. After this apparent success in teaching conservation to nonconservative children, Smedslund compared his 11 training successes to 13 children who had acquired conservation in the "natural" way—that is, without special training. The comparison trials were just like the training trials with one exception. Smedslund cheated. Between prediction and weighing, Smedslund surreptitiously, secretly, and with malice aforethought, pinched off a little bit of the clay and hid it. Conservative predictions that weights would not change were suddenly and surprisingly disconfirmed. The result was that all 11 of the children trained to conserve promptly regressed to their nonconservative ways. However, 6 of the 13 "natural" conservers resisted regression, saying such things as, "We must have lost some on the floor," and so on. Smedslund concluded that the training procedure which appeared to produce conservation had not produced real conservation. This result, of course, is consistent with Piaget's view.

The period of concrete operations

Many of the important properties of the thought of concrete operational children have already been discussed, because they are, in a sense, mirror images of the properties of preoperational thought. Table 6–2 makes this comparison clear.

From concrete operations to formal operations

The last major event in development (according to Piaget) occurs at about age 11 when the child moves from the concrete operational period to the formal operational period. Children in the concrete operational period can reason well about concrete situations—that is, about situations they can see and touch. They do not, however, reason well about imaginary or hypothetical situations. Children in the formal operational period differ from children in earlier periods because they

Table 6-2. Comparison of preoperational and concrete operational thought

Preoperational period Ages 2–7	Concrete operational period Ages 7–11
1. Logical processes Loosely organized (contradiction acceptable)	Logical processes Tightly organized (contradiction unacceptable)
2. Egocentric thought (does not recognize others' points of view)	Socialized thought (recognizes others' points of view)
3. Has not achieved conservation (can consider only one dimension at a time) (lacks an "atomic" theory of matter) (cannot reverse mental operations)	Has achieved conservation (can consider several dimensions simultaneously) (has an "atomic" theory of matter) (can reverse mental operations)

have the capacity for formal scientific thought. That is, they can explore a complex set of hypotheses systematically.

Imagine a child experimenting with a pendulum. The task is to find out what makes the pendulum swing faster or slower. The child has several options—trying pendulum bobs of various weights or strings of various lengths; starting the pendulum at various distances from the resting position; pushing the pendulum at its start with greater or lesser force. Of these four factors, only the length of the string influences the time the pendulum requires for a complete swing, but the child does not know this beforehand.

What we want to understand is how children of various ages try to solve this problem. First let us imagine two concrete operational children. For their first observation, the children pick a light pendulum bob and a short string. They note that the pendulum swings rapidly. Next, they choose a heavy pendulum bob and a long string. They note that the pendulum swings slowly and conclude that heavy pendulums swing more slowly than light ones. What is important here is not that the children drew an incorrect conclusion but rather that they drew a conclusion at all. There were alternative hypotheses which could have accounted for their observations, but they did not consider them. That is, they did not explore the set of alternative hypotheses systematically.

In contrast, let us consider two formal operational children. They observe first a pendulum with a long string and a heavy weight; then, a long string and a light weight; then, a short string and a heavy weight; and finally, a short string and a light weight. They conclude that length makes a difference but weight does not and proceed systematically to rule out the other factors by further observations.

Concrete operational children can deal with the concrete evidence before them and draw conclusions which are consistent with that evidence. What they do not do spontaneously is to imagine the set of alternative hypotheses which are also consistent with the evidence. Because they do not consider the alternative hypotheses, they do not make their observations in a way that allows them to choose systematically among the alternatives. They do not design their experiments properly. The formal operational child, on the other hand, does imagine the set of alternative hypotheses right from the beginning and therefore is able to conduct a systematic scientific study.

As with the other developmental transformations, Piaget believes that the transformation to formal operational thought depends on the development of a complex mental structure arising from the coordination of earlier structures present during the concrete operational period. It is this structure which allows the child to deal systematically with hypothetical states of the world.

SUMMARY

Piaget believes that adult intelligence has its origin in the motor reflexes of the newborn. These reflexes are modified through experience by processes of adaptation and organization. Piaget describes development as occurring in a sequence of four major periods. In the sensorimotor period (0–2 years) the mental structures required for symbolic thought are developed. In the preoperational period (2–7 years) children have symbolic thought but lack some skills required for dealing with concrete problems. For example, they are egocentric and have difficulty in considering more than one aspect of a situation at a time. In the concrete operational period (7–11 years) children can reason well about concrete situations but have trouble dealing systematically with hypothetical situations. In the formal operational period (from 11 on) the person can reason systematically about hypothetical situations and is now capable of scientific thought.

The major theme running through this chapter and the previous one is the view that development is not well understood as the simple accumulation of facts and skills learned through reinforcement (remember Smedslund's experiment). Rather development depends on the acquisition of complex mental structures. By placing the weight of his work and genius behind this view, Piaget has influenced psychologists to consider complex mental structures even though these were not congenial to the Behaviorist approach. In so doing, he has brought psychology closer to a sophisticated view of the mind.

FURTHER READING

Noted in References following, Ginsburg and Opper provide a good introduction to Piaget's theories.

Piaget's observations concerning egocentric and socialized language are presented in *The Language and Thought of the Child,* published in 1974.

The topic of conservation is treated in Piaget's *The Child's Conception of Number,* published in 1965.

REFERENCES

GINSBURG, H., and OPPER, S. *Piaget's theory of intellectual development* (Englewood Cliffs, N.J.: Prentice-Hall, 1969).

HELD, R., and BAUER, J. A. "Visually guided reaching in infant monkeys after restricted rearing," *Science, 155* (1967), 718–720.

MILLER, G. A. *Language and communication* (New York: McGraw-Hill, 1951).

PIAGET, J. *The origins of intelligence in children* (New York: W. W. Norton & Co., Inc., 1963).

PIAGET, J. *The child's conception of number* (New York: W. W. Norton & Co., Inc., 1965).

PIAGET, J. *The language and thought of the child.* Trans. M. Gabain. (New York: New American Library, 1974).

SMEDSLUND, J. "The acquisition of conservation of substance and weight in children, III. Extinction of conservation of weight acquired 'normally' and by means of empirical controls on a balance," *Scandinavian Journal of Psychology, 2* (1961), 85–97.

Chapter 7

Early theories of language and meaning

Questions of meaning keep coming up in our everyday lives. We continually say such things as, "What do you mean?" or, "I know what you mean," or, "Does he *mean* to say that?" Our perceptions, actions, and our speech are all described as meaningful. It is not surprising then that people have persisted in trying to find a satisfactory theory of meaning. The attempts, however, have been beset with difficulties. No real agreement has yet been reached on a theory of meaning. Scientists do not even agree as to whether the term meaning should describe something inside a person or something outside a person. For some, meaning is an image; for others, meaning is a response; for still others, meaning is a set of circumstances in the outside world which causes us to do something. B. F. Skinner, responding to this confusion, has complained that the term "meaning" is vague and not objectively defined and that its use may be misleading. He feels it would be best to banish it from scientific discussion altogether.

Perhaps it is only a saving nature that makes me a nonword-banisher. I think, though, that there are other good reasons as well. First, I do not think that it is such a terrible indictment to say that a word is vague and hard to define objectively. After all, the word *chair* is vague and hard to define objectively. Really! Try to define it. Is a chair something with four legs that you sit on? If so, how do you tell it from a horse? Try to define the boundary between a chair and a bench or a chair and a sofa. These boundaries are really quite vague and ill-defined. *Chair*, then, is a vague though useful word.

The real question about the admittedly vague word *meaning* is this: Is it a useful vague word like *chair*, or is it instead a misleading vague word as Skinner has charged? My own opinion is that the term *mean-*

ing serves important functions in science, and that it cannot as yet be replaced by a more precise term.

Linguists appear to have a clear and compelling need for the word *meaning*. There is a great deal that the fluent speaker knows about language that is not reflected in the grammatical rules of the language. Listeners know that, "Colorless green ideas sleep furiously," is not an acceptable English sentence even though it is quite grammatical. Linguists call such sentences anomalous. Laymen call them meaningless. Further, a native speaker will find a close relation between sentences such as, "The aviator stoned the cop," and, "To pelt the policeman, the flyer used rocks," in spite of their great differences in grammatical structure. The native speaker will say that these sentences "mean the same thing" whereas other sentences which have identical grammatical structures do not mean the same thing at all. Thus, to understand the structure of language, linguists had to go beyond the rules of syntax and include aspects of language related to meaning. The study of these aspects of language is called *semantics*.

Meaning is important not only in the domain of language but in other domains as well. Experiments have shown that people perceive, learn, and remember meaningful material differently from meaningless material.

The evidence from linguistics and from psychology simply confirms our commonsense experience that meaning is a significant aspect of our sensory and linguistic experience. We are all aware of interpreting sentences and assigning meanings to sights and events. It would really be quite surprising if meaning were not somehow useful in describing the results of linguistics and psychology.

THEORIES OF MEANING

A complete theory of language meaning must (1) account for the fact that individual words and events have meaning; and (2) be able to tell us how to find the meaning of word combinations from the meanings of the separate words. The number of meaningful word combinations is simply too large for us to have learned them separately. George Miller (1965) estimates that there are 10^{20} meaningful 20-word sentences in English—many more than anyone could have heard in a human lifetime, or for that matter in the lifetime of the earth. Thus, everyday we hear and understand many sentences which we have never heard before. Part of our linguistic apparatus, then, must be a set of rules by which we combine meanings. An adequate theory of language must include those rules.

No complete theory of meaning is yet available. Nevertheless, psychologists, linguists, and philosophers have been struggling with these problems for a long time. Their efforts, achievements, and failures make an interesting and instructive history.

In this chapter we will review four types of theories of meaning in language:

1. Reference theories
2. Association theories
3. Classical conditioning theories, and
4. Operant conditioning theories.

Meaning and reference

If a child were to come to you and ask, "What does *horse* mean?" you would not hesitate (assuming you did not think the child was pulling your leg) to point to a nearby horse and say, "That's a horse," or "That is what *horse* means." We often treat an external object as the meaning of the word. In the same way, reference theories treat meaning as a relation between language and the world outside the speaker.

George Boole, the 19th-century mathematician, was a reference theorist. For Boole, the meaning of a noun or an adjective was the class of things to which it referred. Thus the meaning of *rock* was the class of rocks and the meaning of *good* was the class of good things. The meaning of a combination of adjectives and nouns was the set of things that are in *all* of the classes referred to by the various words. Boole gives the following example: "Thus, if *x* alone stands for 'white things,' and *y* for 'sheep,' let *xy* stand for 'white sheep'; and in like manner, if *z* stands for 'horned things,' and *x* and *y* retain their previous interpretations, let *XYZ* represent 'horned white sheep,' i.e., that collection of things to which the name 'sheep' and the descriptions 'white' and 'horned' are together applicable" (Boole, 1854, p. 29).

The word *and*, as in "men and women," indicates that the meaning of the combination is obtained by adding classes. The word *except*, as in, "All dogs except Dalmatians," indicates that meaning is obtained by the subtraction of classes.

Boole deals with verbs in two steps. First, he notes that by appropriate modification of the subject, any verb can be replaced by *is* or *are*. Thus, "They hate onions," may be paraphrased as, "They are onion haters," and, "The dog sleepwalks," may be paraphrased as, "The dog is a sleepwalker." Boole then defines expressions of the form "*a* is *b* " to mean that the class *a* is equal to the class *b*. Boole illustrates this with the sentence, "The stars are the suns and the planets," which he interprets as meaning, "The class of stars equals the class of suns plus the class of planets."

While Boole's procedures seem to work well for many common word combinations, there are many cases which cause difficulties. For example, the idea of the intersection of classes works well for some combinations of words but not for others. It works well in the case of "red wagon." We can decide whether or not a thing is red independently of whether or not it is a wagon. We might, for example, determine its color by looking at it through a very blurry window and determine that it is a wagon by looking at a black and white photograph. These independently identified classes may then be combined as Boole suggests to give the correct description.

On the other hand, combination of classes does not seem to work in cases like "good boy" and "big egg." Basically, the trouble is that we cannot decide whether something is good or big without knowing what it is. The operations for deciding whether or not a boy is good are very different from those for deciding whether or not an egg is good. The same can be said of such words as *big* and *small*. By "egg" standards, every boy is big, and by "boy" standards, every egg is small.

Another problem with Boole's system is that every combination which has an empty reference class, that is, a class with no members, means the same thing as every other such combination. Thus, "colorless green," "a gold mountain," and "a U.S. President named Smith" would all have the same meaning. Further, the sentence, "It is impossible to have a colorless green," would be synonymous with the sentence, "It is impossible to have a U.S. President named Smith."

This conclusion is an embarrassment to Boole's system which seems to arise directly from its identification of meaning with referent class. Since the referent class is either empty or not, Boole's system can distinguish things that exist from things that do not. Among things that do not exist, however, it cannot distinguish the possible, for example, a president named Smith, from the impossible, for example, a colorless green. Boole's system would have to be modified greatly to account for all the facts of language.

Association theories of meaning

For most of us, an elephant is a meaningful object. For Titchener (see Chapter 2), an elephant is also a complex assortment of gray and brown patches of light with an odor of hay and, perhaps, peanuts thrown in. How does the particular collection of sensations that we call elephant obtain its meaning? Characteristically, the Associationists answer, "By association." The complex of sensations, of trunk and tail and tusk, keeps turning up—in the circus, in the zoo, and in storybook pictures—until it becomes familiar. The parts come to mean the whole. When some parts are hidden, we can infer them from the rest. When we see the front half of an elephant entering the circus ring, we would be very surprised if it were not soon followed by the back half. The 18th-century philosopher George Berkeley illustrated in his famous description of a coach how meaning might be acquired by association:

"Sitting in my study, I hear a coach drive along the street; I look through the casement and see it; I walk out and enter it. Thus, common speech would incline one to think I saw, heard and touched the same thing, to wit, the coach" (Berkeley, 1929, p. 36).

Berkeley believes that these very different sensations—the sound, sight, and feeling of a coach—are associated because they are frequently experienced together. Therefore they come to be spoken of as the same thing. Notice the similarity of this association process which Berkeley describes to the process Piaget called intersensory coordination in the infant (see Chapter 5).

For the Associationists, then, a sensation acquires its meaning for a person through its history of association with other sensations. Thus, it takes at least two sensations to make a meaning.

Typically, however, a meaningful object will consist not just of two sensations, but rather a whole complex of sensations, each of which means the rest. Words, heard or read, are like any other sensations. They too can acquire a meaning if frequently associated with other sensations. Thus, the word "elephant" can come to mean the whole complex of elephant sensations just as much as the sight of its trunk.

Titchener's theory of meaning.   Titchener was an enthusiastic advocate of the Associationist doctrine of meaning. His own position on meaning, however, includes much more than the Associationist doctrine. Among the most charming of Titchener's writings are his reports of his own introspections as to the meanings of words. Concerning the word *but*, Titchener says: "My feeling of *but* has contained . . . a flashing picture of a bald crown, with a fringe of hair below, and a massive black shoulder, the whole passing swiftly down the visual field from northwest to southeast" (Titchener, 1909, p. 17). In describing his introspections on the meaning of the word "meaning," Titchener reports seeing the point of a blue-gray scoop digging into a mass of plastic material. He suggests that the image arose from his teacher's exhortations to "dig out the meaning" (Titchener, 1909, p. 18).

For Titchener, the sensations most important for meaning are muscle sensations and word images. He believes that meaning is, originally, muscle sensation. When we are faced with some situation, we adopt some bodily attitude toward it, perhaps alertness or defense. The characteristic muscular sensations of the attitude are for Titchener the meaning of the situation.

Of word images, Titchener says, "And words themselves, let us remember, were at first motor attitudes, gestures, kinesthetic contexts: complicated, of course, by sound . . . but still essentially akin to the gross attitudes of primitive attention" (Titchener, 1909, p. 19). While words later acquired meaning content as visual and auditory sensations, Titchener felt that their historic origin in gesture made them especially suitable as vehicles of thought. As a person's language skills increase, Titchener felt, the kinesthetic aspect of meaning may become more prominent. He believed that the meaning of a printed page may consist of the feelings accompanying internal speech.

CLASSICAL CONDITIONING THEORIES

With the advent of Behaviorism, conditioned responses replaced associations as the essential ingredient in theories of meaning. Early Behaviorists such as Watson (see Chapter 3) based their theories on a simple but appealing analogy. In classical conditioning, the sound of a bell after many pairings with food comes to elicit salivation in much the same way that the presentation of the food had done. It is as if the bell had come to "mean" food to the animal. Following this lead, the early Behaviorists proposed that words acquire their meaning by conditioning. For example, a word such as *rain*, often paired with the occurrence of physical rain, comes to produce the same responses that physical rain does, e.g., running for cover, opening umbrellas, cancelling picnics, etc. For these theorists, the critical relation is that a word means a situation *because* the word elicits the same responses as does the situation. Thus, the announcement "supper" is meaningful because it produces the same responses as showing people that supper is on the table. This theory is called substitution theory.

Later Behaviorists have abandoned substitution theory because people do not act as if words were simply conditioned substitutes for the things that they refer to. Saying the word *apple* does not produce noticeable apple picking or apple chewing movements in most of the people that we would care to associate with. As we saw in Chapter 3, efforts to find traces of such movements in small muscular contractions met with very little success.

Mediation theory

To continue to use the conditioned response in the description of meaning and at the same time to avoid the problems of substitution theory, modern Behaviorists have developed mediation theory. The basic ideas of mediation theory, taken from the account given by C. E. Osgood, are these:

Suppose that some stimulus, say the rainstorm mentioned above, reliably produces a pattern of behaviors, such as crouching, covering the head, running for cover, and so on. Suppose also that the word *rain* is repeatedly paired with the occurrence of rainstorms. According to mediation theory, the word *rain* will not become conditioned to the entire rainstorm behavior pattern. Rather, it will be conditioned only to that portion of it which is "the most readily conditionable, least effortful, least interfering" part of the total pattern. The portion conditioned to the word is called 'the mediation response' " (Mowrer, 1954, p. 664). Thus, the mediating response for rain is likely to be some minor muscular tensions, related say, to crouching, but which do not interfere with other ongoing activities.

According to mediation theory, to acquire meaning is really to acquire a mediating response. A mediating response may be said to refer to a situation because it is a part of a person's response to that situation. Different situations, because they elicit different total response patterns, result in characteristically different mediating responses. Thus, there are, actually and potentially, a great many distinct mediating responses, each referring to a different situation.

The mediating response has two important properties. First, being the least effortful part of the total pattern, it may be of very small magnitude, and hence very hard to observe. By postulating the unobservable mediating response, the mediation theorists have solved the problem of substitution theory in a direct if not a subtle way.

The second important property is that each mediating response produces a distinctive pattern of stimulation. Since they are, by and large, so small as to be unobservable, mediating responses are not useful instrumentally. That is, one does not employ a mediating response to move a chair or lift a rock. What function then do they serve? The main function of a mediating response is to produce stimuli which can be conditioned to useful instrumental acts. For example, the mediating response to the word *rain* (some unobservable vestige, say, of a crouching response) can be conditioned to useful acts such as taking an umbrella before leaving the house. Listeners may be said to react meaningfully to the word *rain* because they respond to it with instrumental acts appropriate to a rainstorm. They are able to do so through the action of the mediating response and the pattern of stimulation which it elicits.

The mediating mechanism is used to explain many phenomena related to the use of language, such as semantic generalization. Semantic generalization is the phenomenon in which words similar in meaning are treated more alike than words similar in form. A newly learned response, such as an eye blink conditioned to the word *hit* may generalize more strongly to the word *strike* than to the physically more similar word *sit*. The mediation theory explanation is that *hit* and *strike*, since they refer to similar actions, have similar mediating responses and hence, similar associated stimulus patterns. The eye blink, conditioned to the stimulus pattern for *hit*, generalizes readily, therefore, to the stimulus pattern for *strike*.

   Mediation theory also provides an explanation of semantic satiation. Semantic satiation is the loss of meaning which occurs when a word is repeated over and over. You may demonstrate this for yourself by repeating a word such as *hum* or *lull* again and again. Essentially, the explanation given is that when a word is repeated out of context, the mediating response extinguishes, and hence, meaning is lost.

   Osgood's theory of assigns.   One of the objections that can be raised to mediation theory is that while some words may obtain their meanings through their relation to practical situations, many, such as *Antarctica* and *Napoleon* do not. Osgood (1953) proposed to take such words into account by his theory of assigns. According to this theory, meanings are assigned to these words by association with other words rather than with practical situations. He suggests that the word *alien,* for example, acquires its unsavory significance by association in sentences like, "We don't want any aliens poisoning our country," and, "That troublemaker is an alien and ought to be shipped back where he came from."

   Being in the proximity of unpleasant words is not enough to give a word an unpleasant meaning when the words are in the context of a sentence, however. In the example below the A sentences give a distinctly poorer impression of Grundges than do the B sentences. Nevertheless, more unpleasant words are contained in the B sentences than in the A.

A

Grundges love dictatorship and injustice.
Grundges cause pain and stop healing.
Grundges are covered with fleas and have bad breath.
When her Grundge died, my sister laughed and sang.

B

Grundges hate dictatorship and injustice.
Grundges stop pain and cause healing.
Grundges repel fleas and prevent bad breath.
When her Grundge died, my sister cried and gnashed her teeth.

   To explain why the A sentences give a bad impression of Grundges and the B sentences give a good one requires a theory which can explain why the words "cause pain and stop healing" have a bad meaning and the words "stop pain and cause healing" have a good one. The theory must be able to explain why a sentence which consists of nothing but pleasant words, like, "Your best friend is in your home making love to your wife," can, when it is announced under the right circumstances, have such a remarkable unpleasant effect. In short, what is needed is a theory which can deal with the grammatical *and* semantic complexities of the language. It seems unlikely that mediation theory, which has trouble even with the combination of adjectives and nouns, can fill this need.

Predication. Closely related to mediation theory is O. H. Mowrer's (1954) theory of predication. Up until now, we have been discussing relatively slow processes in which words acquire meaning by occurring repeatedly in certain situations or with certain other words. Now we must discuss the extremely rapid process by which a single presentation of a sentence transfers information from the predicate of the sentence to its subject. At this point, it may not surprise you to find Behaviorism's workhorse, classical conditioning, being pressed into service again. Mowrer states his theory this way:

> What then, is the function of the sentence, "Tom is a thief"? Most simply and most basically, it appears to be this. *Thief* is a sort of "unconditioned stimulus" . . . which can be translated into, or defined by, the phrase, "a person who cannot be trusted," one who "takes things, steals." When, therefore, we put the word, or sign, *Tom,* in front of the sign *thief,* . . . we create a situation from which we can predict a fairly definite result. On the basis of the familiar principle of conditioning, we would expect that some of the reaction evoked by the second sign, *thief,* would be shifted to the first sign, *Tom,* so that Charles, the hearer of the sentence, would thereafter respond to the word, *Tom,* somewhat as he had previously responded to the word *thief* (Mowrer, 1954, p. 664).

Mowrer's theory has two major weaknesses which make it quite unacceptable. First, it has been shown that very little classical conditioning takes place unless the conditioned stimulus occurs before the unconditioned stimulus (see Chapter 3). If Mowrer's theory were correct, then, we would expect meaning to be transferred in a sentence in only one direction; that is, from the latter words to the earlier ones. This is plainly not the case, for the sentence, "The thief is Tom," blackens Tom's character just as badly as, "Tom is a thief."

The second weakness has to do with the problem of combining meanings, a weakness shared by mediation theory. If Mowrer's theory were correct, the sentence, "Tom is a perfect idiot," should make Tom seem both perfect and an idiot.

Skinner's analysis of language

As we saw in Chapter 3, Skinner was very successful in controlling the behavior of animals in isolated environments by manipulating their stimuli and their schedules of reinforcement. In his book *Verbal Behavior* (1957), he set out very seriously to apply his style of analysis to the human language functions of speech, reading, and writing. That is, he attempted to identify the stimuli and the conditions of reinforcement which control the strength of these behaviors.

Skinner suggested that the strength of a verbal response could be measured by, among other things, the probability of its being said, the energy and speed with which it is said, and the speaker's tendency to repeat it. Thus, a child, familiar with the factors controlling the father's speech, knows that when he sees the wreckage in the child's room, he will *probably* say, "Clean up your room." Furthermore, the child knows that, if there is delay, the father will repeat this command with greater and greater frequency until finally he delivers an ear-piercing, "Clean up your room!!!" in a rich contralto. These symptoms reflect the strength of the verbal behavior and, of course, the strength of the factors which control that behavior.

For Skinner, the special character of verbal behavior is that it is reinforced through the mediation of other people. Words have no direct effect on the insensate world. Saying, "Start, damn you!" to your car is not nearly as effective as nonverbal behaviors such as keeping it supplied with gas. Saying, "Excuse me," to department store dummies is never reinforced by the dummy and is often regarded with a very aversive sort of amusement by passersby. Language, whether written or oral, typically depends on real live people for its reinforcement (although in some few cases, a particularly sympathetic dog may do).

People reinforce verbal behavior in many ways. They may give the speaker what he asks for as when he says, "Please pass the soup," or, "Stick 'em up." They may give their attention and perhaps even laugh at the appropriate places when the speaker tells a story. They may say, "That's right!" for a well-made point.

Skinner categorizes verbal behaviors on the basis of the conditions of stimulation and reinforcement which control them. One important category is the *mand*—a name Skinner derived from the words *command* and *demand*. This category includes commands, demands, and requests of all sorts. The mand is a verbal behavior which specifies its reinforcement. We use it when we want something, e.g., "Please pass the guacamole," or when we want to avoid something, e.g., "Get this wretch out of my sight!" The strength of a mand will depend on how much we want the reinforcement it specifies. The longer it has been since lunch, the stronger are mands such as, "Let's eat!" and, "How about dinner?" As we saw above, the father's mand, "Clean up your room," increased in strength the longer he waited for action.

Another of Skinner's categories is the *tact*. The tact is a verbal response which describes something. Skinner invented the term *tact* to suggest making contact with the physical world. Since tacts describe things, they are at least partly under the control of stimuli in the environment. For example, we are much more likely to say, "Oh, there is George," when George is, in fact, there. People who violate this principle very often are put in special places to live until they get better. Tacts are under the control of the stimulus environment because the speaking community insists. Parents teach children to say "green" when they are considering something green, and to say "horse" when there is a horse to pay attention to. Saying "doggie" to anything with four feet is cute at age two but it is a real liability at age 22. The community insists on accurate description because accurate descriptions are useful and inaccurate ones are not. False alarms, of all sorts, waste time and effort.

Skinner defines a number of other categories of verbal behavior including auto-clitics, and textual behavior. Unlike tacts, which are controlled by publicly observable stimuli, auto-clitics are controlled by stimuli which only the speaker can observe. For example, it is typically only the speaker who can judge the accuracy of statements such as, "I was just going to say that," and, "I'm not sure whether I like this wine or not." Textual behavior is reading.

Critique of Skinner's system

Skinner's analysis of language received severe criticism right from the start. The linguist Noam Chomsky, in a long and caustic review (1959), concluded that rather than providing a scientific analysis of language, Skinner had simply restated some traditional views dressed up in such terms as *stimulus control, response strength,* and *reinforcement.* These terms sound scientific but are actually less accurate than the traditional terms they replaced.

As an example of stimulus control, Skinner suggested that when a person looks at a painting and says, "Dutch," the response is under the control of extremely subtle properties of the painting. Chomsky pointed out that if the person had said, "Clashes with the wallpaper," "I thought you liked abstract work," "Never saw it before," "Tilted," "Beautiful," "Hideous," or anything else that might occur to the person, Skinner would have had to assert that the response was under the control of some other subtle property of the painting. Chomsky's point is that in most complex situations, we really cannot predict accurately what aspects of the world a person will respond to. The kind of stimulus analysis which is adequate for a rat or a pigeon in a Skinner Box is completely inadequate for describing human speakers in complex environments.

Chomsky also criticizes Skinner's use of the concept response strength. He points out that to impress the owner of a picture favorably, you should not stand in front of it and shriek, "Beautiful," in a loud high pitched voice rapidly and repeatedly, although to do so should certainly indicate high response strength according to Skinner's criteria. Again, the problem according to Chomsky is that a term such as response strength, which is adequate for describing the behavior of simple animals in simple environments, is not adequate to describe complex human situations.

Further Chomsky objects to the way in which Skinner uses the term *reinforcement*. In Skinner's animal laboratory, a reinforcement is an observable event which the experimenter controls, such as the delivery of a food pellet. Skinner manipulates the reinforcement schedule and demonstrates predictable changes in the animals' behavior. In *Verbal Behavior*, the term reinforcement is used much more loosely. Skinner often explains behaviors as being controlled by reinforcements which are private and unobservable. For example, he speaks of automatic self-reinforcement which results from making pleasant or familiar sounds, for example, a child making train noises, and of the reinforcement an author receives by anticipating the approval of a future generation of readers. Used in this way, the term no longer has the explanatory power of objective reinforcement. In fact, it appears to have no explanatory power at all. Whenever we observe someone doing something, we can always say that it is automatically self-reinforcing, or if we are feeling traditional, we can say instead, "Well, I guess he just likes to do it." The two explanations are equally uninformative.

Skinner set out to show that the strength of a verbal response was controlled by the stimulus environment and the schedule of reinforcement in much the same way that a rat's responses are controlled in a Skinner Box. Unfortunately, in following Skinner's demonstration, we have had to accept invisible reinforcements, unanalyzable stimuli, and an inappropriate definition of response strength. It is as if Skinner offered us a grilled cheese sandwich but forgot to include the cheese and the bread.

A major stumbling block common to all of the theories of meaning we have discussed was their inability to solve the problem of combining word meanings. None of the theories was at all adequate to handle the range of grammatical relations found in natural language. They could not, for example, differentiate between "Grundges cause pain and stop healing" and "Grundges stop pain and cause healing." Progress on this problem had to await the development of much more sophisticated theories of grammar.

Near the end of his critique of Skinner's theory of language, Chomsky, in a rather offhanded way, dropped another bombshell that was to shake the psychological world. He suggested that innate factors must play an important role in the child's acquisition of language. Chomsky felt that children acquired language at a rate that was far too rapid to be accounted for by learning alone. He believed, therefore, that children must have a highly specific inherited predisposition to acquire language—a predisposition that allows them to discover the grammar of their language, whether it be English, German, or Swahili, on the basis of very little experience. It is as if children have some linguistic knowledge already "wired in" at birth.

By taking this position, Chomsky came surprisingly close to Descartes' doctrine of innate ideas. For Chomsky, though, the innate ideas were not ideas of God or of the geometrical axioms; rather, they were ideas of the rules which underlie all languages—the laws of universal grammar.

Chomsky's criticism of Skinner dramatized the failure of the earlier theories. His own revolutionary work on grammar (see Chapter 9) pointed the way to new approaches to the difficult problems of word combination. Perhaps, in addition, the fact that Behaviorism had been dominant in American psychology for 40 years made some anxious for new approaches.

SUMMARY

Psychologists have attempted to account for the meanings of words and word combinations for some time. Important among the earlier theories are:

1. *Reference theories:* the meaning of an utterance (word or word combination) is the reference class of the utterance.
2. *Association theories:* the meaning of an utterance is the set of events which have happened close in time to the utterance.
3. *Classical conditioning theories:* the meaning of an utterance is the response which is classically conditioned to it.
4. *Operant conditioning theories:* the meaning of an utterance is the set of conditions which determine its strength as an operant response.

None of these theories is able to deal adequately with the problem of combining word meanings.

FURTHER READING

As noted in References following, Roger Brown's delightful book, *Words and Things,* is worth reading in its entirety. Chapter 8 is of special relevance to the material of this chapter.

Osgood presents the case for his own theory of meaning in Chapter 16 of his book, *Method and Theory in Experimental Psychology.*

Chomsky presents his views on innate factors in language and on many other things in *Language and Mind.*

Bever argues that innate factors involved in language learning are not specific to language but underlie human cognitive processes generally. His position is presented in "The cognitive basis for linguistic structures," in J. R. Hayes (Ed.), *Cognition and the Development of Language* (1970).

REFERENCES

BERKELEY, G.   "An essay toward a new theory of vision," *Berkeley selections,* ed. Mary W. Calkins. New York: Charles Scribner's Sons, 1929.

BEVER, T. G.   "The cognitive basis for linguistic structures." In J. R. Hayes (Ed.), *Cognition and the development of language.* New York: Wiley, 1970.

BOOLE, G.   *The laws of thought.* New York: Dover Press, 1854.

BROWN, R.   *Words and things.* Glencoe, Illinois: The Free Press, 1958.

CHOMSKY, N.   "A review of B. F. Skinner's *Verbal behavior,*" *Language,* 35 (1959), pp. 26–58.

CHOMSKY, N.   *Language and mind.* New York: Harcourt, Brace, & World, 1968.

MILLER, G. A.   "Some preliminaries to psycholinguistics," *American Psychologist, 20* (1965), pp. 15–20.

MOWRER, O. H.   "The psychologist looks at language," *American Psychologist, 9* (1954), pp. 660–694.

OSGOOD, C. E.   *Method and theory in experimental psychology.* New York: Oxford University Press, 1953.

SKINNER, B. F.   *Verbal behavior.* New York: Appleton-Century-Crofts, 1957.

TITCHENER, E. B.   *Lectures on the experimental psychology of the thought-processes.* New York: Macmillan, 1909.

Chapter 8

The impact of the computer
on psychology

The development of the computer had an enormous impact on psychology. One might *expect* that the scenario would run something like this:

Scene 1. A scientist is sitting in front of a complex array of flashing lights and bubbling test tubes. [We can tell he is a scientist because he has a white coat and bears a strange resemblance to Albert Einstein and Vincent Price.] He says, "Knight takes rook, check. Your move, Hal." A strange voice without intonation, obviously that of a computer, drones, "I see that you have fallen for my trap, Professor Einprice. Your circuits are not computing well today. Queen to Queen Bishop 5, checkmate."

(FADE)

Scene 2. Two gentlemen in the reading room of an elegant London club. The older gentleman says, "I see that Einprice has turned his computer into an artificial chess master. Quite a surprise, what!" The younger gentleman replies, "Oh, immensely exciting! Don't you see? It means that man's mind needn't be the fuzzy spiritual thing we always thought. It can be a mechanism just like the rest of nature!" In the background an ecclesiastic crosses himself and mutters, "There are some things that the human mind should not explore!"

This scenario has some plausibility, but *it's not the way things happened*. The idea that man is a mechanism had been around for a long time before the computer appeared. Further, most psychologists, whether they were raised in the tradition of Freud, Wertheimer, or

Skinner, already believed that the human mind is a mechanism. The idea has been around at least since 1748, when the French philosopher Julien Offroy de La Mettrie proposed it in his book, *L'Homme Machine*.

The real impact of the computer was to give psychologists a new way to represent mental processes through information-processing models. Our main task in this chapter will be to explain what information-processing models are and why they are useful.

Before information-processing models were introduced, most psychological models belonged to one of two classes: black-box models and physiological models. [Hull's use of S-R chain models (see Chapter 3) is an exception to this generalization.] Black-box models handle internal mental processes by firmly ignoring them. The person is viewed as an unopenable black box receiving inputs (stimuli) and emitting outputs (responses). The psychologists' task is to find the relations between the inputs and the outputs and *not* to worry about what goes on in between. As we saw in Chapter 3, this is the position strongly favored by the Skinnerians, who view their task as reporting the relations of inputs, for example, stimuli and schedules of reinforcement, to outputs, for example, responses, and *not* worrying about what goes on inside.

Physiological models attempt to account for mental processes through neural and chemical mechanisms which connect the organism's input to its output. As we saw in Chapter 4, the Gestalt psychologists favored physiological models. It seems reasonable to believe that physiological models will eventually account for most psychological phenomena. We are still, however, very far from that goal. The progress of developing workable physiological models has been hampered by the difficulty of obtaining information about relevant neural mechanisms.

To understand the alternative that information-processing models have provided for psychology, we should first understand what computers are and how information processing models apply to them.

THE DEVELOPMENT OF THE COMPUTER

As early as Roman times, Heron of Alexandria described a device for measuring the distance traveled by cart. It consisted of a sequence of pegged counting wheels such as is shown in Figure 8–1. The lowest wheel was attached to the axle of the cart. Each time the lowest counting wheel rotated, the next higher counting wheel would be moved one peg ahead—that is, a fraction of a revolution. In the same way, each rotation of the second wheel would move the third wheel one peg ahead. Heron's device, then, would count and remember cartwheel revolutions. By looking at the positions of the counting wheels at the beginning and end of a trip, one could determine the number of

Figure 8—1. Heron's pegged counting wheels

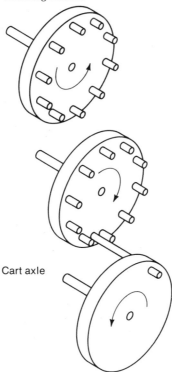

Cart axle

cartwheel revolutions required by the trip, and therefore the distance covered.

The mathematician Pascal applied the principle of the pegged counting wheel to adding and subtracting numbers when he invented the first calculator in 1642.

These early machines were very primitive. Hundreds of years of technical development were required to produce the convenient reliable desk calculators of today. Even the best of modern desk calculators, though, have very little to interest the psychologist because they don't seem at all "intelligent" in the way that computers do. The reason is easy to explain.

Suppose that you have two assistants—P. D. Quick and Ernest Dull—who help you run your million dollar business. You are on the phone to Hong Kong and you need a calculation. You need the value of the expression,

$$\sqrt{(27 + 14)} \times [0.6 \ (15) + 2]$$

You call for P. D., but he is in the library revising the theory of relativity. You know you could have given him the expression and he would have calculated the answer while you continued your conversation with the Hong Kong office. But, alas! You will have to rely on Ernest. You call him in and say, "Now, Ernest, this is what I want you to do. First add 27 to 14 and give me the answer. I'll remember it for you. 41? OK, now multiply 15 by 0.6 and give me the answer." Eventually, the computation gets done. Now, even though both assistants can give you the right answer, it is clear why you regard P. D. as smarter than Ernest. Ernest depends on you completely for memory and for determining the sequence of operations, while P. D. can handle these things for himself. This is just the difference that makes calculators seem dumber than computers. Computers can store lots of information and can control their own sequence of operations. Calculators typically do neither of these things. Clearly calculators are instruments controlled by an intelligence external to themselves. Since computers incorporate some of these control functions inside themselves, they seem far more intelligent.

The next important development in the *idea* of the computer came from the eccentric British mathematician, Charles Babbage. Babbage's Analytic Engine was to be a true digital computer in the sense we will discuss below. (It never actually got off the drawing board.) Data were to be introduced on punched cards. It was to have a memory of 1,000 50-digit numbers. It would carry out any arithmetic operations, and it could modify its instructions on the basis of how the computation was going. This last feature, which Babbage described as "eating its own tail," is extremely important since it would allow the machine *to regulate itself.* This is an essential feature of all modern computers.

The first computer which actually worked was Howard Aiken's Mark I, a digital computer consisting of electromagnetic relays. It went into operation in 1944. Since then numerous improvements in design and components have increased the speed of computers enormously. Vacuum tubes replaced relays and were in turn replaced by transistors. As Apter (1970) notes, the speed of Babbage's machine might have been measured in seconds, the speed of vacuum-tube machines in milliseconds (10^{-3}), the speed of machines using transistors in microseconds (10^{-6}), and the speed of recent machines in nanoseconds (10^{-9}). Computers, then, have increased in speed a million times in the last 25 years.

One very important design advance was the stored program first used in 1949 in the EDVAC computer designed by Mauchly, Eckert, and Von Neuman. Stored programs have two advantages. The first is speed. Reading instructions is much faster when they are stored in computer memory than when they are stored externally on cards or magnetic tape. The second advantage is flexibility. With a stored program, it is practical to instruct the computer to change its own instructions. A simple example will illustrate how useful this feature is to the programmer. Suppose that we wanted to add up the digits from 1 to 1000. We could instruct the computer as follows:

Step	Instruction
1	Add 1 to the running total
2	Add 2 to the running total
3	Add 3 to the running total
.	.
.	.
.	.
1000	Add 1000 to the running total
1001	Print out the answer and stop

This would be a very tedious program to write. By instructing the computer to change its own instructions, however, our task becomes much easier. We can do the same job in just five steps:

Step	Instruction
1	Set n to 1
2	Add n to the running total
3	If $n = 1000$, print out the answer and stop
4	Add 1 to n
5	Go to step 2

If you have trouble understanding the five step program, try working through the steps, doing exactly what the instructions tell you, and keeping track of n and the running total. If you still have trouble, just remember the main point—when the computer is able to modify its own instructions, the programmer can write much shorter programs. The ability to make rapid self-modification is an important aspect of the machine's "intelligence."

The structure of a modern digital computer is shown in Figure 8–2. It has four major parts or sections: input-output, memory, processing, and control. To use the machine, a person inserts data and instructions

Figure 8–2. Structure of a modern digital computer

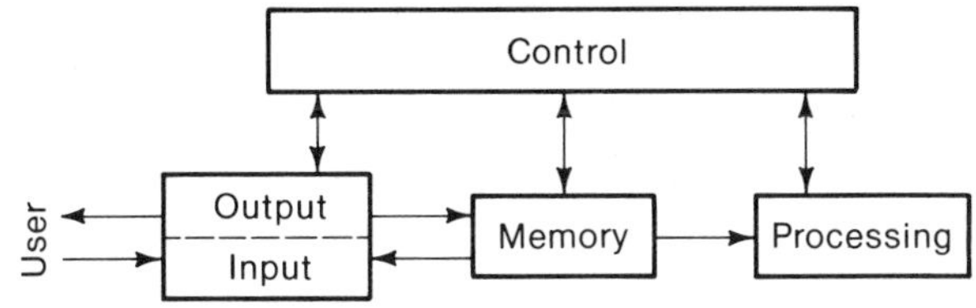

through an input device such as a teletype or a magnetic tape. If he uses a teletype or similar machine, he simply types the information which he wants the computer to have on the teletype. A special program (already in the computer memory) takes the information from the teletype and stores it in memory.

The computer memory consists of a large number of memory registers, places for storing numbers. Each memory register has an "address." For example, the first register will have the address 0001, the second, 0002, and so on. The organization of a typical computer memory is shown in Figure 8–3.

Figure 8–3.   Computer memory

Memory address	Content of memory register	
0001	0006	0571
0002	0007	1371
0003	0000	0918
0004	0000	0003
0005	0000	0000
—	—	—
—	—	—
0010	0020	0000
0011	0003	0001
0012	0003	0002
0013	0003	0003
0014	0005	0004
0015	0007	0005
0016	0040	0000
—	—	—
—	—	—
9998	0000	0000
9999	0000	0000

Suppose you want the computer to find the average of a set of numbers. First you give the machine the numbers you want averaged—the data—and a set of instructions for finding the average (the program). Your data and the program for computing averages are both stored in the computer memory in the same form, that is, as numbers.

In Figure 8–3 the numbers to be averaged—60,571, 71,371, and 918—are stored in the first three registers. The count of the numbers—3—is stored in register 4. The program for averaging the numbers is stored in registers 0010 through 0016. These locations for data and program are arbitrarily chosen by the programmer. Any free locations in memory would do.

The instructions look just like the data in that both are in numerical form, but we want them to be interpreted differently. We want the processing section to interpret the first part of each number as an action it would take and the second part as the address of the memory register that it would take the action on. For example, the 0003 part of the instruction in register 11 should be interpreted as "add" and the 0001 part as the address of the number which is to be added. Similarly, the 0005 part of the instruction in register 14 should be interpreted as "divide by" and the 0004 part as the address of the divisor. The number to be divided and the number to be added to are stored in a special working memory register.

The computer's control section controls the actions of the other sections. Suppose that we tell the control section, "start at register 0010." It will then direct the processing section to execute the instruction in register 0010. In this case, the instruction is to clear (erase) the working memory register. When this has been done, the control section in normal sequence directs the execution of instructions 0011, 0012, 0013, and so forth, in sequence, until it comes to the "Halt" instruction, 0040 0000, in register 0016. For some instructions, however, the normal sequence is changed. For example, an instruction may say, "If the quantity in the working memory register is negative, go to instruction 0092." In this case, if the running total is negative, control directs the execution of instruction 0092. If the running total is positive, however, it continues with the next instruction in the normal sequence.

Not only are recent machines faster than those of the 1950s, but they are also easier to use. Early machines were programmed by typing in a complex sequence of numbers. For example, to instruct the machine to add 43 to the working memory, we would have typed in something like 0003 0271, which the machine interpreted as "add the contents of register 271." Of course, we would have previously stored the number 43 in register 271. Today it is possible to program computers using a programming language which is very similar to English. For example, to instruct the machine to add 43, we can now simply type "add 43."

The instructions of the programming are translated by a special computer program into lists of numbers which control the computer, the machine's language. The result is that people can program in a language they understand (words), the computer receives the instructions in a language it understands (numbers), and a great deal of human effort is saved. Programming languages have names such as FORTRAN, ALGOL, BASIC, APL, and LISP.

Computers have come upon us with apparent suddenness because a very powerful idea awaited technological developments before it could be applied effectively. Most important were the developments in electronics—vacuum tubes, transistors, magnetic core memories, and so on, and in computer design. Also important, however, was the development of computer languages similar to English which made computers easier to use.

INFORMATION-PROCESSING MODELS

As we indicated above, what the advent of the computer really did was to give psychologists a new way to represent mental functioning—the information-processing model. To understand what information-processing models are, let us consider how such models are used to describe computer operations.

Suppose that we have two computers of very different vintage—an old, large, slow job made from relays and a new, compact, fast computer using transistors and magnetic core memory. If we program the two machines to give us the cube root of 29 by the logarithm method, they will give us the same answer—3.072. . . . The physical events which were involved at each stage of computing the answer, however, were entirely different. In one case the problem and instructions were represented as relay settings—as a set of positions of relay arms. In the other case, they were represented in the magnetic state of scores of tiny magnetic donuts with no physical resemblance to a relay. Despite the obvious physical differences between the two computational procedures, however, there is a very important sense in which the two procedures are the same. In solving the problem, each computer processed the information which we provided (namely, that we wanted the cube root of 29 by the logarithmic method) through the stages shown in Figure 8–4. Thus, the information processing was the same even though the physical events underlying the information processing were very different.

Figure 8–4.
Information-processing model
of logarithmic method

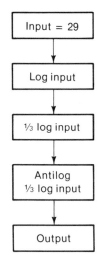

Input = 29

Log input

⅓ log input

Antilog
⅓ log input

Output

If we were now to program the two computers to find the cube root of 29 by Newton's method, rather than by the logarithmic method, both of the computers would process information differently from the way they did before. But again, despite their physical differences, both computers, when they are using Newton's method, can be described as carrying out the same sequence of information-processing steps. The partial results which Computer A obtains on its way to the final solution would correspond exactly to the partial results obtained by Computer B.

Information-processing models, then, ignore the physical representation of the information being processed. They make no distinctions between a number represented by a sequence of relay settings, by the magnetic state of a sequence of magnetic cores, or by the excitation of a set of neurons in a human brain. Information-processing models are concerned with how information is transformed. An information-processing model is concerned about whether a number is subtracted, squared, or logged, but not with the particular physical system by which that number is represented. Pegged counting wheels, relays, transistors, and neurons are all the same to it.

Now, back to the main question of this section: "What sort of alternative is it that information-processing models offer for psychology?" First, they provide an alternative to the black-box model which ignores internal processes. The fact that computers are complex and yet have objectively describable inner processes seems to have given us confidence that humans may have describable inner processes as well. We can use information-processing models, then, to propose descriptions for the contents of the unopenable black box.

Second, they provide an alternative to the physiological model. A physiological model is not an information-processing model either because it is tied to specific physical mechanisms. That is, a physiological model must involve physiological hardware such as receptors, cerebral neurons, or hormones. Unlike information-processing models, physiological models specify the particular physical means by which information is represented.

Progress in physiological psychology, while impressive, has been slow. It is not unreasonable to believe that we will achieve an adequate information-processing model of human thought processes long before we will find an adequate physiological model. Good physiological models are many years in the future, but information-processing models are achievable now.

Examples of information-processing models in psychology

The work of Posner and Mitchell (1967) provides us with an excellent example of the way information-processing models can be used to advantage in psychology. Posner and Mitchell asked people to do some very simple discrimination tasks involving upper and lower case letters. Pairs of letters were flashed on a screen and subjects were asked to respond to them as rapidly as possible. They were to press a "same" button if both letters were vowels or both were consonants and to press a "different" button if one letter was a vowel and the other a consonant. Notice that there are three different situations in which subjects were asked to press the "same" button:

1. Cases of *physical identity*, for example, AA and bb,
2. Cases of *name identity*, for example, aA and Hh, and
3. Cases of *category identity*, for example, AE, bH.

Table 8–1 shows the mean response times (the time from the appearance of the letters to pressing of the correct button) for the three "same"

Table 8–1. Response times in a letter discrimination task

Physical identity	Name identity	Category identity	Different
549	623	801	801

Source: Redrawn from data presented in M. I. Posner and R. F. Mitchell, "Chronometric Analysis of Classification," *Psychological Review, 74* (1967), p. 403.

situations and for the "different" situation. On the basis of these and other data, Posner and Mitchell proposed the information-processing model represented in Figure 8–5. In words, the Posner and Mitchell model is this: In making judgments subjects may employ three distinct information processes. First, they compare the physical appearance of the letters. If the letters are physically identical, they respond "same"; if not, they compare the names of the letters. If the names are the same, subjects respond "same." If not, they compare the categories of the letters. If the categories are the same (both vowels or both consonants), they respond "same." Otherwise, they respond "different."

What the model does is to specify the order in which people will process information in making same and different judgments. Notice that the model makes no reference to the physiological mechanisms which must underlie these information processes.

Another more elegant information processing model is that proposed by Groen and Parkman (1972) to account for the way in which first graders add numbers. The model is diagrammed in Figure 8–6. The model holds that when children add two numbers, say 3 and 5, they will first determine which of the numbers is the larger and which the smaller. They will then count up from the larger number, that is, suc-

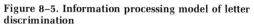

Figure 8–5. Information processing model of letter discrimination

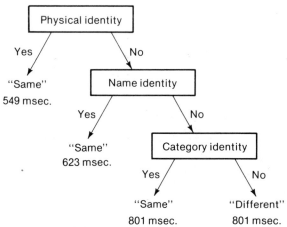

Source: Redrawn from M. I. Posner and R. F. Mitchell, "Chronometric Analysis of Classification," *Psychological Review,* 74 (1967), p. 404.

cessively add ones to the larger number, the smaller number of times. Thus, they will take 5 and add ones to it three times to get the answer 8. Groen and Parkman assume that it takes a fixed amount of time to find the larger and the smaller of the two numbers and another fixed amount of time to count up by one digit. It follows that the time required to add two numbers will increase as the smaller of the two numbers increases. Thus, adding 8 and 1 will involve one count, while adding 5 and 3 will involve three counts. Figure 8–7 shows that generally Groen and Parkman's model fits the data well. A few number pairs, however, such as 1 and 1 or 3 and 3 are added relatively quickly and the time does not appear to depend on the size of the smaller number. Groen and Parkman suggest that the children have learned these particularly simple number pairs by rote and that in these cases addition is done by remembering the answer rather than computing it.

Figure 8–6. Groen and Parkman's minimum model

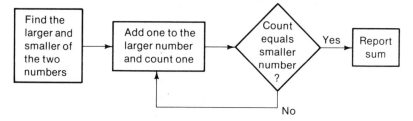

Figure 8—7. Overall mean latencies to each problem as a function of the minimum addend

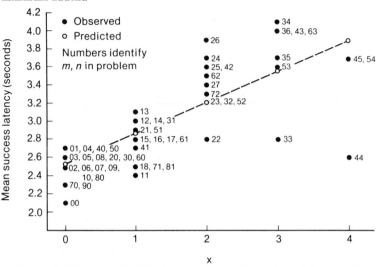

Notice that the Groen and Parkman account of children's addition is quite different from the more traditional view that learning arithmetic is strictly a matter of rote memorization. They hold that while children know some answers by rote, in most cases, they compute the answer anew rather than remembering it.

There are now many very interesting information-processing models in psychology. Good examples include Chase and Clark's (1972) model of how people compare pictures and sentences; Carpenter and Just's (1975) model of the processes involved in comprehending negatives in sentences; Hunt's (1974) model of how people solve visual analogy problems; and Greeno's (1976) model of geometry problem solving.

For the simpler models such as those of Posner and Mitchell (1967) and Groen and Parkman (1972), it is easy enough just using pencil and paper to understand the implications of the models. For more complex models, however, it is not so simple. Fortunately, the psychologist can again call on the computer for aid. Since an information-processing model is not concerned with the mechanism which does the processing—that is, it does not matter to the model whether the processing is done by neurons or transistors—it is natural to use computers to simulate complex models of human information processing. There are a number of advantages in using computer simulation to test a model. Among these are speed and objectivity. A computer can explore the implications of a complex model far more rapidly than can an unaided human. Further, computers are objective in carrying out directions. They require very explicit instructions from us and then they do exactly what we tell them. The results are sometimes surprising or embarrassing, or both. Thus, if we tell people to go outside and open the door, they will interpret our instructions and do what they believe we meant them to do. The computer will do exactly what it is told—it will crash through the door and then open what remains of it.

By demanding explicit instructions, computers force us to be very clear and explicit about our theory. If we tell our theory to humans, they may fill in the vague parts from their own knowledge or ignorance. The computer never does this. It does not know any psychology and thus forces us to deal with any vagueness that we may have let slip into our theory.

Feigenbaum and Simon have developed a very influential information-processing model of human memory called EPAM—for Elementary Perceiver and Memorizer—(Simon and Feigenbaum, 1964; Feigenbaum and Simon, 1962; Gregg and Simon, 1967). EPAM is a computer program which learns and remembers things.

To illustrate how EPAM works, let us assume that you and EPAM are sitting in your office awaiting the arrival of a sequence of three visitors: Smith, Jones, and Robinson. As a socially conscious person and a socially conscious computer program, respectively, the two of you want to learn to associate each visitor's name with his face as quickly as possible. Further, the two of you share a tendency, when recognizing people, to notice eyebrows first, nose second, and chin third. Finally, the two of you are quite impatient and try to recognize people on the basis of as little information as possible. While neither of you knows it as yet, Smith has bushy eyebrows, a big nose, and receding chin; Jones has bushy eyebrows, a small nose, and prominent chin; and Robinson has bushy eyebrows, a small nose, and a receding chin.

Smith arrives first. You notice his bushy eyebrows, and store a visual image of his face and a sound image of his name. When next you see a person obscured by darkness except for his bushy eyebrows, you will think of Smith's face and name. EPAM also notices his bushy eyebrows, and begins to build a discrimination net. The discrimination net consists of test nodes with tests such as, "What kind of eyebrows does he have?" and, "What kind of nose does he have?" and terminal nodes at which are stored visual images of faces and sound images of names. The net which EPAM builds as a result of meeting Smith is shown in Figure 8–8. Test nodes are shown as circles and terminal nodes as squares.

If EPAM were to meet Smith again, it would note the bushy eyebrows, move down the "bushy" branch of the net to the terminal node,

Figure 8–8. Net EPAM builds as a result of
meeting Smith

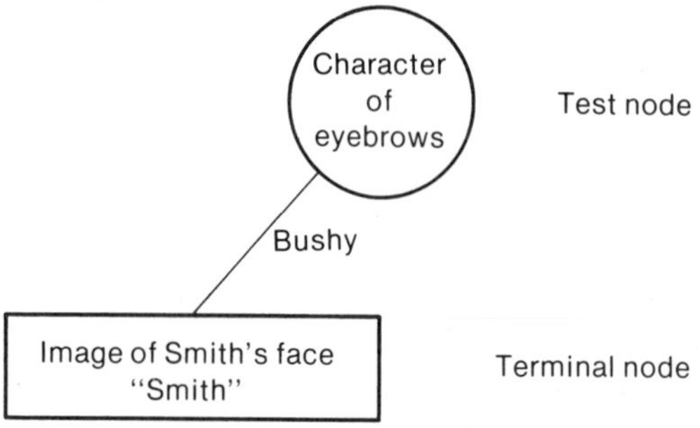

match Smith's face against the stored image and thus successfully
"recognize" Smith.

Now Smith leaves and Jones is ushered in. You look up quickly, see
Jones' bushy eyebrows and think for the moment that you are meeting
Smith again. Then you notice that Jones' face doesn't match your remembered image of Smith and recognize your mistake. To avoid making
the same mistake again, you take care to notice that while Smith has
a big nose, Jones has a small one.

Meanwhile EPAM has also noticed Jones' bushy eyebrows and has
sorted down through its discrimination net to the terminal node where
the image of Smith's face is stored. Since Jones' face does not match the
image of Smith's face, however, the recognition process has failed. As a
result, EPAM adds a new test to its net to discriminate between Smith
and Jones, in this case, a "nose" test, and creates a new terminal node
for Jones as shown in Figure 8–9.

Next Robinson comes in. You notice the bushy eyebrows and small
nose and think "Jones." But Robinson's face doesn't match your remembered image of Jones. To avoid this error in the future, you notice that
Robinson has a receding chin while Jones has a prominent one.

EPAM also notices Robinson's bushy eyebrows and small nose and
sorts down its discrimination net to the terminal node where it has
stored the image of Jones' face. It notices that Robinson's face doesn't
match the image and therefore that recognition has again failed. As a
result, it modifies its discrimination net by adding a "chin" test to its
net as shown in Figure 8–10.

The EPAM model exists (in various versions) as a computer program
and has been used to account for many aspects of human verbal reasoning. For example, Feigenbaum and Simon (1962) have used EPAM to
account for the serial-position effect. The serial-position effect is the
tendency for people to learn the beginning and the end of a list of words

Figure 8–9. EPAM adds a new terminal mode for Jones

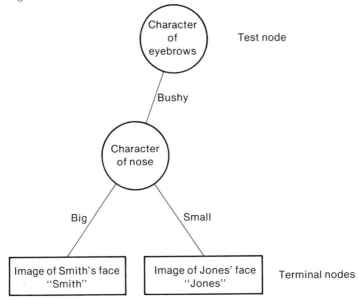

Figure 8–10. EPAM adds a new terminal node for Robinson

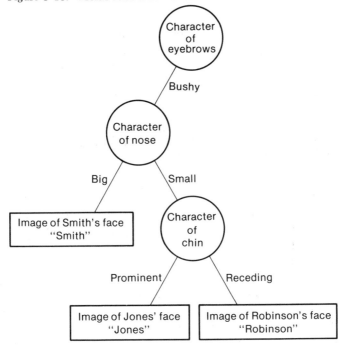

more easily than they learn the middle of the list. Since the model exists as a computer program, Feigenbaum and Simon were able to derive the prediction of the model by actually having the EPAM program learn a number of lists of words. The information-processing model which the program embodies will determine how difficult it is for EPAM to learn the words at each of the positions in the lists. The number of errors which EPAM makes can be compared position by position to the numbers of errors people make. If the EPAM model is a good one, it should be difficult to distinguish EPAM's learning behavior from that of a human. Figure 8–11 shows error curves for EPAM and for humans learning a 14-syllable list.

Figure 8–11.   Serial position effect for EPAM and for humans

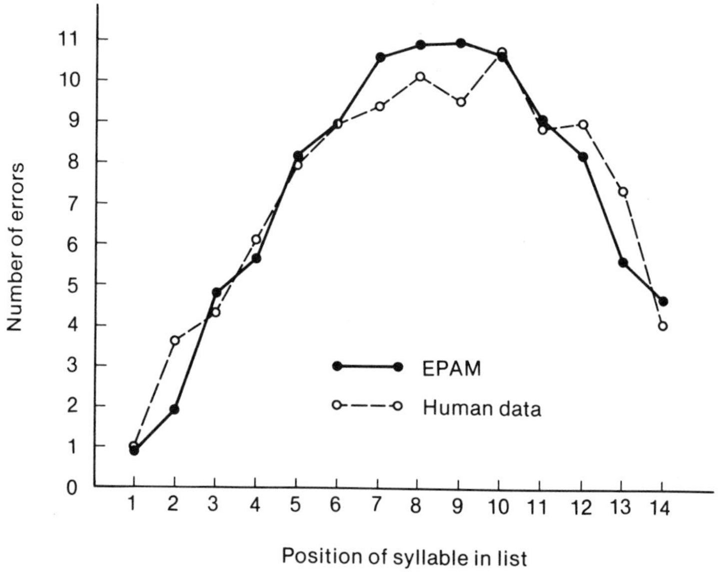

Position of syllable in list

Source: Based on data presented in E. A. Feigenbaum and H. A. Simon, "A Theory of the Serial Position Effect," *British Journal of Psychology*, 53 (1962), p. 313.

EPAM has been used by Simon and Gilmartin (1973) as the learning portion of their MAPP program. The MAPP program embodies an information-processing model of the chess player's skill in perceiving a position in a chess game.

We should point out that the purpose of computer simulation is *not* to get a computer to behave like a person. The purpose is to help us to understand how people behave by providing a quick and objective test of a psychological theory. If the program behaves in the way people do, the theory is supported. If not, the theory must be revised. The important result of a computer simulation is not a computer that behaves like a person. Rather it is increased knowledge about the functioning of the human mind.

COMPUTER SIMULATION AND ARTIFICIAL INTELLIGENCE

The development of the computer has suggested a new technique for analyzing mental phenomena—the information-processing model—and has provided a powerful objective method for testing these models—computer simulation. Psychology has gotten more from the computer revolution, though, than just information-processing models and computer simulation. In addition, it has been enriched by discoveries in the field of artificial intelligence. Artificial intelligence is the discipline concerned with programming computers to do complex tasks which in the past have been assumed to require human intelligence.

Though their goals are very different, computer simulation and artificial intelligence are frequently confused. A computer simulation is a test of a theory about human performance of some task, say in memory or problem solving. The test succeeds if the computer performs the task *the way people do* and fails otherwise. In artificial intelligence, however, the goal is to get the computer to do the task in the best way it can. Usually the best way for the computer to do the task is not the way humans do it.

Even though studies in artificial intelligence are not *aimed* at understanding human thought processes, still psychologists can make use of them for just this purpose. A geographical analogy will help to illustrate this point. If we were planning to explore the wilds of a little known territory, we would want to talk to others who had explored that territory even if their explorations did not cross our intended path. We could learn of the special difficulties the territory presented to the explorer—diseases, impassable mountains, lack of critical resources—and perhaps some hints about how these difficulties can be overcome.

Heuristic search and the Logic Theorist

An important idea that psychology has borrowed from computer science is *heuristic search*. In oversimplified terms, heuristic search is intelligent search. It involves using your knowledge to guide your search for something to those places where it is most likely to be. The importance of heuristic search was first brought to the attention of the scientific world through a dramatic demonstration of its power in the Logic Theorist, a program for discovering proofs in logic, devised by Newell and Simon (1956).

Logic Theorist, or LT, as we will call it hereafter, was genuinely an exploration in artificial intelligence. The objective was to get the computer to discover proofs in logic. It was *not* intended to be and it was not a simulation of the processes by which humans discover proofs in logic.

Since many readers are not familiar with the technical aspects of logic, we will discuss the operation of LT in terms of principles and avoid details. Excellent discussions by Newell and Simon (1956, 1972) will provide the interested reader with a deeper and more detailed description.

Discovering proofs in logic is very much like discovering proofs in geometry. One starts with a small set of axioms, that is, elementary statements which are assumed to be true without proof. The first theorems are deduced from the axioms alone and later theorems from the axioms together with the earlier theorems. In all cases, proofs are carried out using strict rules of inference.

Figure 8–12 is a schematic representation of the process by which theorems are derived from axioms and from theorems proved earlier. Theorem T11 is derived directly from axioms 1 and 2, and theorem T22 from theorem T11 and axiom 3. The theorems are classed as one-step theorems, two-step theorems, three-step theorems, etc., depending on the number of steps of inference required to derive them from the axioms.

Figure 8–12.   Schematic representation of the process by which theorems are derived from axioms and theorems proved earlier

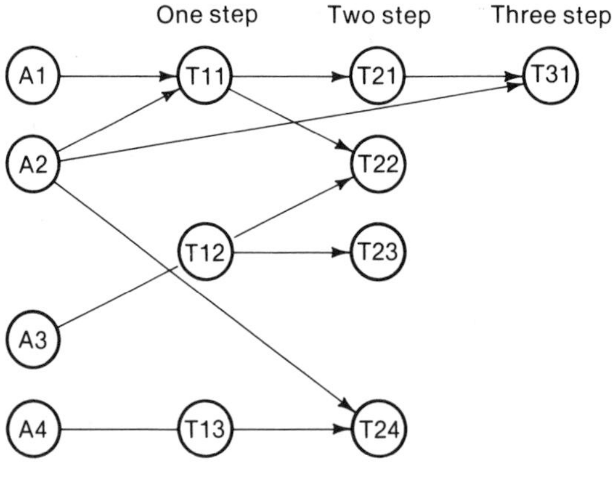

Exhaustive search

There is a charming fantasy which illustrates the idea that order can be selected from chaos. The fantasy is that if we were to allow a thousand monkeys to type away at a thousand typewriters for long enough, they would eventually type out all of the volumes in the British museum. While the fantasy is startling to some, the underlying idea is a correct one. If the monkeys had enough time, they *would* type out all of the volumes in the British museum. The practical problem lies in letting them have enough time. Let us try to set a lower limit on the amount of time that would be required. First, let us assume that we will be satisfied if we get all of the sentences which are 100 letters or less in length. Second, let us assume that through careful training we have gotten our monkeys to search systematically rather than randomly for sentences. That is, when they type strings of letters, they start with aaa. . . .aa, then type aaa. . . .ab, aaa. . . .ac, and so forth, through zzz. . . .zz. This systematic procedure is more efficient than random typing because it insures that no strings will be duplicated. Further, let us assume that our well-trained monkeys each types 120 words or 600 letters or six 100-letter strings per minute. Now, if we had a thousand such monkeys, and we let them type day and night for a million years, they would produce about 3×10^{15} 100-letter strings. But this is a very small proportion of the total number of 100-letter strings. If we allow 26 letters and a space as the allowable symbols, then there are 27^{100} possible strings 100 letters long or about 10^{140} strings—a number monstrously larger than the number of strings our monkeys can produce in a million years of typing. Clearly, if we are at all impatient, we are not going to want to wait for our monkeys to finish their typing job.

We could turn our monkeys' efforts to generating logic theorems by providing them with special typewriters which type only logic expressions. It should be clear, though, from our experience in trying to get the monkeys to generate sentences, that this is a *very* inefficient procedure. For comparison with LT, Newell and Simon (1972) have suggested a procedure which resembles the exhaustive search procedures used by the monkeys. They call it the *British Museum Algorithm* (BMA). The British Museum Algorithm first generates all of the theorems which can be derived from the axioms in one step. Next it generates all of the theorems which can be derived in two steps, and so on. Figure 8–13 shows how many theorems the British Museum Algorithm generates in various numbers of steps.

LT versus the British Museum Algorithm

Now, not all logic theorems are "interesting" even by logician's standards. Logic textbooks certainly do not present all possible logic theorems, nor do they even present all of the simpler theorems. Rather, they are very selective and present only those theorems which are especially useful either for applications or for providing more logic theorems.

Newell and Simon (1956) were interested in LT's ability to prove interesting theorems. As a test, they set it the task of proving the theorems in an early chapter of Whitehead and Russell's classic work on

Figure 8–13. Number of proofs generated by
first few steps of British Museum Algorithm

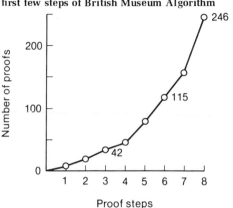

Proof steps

Source: A. Newell, and H. A. Simon, *Human Problem Solving.* Englewood Cliffs, N.J.: Prentice-Hall
1972, p. 109.

logic, *Principia Mathematica* (1935). Before examining LT's performance, though, we will first ask how the British Museum Algorithm
performs this same task.

When the British Museum Algorithm starts working, one of the first
42 theorems it proves is an interesting one—Whitehead and Russell's
theorem 2.01. Then three more of their theorems turn up by the time it
has cranked out the first 115 theorems—Whitehead and Russell's
theorems 2.02, 2.03, and 2.04. However, only two more of their
theorems—2.05 and 2.07—turn up in the first thousand theorems
proved. Newell and Simon estimate that the remaining theorems of the
chapter (58 in number) are hidden among some $10^{1,000}$ other theorems
which the British Museum Algorithm might prove. They estimate
therefore that it would take "eons of eons" of computing time for the
British Museum Algorithm to prove the remaining theorems in the
Whitehead and Russell chapter.

LT was tested on the first 52 of the theorems of the chapter. Of these,
it succeeded in proving 38, or 73 percent. About half of these theorems
were proved in less than a minute, most of the rest took from 1 to 5
minutes, and a few took up to 45 minutes.

LT's advantage—Heuristic search

The main reason LT is so much more successful than the British
Museum Algorithm is that it is much more selective in searching for
proofs than is the British Museum Algorithm. While BMA tries everything it can to find a theorem, LT only tries those approaches that seem

promising. The result is that BMA wastes a great deal of time exploring blind alleys which LT chooses not to enter.

Two of the processes LT uses which make its search selective are *similarity testing* and *matching*. LT works by applying rules of inference to the already proved theorems in an attempt to transform them into the desired theorem. LT, however, will not try to transform just any theorem. Before it attempts a transformation, LT applies a similarity test. If the already proved theorem is very different from the theorem LT is attempting to prove, LT will drop it from consideration and search for another already proved theorem which can pass the similarity test. Since transformation is more likely to succeed between similar theorems than between dissimilar ones, the similarity test allows LT to concentrate its efforts where they are most likely to succeed.

When LT finds a known theorem which passes the similarity test, the attempt to transform it into the desired theorem is guided by the *matching* process. We will use a very crude analogy to describe how the matching process works and why it helps.

Suppose that you want to determine if the letters abcdef are an anagram for the word *gadfly*. BMA would generate all possible combinations of the letter sequence (720 of them) and then notice that *gadfly* was not one of them. This would require 720 complex comparisons. LT's matching process would start with A and match it against the A in gadfly. This requires not more than 6 simple (one letter) comparisons. Then it would consider the B and fail to match it, again requiring not more than 6 simple comparisons. At this point it would report, "No, the letter string is not an anagram for gadfly," and stop—a much quicker process than that used by BMA.

The matching process helps because it breaks the search for a solution into parts and does the parts one at a time—when any part fails, the search process is stopped.

The idea of heuristic search has proved extremely useful to psychologists trying to understand human problem solving. People are quite slow compared to computers. Therefore trial and error and exhaustive search are even less attractive problem-solving procedures for people than they are for machines. To solve any very complex problem, people must use heuristic search. In Chapter 10, we will discuss some heuristic search procedures which are especially useful for describing human problem solving.

SUMMARY

The development of computers had three major effects on psychology:

1. It provided psychologists with a powerful theoretical tool—the information-processing model—which could serve as an alternative to black-box and physiological models.

2. It provided psychologists with a powerful practical tool—computer simulation—for testing complex psychological theories; and
3. It provided psychologists with a very valuable source of ideas for psychological theories through developments in the field of artificial intelligence.

FURTHER READING

Feigenbaum and Feldman (see References following) include a number of the important early papers in this field in their book, *Computers and Thought* (1963).

REFERENCES

APTER, M. J.   *The computer simulation of behavior.* New York: Harper & Row, 1970.

CARPENTER, P. A., and JUST, M. A.   "Sentence comprehension: A psycholinguistic processing model of verification," *Psychological Review, 82* (1975), pp. 45–73.

CHASE, W. G., and CLARK, H. H.   "Mental operations in the comparison of sentences and pictures," *Cognition in learning and memory.* Ed. L. Gregg. New York: Wiley, 1972.

FEIGENBAUM, E. A., and FELDMAN, J.   *Computers and thought.* New York: McGraw-Hill Book Company, Inc., 1963.

FEIGENBAUM, E. A., and SIMON, H. A.   "A theory of the serial position effect," *British Journal of Psychology, 53* (1962), pp. 307–320.

GREENO, J. G.   "Cognitive objectives of instructions: Theory of knowledge for solving problems and answering questions," *Cognition and instruction.* Ed. D. Klahr. Hillsdale, N.J.: Lawrence Erlbaum, 1976.

GREGG, L. W., and SIMON, H. A.   "An information-processing explanation of one-trial and incremental learning," *Journal of Verbal Learning and Verbal Behavior, 6* (1967), pp. 780–787.

GROEN, G. J., and PARKMAN, J. M.   "A chronometric analysis of simple addition," *Psychological Review, 79* (1972), pp. 329–343.

HUNT, E.   "Quote the Raven? Nevermore!" *Knowledge and cognition.* Ed. L. Gregg. Potomac, Maryland: Lawrence Erlbaum, 1974.

NEWELL, A., and SIMON, H. A.   "The logic theory machine: A complex information-processing system," *I.R.E. Transactions on Information Theory, 2* (1956), pp. 61–79.

NEWELL, A., and SIMON, H. A.   *Human problem solving.* © 1972, p. 109. Reprinted by permission of Prentice-Hall, Inc., Englewood Cliffs, N.J.

POSNER, M. I., and MITCHELL, R. F.   "Chronometric analysis of classification," *Psychological Review, 74* (1967), pp. 392–409.

SIMON, H. A., and FEIGENBAUM, E. A.   "An information-processing theory of some effects of similarity, familiarization, and meaningfulness in verbal learning," *Journal of Verbal Learning and Verbal Behavior, 3* (1964), pp. 385–396.

SIMON, H. A., and GILMARTIN, K.   "A simulation of memory for chess positions," *Cognitive Psychology, 5* (1973), pp. 29–46.

WHITEHEAD, A. N., and RUSSELL, B.   *Principia mathematica,* vol. I, 2d ed. Cambridge: The University Press, 1935.

SECTION III

RESEARCH IN COGNITIVE PSYCHOLOGY

In the last four chapters we have presented three themes which we feel are especially important in the evolution of cognitive psychology.

1. Piaget exemplified the growing awareness among psychologists that complex mental structures were essential to psychological theories.
2. The Behaviorists' failure to make progress in describing language led many to believe that a new theoretical approach was desirable.
3. The development of information-processing models provided a new approach which facilitated the description of complex mental structures.

Newell and Simon presented the first statement of the new approach in 1958 in their paper, "Elements of a theory of human problem solving." Chomsky published "A review of B. F. Skinner's Verbal Behavior" in 1959. These two events, occurring close in time, provided a strong impetus for many to turn to cognitive psychology.

In the next four chapters, we will discuss research in four very active areas of cognitive psychology to illustrate the power of the new approach.

Chapter 9

Modern approaches to language

Linguists have traditionally distinguished between the grammar of a language and its semantics or meaning. The sentence, "Colorless green ideas sleep furiously," is perfectly grammatical. Its grammatical structure—adjective, adjective, noun, verb, adverb—is shared by more sensible sounding sentences such as, "Big white sheep walk slowly." The problem with the sentence is in its semantics. We know that a real-world object cannot be both colorless and green, that ideas neither have color nor do they sleep, and that sleeping is typically not done furiously. We cannot match these words to things and actions in the real world, and so the sentence does not mean anything to us. On the other hand, the sentence, "Me no spoke so good English," while it violates many grammatical rules, is understandable and meaningful. Clearly grammar and semantics can be judged separately.

Chomsky's most important contributions have been to the analysis of grammar. It is fair to say that he has initiated the modern phase of grammatical study. In the modern view, a grammar is a set of rules which serves two functions. First, it differentiates grammatical sentences from ungrammatical strings of words. Second, it identifies grammatical relations among the various parts of the sentence. For example, it identifies such relations as subject, verb, and direct object.

An important property of modern grammars is that they are generative; that is, they consist of sets of rules which generate sentences in the same way as the axioms of geometry generate theorems. There are many different forms such a set of rules might take. One popular form is called a "phrase structure" grammar. The set of rules in Figure 9–1 is an example of a simple phrase structure grammar which generates a set of English sentences from an initial symbol S (for sentence). The rules of the grammar are called rewrite rules because they are read, "X

Figure 9–1.   An example of a phrase structure grammar

S ⟶ noun phrase (NP) + verb phrase (VP)
NP ⟶ determiner (D) + noun (N)
VP ⟶ verb (V) + noun phrase (NP)
D ⟶ the, a
N ⟶ cat, dog, mouse, etc.
V ⟶ hit, bit, shot, etc.

Source: J. R. Hayes, ed., *Cognition and the Development of Language*. New York: John Wiley & Sons, Inc., 1970, p. 2.

may be rewritten as Y." For example, the first rule is read, "S may be rewritten as NP + VP."

The tree diagram in Figure 9–2 shows how the rules may be applied in succession to generate an English sentence. The part of the diagram

Figure 9–2.   Tree diagram applying rules in succession to generate an English sentence

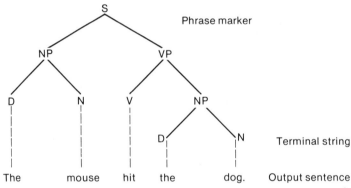

Source: J. R. Hayes, ed., *Cognition and the Development of Language,* New York: John Wiley & Sons, Inc., 1970, p. 2.

above the dashed line is called the phrase marker of the sentence. The lowest line of the phrase marker, just above the output sentence, is called the terminal string.

In a phrase structure grammar, the phrase marker provides a complete description of the grammatical relations among the parts of the sentence. We can determine, for example, whether a noun is the subject, the direct object, or the indirect object of a sentence simply by knowing where it fits in the phrase marker.

The important fact about a generative grammar is that it is perfectly explicit. Such grammars, unlike traditional grammars, spell out *all* of the rules for deciding whether a sentence is grammatical or not. Nothing is left to the reader's linguistic intuition.

The rules which we illustrated above are of the type called phrase structure rules. Chomsky (1965) argues that phrase structure rules are not sufficient in themselves to yield an adequate grammar. He claims that a grammar must also contain rules of another type called transformation rules.

A transformation rule is a rule which takes the terminal string of a phrase marker and modifies it to produce a new string. Figure 9–3 shows in simplified form how a passive transformation rule might modify the terminal string in Figure 9–2 to yield a passive sentence.

Figure 9–3. A transformation rule modifying the terminal string

D_1 + N_1 + V + D_2 + N_2 → D_2 + N_2 + was + V + by + D_1 + N_1
The   mouse   hit   the   dog.   The   dog   was   hit   by   the   mouse.

Source: J. R. Hayes, ed., *Cognition and the Development of Language*, New York: John Wiley & Sons, Inc., 1970, p. 3.

Chomsky argues for the inclusion of transformation rules in the grammar because they simplify the description of some common grammatical relations. Consider the four sentences shown in Figure 9–4. Clearly these sentences are closely related. If the grammar con-

Figure 9–4. Sentences illustrating grammatical transformations

SAAD (Simple Active Affirmative Declarative) . . . .   The mouse hit the dog.
Passive . . . .   The dog was hit by the mouse.
Negative . . . .   The mouse did not hit the dog.
Question . . . .   Did the mouse hit the dog?

Source: J. R. Hayes, ed., *Cognition and the Development of Language*, New York: John Wiley & Sons, Inc., 1970, p. 3.

tained only phrase structure rules, the four sentences would have very different-appearing phrase markers and these would in no way reveal this close relationship. If the grammar contained transformation rules as well, however, all four sentences could be derived (by the application of active, passive, negative, or interrogative transformations) from the *same* underlying phrase marker, such as the one shown in Figure 9–1. The identical phrase marker would represent the core of sameness among these sentences, and the different transformations which modify it could represent the differences.

Chomsky describes the transformation rules as belonging to the surface structure of the grammar because they determine immediately apparent details such as the word order of the spoken sentence. The phrase structure rules, on the other hand, belong to the deep structure because they reflect underlying structural properties. In the example above, we saw that the phrase markers reflected underlying similarities among sentences which were superficially quite different. In ambiguous sentences, on the other hand, the phrase markers will reflect underlying differences between sentences which appear superficially identical. The simplified phrase markers in Figure 9–5 reveal the structural differences in the two sentences which have the form, "They are playing cards."

Figure 9–5. Structural differences between two superficially identical sentences

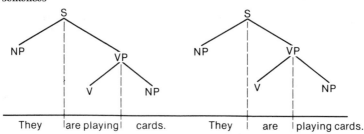

Source: J. R. Hayes, ed., *Cognition and the Development of Language*, New York: John Wiley & Sons, Inc., 1950, p. 4.

GRAMMAR AS A MODEL OF HUMAN LANGUAGE PROCESSES

Impressed by the success of the new grammatical theories, psycholinguists were anxious to borrow what they could from the grammarians for application to their own problems. So, with an eye to sharing the scientific wealth, psycholinguists launched a vigorous experimental program to find psychological correlates for grammatical structures. They wanted to determine, for example, if there were psychological processes corresponding to transformations or to the rewrite rules of phrase structure grammars.

We should note that there is a major issue here. A grammar may or may not correspond to the psychological processes by which sentences are generated. Grammars were intended by linguists as descriptions— descriptions of the structure of sentences. A description may, or may not, correspond to the processes by which the thing described was generated. An anatomical description of a cat, for example, bears no simple relation to the processes by which cats are generated. A recipe for lasagne, however, is exactly a description which specifies the processes for generating lasagne. The issue, then, is whether a grammar is an anatomy of a sentence or a recipe for a sentence.

Brown (1965) proposed a form of the recipe hypothesis in connection with his research on the language of young children. He proposed that the phrase structure grammars which describe the speech of his young subjects be viewed as models for the mechanism which the subjects actually use to generate sentences.

The best evidence for the recipe hypothesis comes not from studies of phrase structure rules but rather from studies of transformations. The experiment of Miller, McKean, and Slobin on transformations (1962) illustrates one rather direct approach to the recipe problem. They tested the idea that it is easier for people to match sentences which differ by one transformation than sentences which differ by two transformations. Subjects were given two lists of sentences. The second list consisted of grammatical transformations of the sentences in the first list but arranged in different order from those in the first list. The subjects' task was to match the sentences with their transformations as fast as they could. In some conditions only one transformation was required. For example, to get from, "Joe hit the ball," to, "The ball was hit by Joe," requires only the passive transformation. Other conditions require two transformations. For example, to get from, "Joe hit the ball," to, "The ball was not hit by Joe," requires both passive and negative transformations. Examples in which no transformations were required were included to provide baseline data. The measure of performance was the time required to match all of the sentences minus the baseline time.

The rationale of the experiment was this: According to the recipe hypothesis, a longer grammatical derivation implies a longer sequence of psychological processes. A longer sequence of psychological processes, in turn, requires more time. Thus, matching sentences which are two transformations apart should take more time than matching sentences which are one transformation apart.

The results were quite encouraging for the recipe hypothesis, as Figure 9–6 shows. The double arrow indicates that the results are averaged over both directions of the transformation, for example passive to negative and negative to passive. Other experiments have confirmed these results in their essential features (Miller and McKean, 1964).

Figure 9–6. Results from a transformation experiment supporting the recipe hypothesis

	Seconds longer than base search time
SAAD ↔ Negative	1.1
SAAD ↔ Passive	1.4
Passive ↔ Passive, negative	1.7
Negative ↔ Passive, negative	1.9
SAAD ↔ Passive, negative	2.7
Negative ↔ Passive	3.5

Source: J. R. Hayes, ed., *Cognition and the Development of Language*, New York: John Wiley & Sons, Inc., 1970, p. 6.

Another approach to the recipe problem is illustrated in the extremely clever experiment of Savin and Perchonock (1965). This experiment tested two hypotheses simultaneously. First, it tested the recipe hypothesis in the following form: Remembering a transformation of many steps requires more memory slots than remembering a transformation of few steps. Second, it tested Savin and Perchonock's hypothesis that sentences are stored as an underlying SAAD sentence plus transformations. Thus, "The ball was not hit by Joe," would be stored as, "Joe hit the ball," plus "negative" plus "passive."

The subjects' task in the experiment was to listen to a short sentence followed by a list of unrelated words, and then immediately to repeat as much as they could of what they had just heard. The subjects almost always correctly remembered the sentence and some but not all of the unrelated words. The number of unrelated words remembered, then, was a good measure of how much memory was occupied by the sentence.

There again the results were quite encouraging for the recipe hypothesis. Subjects remembered an average of 5.27 unrelated words when the sentence was an SAAD. They remembered between 4.30 and 4.78 unrelated words when the sentence required one additional transformation, and they remembered between 3.48 and 4.02 unrelated words when the sentence required two additional transformations.

The two experiments which we have described in detail represent a large number of such studies which have given predominantly positive results. As a whole they have made quite a strong case for the recipe hypothesis.

Despite these early encouraging results, the recipe hypothesis has proved to be a disappointment. Fodor and Garrett (1966) have listed several reasons for doubting it in their critical review. First and most important is the fact that a number of experiments have failed to show the expected results; e.g., Mehler (1963), Miller and McKean (1964), Bever, Fodor, Garrett, and Mehler (1966). Most researchers have now abandoned the recipe hypothesis concerning phrase structure and transformational grammars. These grammars are viewed as providing a very useful anatomy of sentences but not a recipe for generating them. The search for the psychological processes underlying language generation has moved in other directions, as we will see below.

ARTIFICIAL INTELLIGENCE RESEARCH ON LANGUAGE UNDERSTANDING

Researchers in artificial intelligence have carried out an enormous amount of work on language understanding. We will discuss just two projects here, both of which illustrate something about the role of semantics in language. One is Weizenbaum's program ELIZA (1966), which shows how far one can go with very little knowledge. The other is Winograd's program SHRDLU (1970), which makes very good use of semantic knowledge in understanding a limited world of children's blocks.

ELIZA—A Computer Therapist

ELIZA is a program designed to carry on conversations with people (through a typewriter) much in the manner of a nondirective therapist. In the dialogue below (reported by Weizenbaum, 1966, pp. 36–43), the first to speak is a young lady. The computer's responses are printed entirely in capitals, that being the only way computers print.

Dialogue 1

Men are all alike.
IN WHAT WAY
They're always bugging us about something or other.
CAN YOU THINK OF A SPECIFIC EXAMPLE
Well, my boyfriend made me come here.
YOUR BOYFRIEND MADE YOU COME HERE
He says I'm depressed much of the time.
I AM SORRY TO HEAR YOU ARE DEPRESSED
It's true. I am unhappy.
DO YOU THINK COMING HERE WILL HELP YOU NOT TO BE UNHAPPY
I need some help, that much seems certain.
WHAT WOULD IT MEAN TO YOU IF YOU GOT SOME HELP
Perhaps I could learn to get along with my mother.
TELL ME MORE ABOUT YOUR FAMILY
My mother takes care of me.
WHO ELSE IN YOUR FAMILY TAKES CARE OF YOU
My father.
YOUR FATHER
You are like my father in some ways.
WHAT RESEMBLANCE DO YOU SEE
You are not very aggressive but I think you don't want me to notice that.
WHAT MAKES YOU THINK I AM NOT VERY AGGRESSIVE
You don't argue with me.
WHY DO YOU THINK I DON'T ARGUE WITH YOU
You are afraid of me.
DOES IT PLEASE YOU TO BELIEVE I AM AFRAID OF YOU

My father is afraid of everybody.
WHAT ELSE COMES TO MIND WHEN YOU THINK OF YOUR FATHER
Bullies.
DOES THAT HAVE ANYTHING TO DO WITH THE FACT THAT YOUR
  BOYFRIEND MADE YOU COME HERE

After reading this dialogue, many find it hard to believe that ELIZA understands almost nothing of what is said to it. In fact, ELIZA understands almost nothing of what is said to it. It would respond just as glibly to sentences such as, "My mumble bzzz grumble grumble," as to sensible English.

What ELIZA does is to examine the sentences which humans type to it to find keywords it can respond to. These include personal pronouns such as I, me, you, family related words, question words such as how and what, and a relatively small number of other word groups.

If you were being interviewed by ELIZA and you typed the sentence, "It's obvious that you really detest me," ELIZA would recognize the keywords "you" and "me." It would then divide your sentence into four parts, as follows:

It's obvious that   you   really detest   me.

       1   2   3   4

ELIZA constructs its reply starting with the stock phrase, "WHAT MAKES YOU THINK THAT I. . ." It then copies part 3 of your sentence and adds the word "YOU" to the end to yield the very sensible reply,
"WHAT MAKES YOU THINK THAT I REALLY DETEST YOU?"

If you had typed, "Am I too dependent?" ELIZA would recognize the keywords "am" and "I." In this case it constructs its reply of the stock phrase, "DO YOU BELIEVE YOU ARE. . ." to which it adds your words, "TOO DEPENDENT."

If you type a question involving the words "how" or "what," ELIZA will parry with, "WHY DO YOU ASK?" OR "IS THAT AN IMPORTANT QUESTION?"

When ELIZA fails to find a keyword, it does one of two things. Either it replies with an innocuous phrase such as "PLEASE GO ON," "THAT'S VERY INTERESTING," or, "I SEE," or it draws on its memory. We should note that ELIZA stores in its memory any statement the human types which contains the word "my." Thus, in the dialogue above, among other things, ELIZA stored, "My boyfriend made me come here." When it found no keyword in the reply, "Bullies," it reached into its memory at random to construct, "DOES THAT HAVE ANYTHING TO DO WITH THE FACT THAT YOUR BOYFRIEND MADE YOU COME HERE?"

ELIZA's ability to make sensible replies in Dialogue 1 depends in a large measure on the fact that the human it is conversing with is talking sense to it. The same rules which allowed ELIZA to appear so sensible before would lead to the following dialogue if we were to talk nonsense to it.

Dialogue 2

My mumble bzzz grumble grumble.
THAT'S VERY INTERESTING.
Ugh, you izzle flerp me.
WHAT MAKES YOU THINK THAT I IZZLE FLERP YOU?
Gorch.
DOES THAT HAVE ANYTHING TO DO WITH THE FACT THAT YOUR
   MUMBLE BZZZ GRUMBLE GRUMBLE?

SHRDLU

Clearly, the fact that a computer program (or anyone else) can be pleasantly conversational is no guarantee that it understands what we say to it. It would be a far better test of understanding if the program took some appropriate action on the basis of what we told it. Winograd's program SHRDLU is able to pass this sort of test of understanding. SHRDLU will correctly carry out instructions in natural language about a set of children's blocks. Here again the human's questions and directions are in lower case and SHRDLU's responses are in upper case. The world of blocks and the changes that SHRDLU makes to it are displayed on a TV screen as shown in Figures 9–7 to 9–10.

Dialogue 3

1. Pick up a big red block.
   OK.

   The system answers "OK" when it carries out a command. In order to pick up the red block, it had to clear it off by finding a space for the green one and moving the green one away. Figure 9–7 shows the scene when the command was given, and Figure 9–8 shows the end result.

2. Grasp the pyramid.
   I DON'T UNDERSTAND WHICH PYRAMID YOU MEAN.

   When SHRDLU doesn't understand, it does nothing.

3. Find a block which is taller than the one you are holding and put it into the box.
   BY "IT," I ASSUME YOU MEAN THE BLOCK WHICH IS TALLER THAN THE ONE I AM HOLDING.
   OK.

Figure 9–7.

Pick up a big red block.

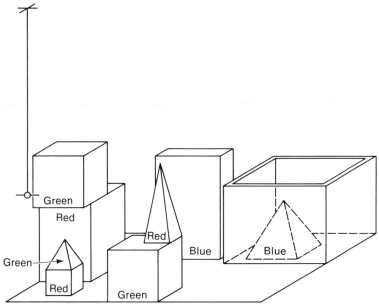

Source: T. Winograd, "Procedures as a Representation for Data in a Computer Program for Understanding Natural Language," Doctoral dissertation, M.I.T., 1970, p. 36.

4. What does the box contain?
    THE BLUE PYRAMID AND THE BLUE BLOCK.

5. What is the pyramid supported by?

    > *Earlier the system responded to "the pyramid" by saying, "I don't understand which pyramid you mean." Now, it knows that we must mean the one which was just mentioned.*

    THE BOX.

6. How many blocks are not in the box?
    FOUR OF THEM.

7. Is at least one of them narrower than the one which I told you to pick up?
    YES, THE RED CUBE.

8. Is it supported?
    YES, BY THE TABLE.

9. Can the table pick up blocks?
    NO.

10. Can a pyramid be supported by a block?
    YES.

    > *The deductive system finds an actual example; so it knows this is possible.*

Figure 9–8.

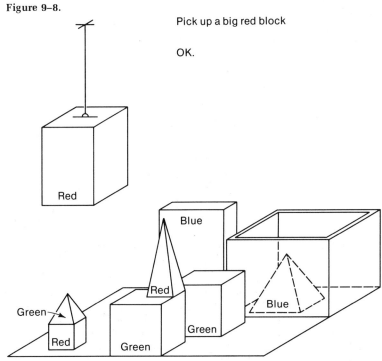

Pick up a big red block

OK.

Source: T. Winograd, "Procedures as a Representation for Data in a Computer Program for Understanding Natural Language," Doctoral dissertation, M.I.T., 1970, p. 38.

11. Can a pyramid support a pyramid?
     I DON'T KNOW.
12. Stack up two pyramids.
     I CAN'T.
          SHRDLU tries and fails.
13. The blue pyramid is nice.
     I UNDERSTAND.
          This data is added to the data base.
14. I like blocks which are not red, but I don't like anything which supports a pyramid.
     I UNDERSTAND.
          Two new theorems are created for proving things about "liking."
15. Do I like the box?
     NO.
16. Do I like anything in the box?
     YES, TWO THINGS: THE BLUE BLOCK AND THE BLUE PYRAMID.

Figure 9–9.

Will you please stack up both of the red
blocks and either the green cube or a pyramid.

OK.

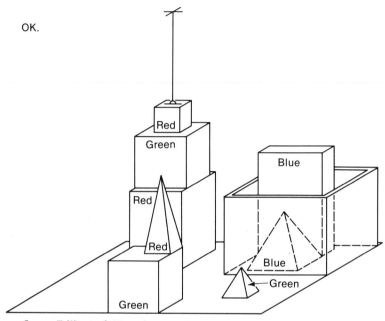

Source: T. Winograd, "Procedures as a Representation for Data in a Computer Program
for Understanding Natural Language," Doctoral dissertation, M.I.T., 1970, p. 45.

17. Will you please stack up both of the red blocks and either a green cube or a
    pyramid?
    OK.
18. Which cube is sitting on the table?
    THE LARGE GREEN ONE WHICH SUPPORTS THE RED PYRAMID.
19. Is there a large block behind a pyramid?
    YES, THREE OF THEM: A LARGE RED ONE, A LARGE GREEN CUBE
    AND THE BLUE ONE.
20. Put a small one onto the green cube which supports a pyramid.
    OK.
21. Put the littlest pyramid on top of it.
    OK.
22. Does the shortest thing the tallest pyramid's support supports support
    anything green?
    YES, THE GREEN PYRAMID.
23. What color is it?

Figure 9–10.

Put the littlest pyramid on top of it.

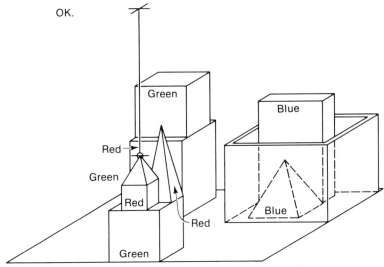

Source: T. Winograd, "Procedures as a Representation for Data in a Computer Program for Understanding Natural Language," Doctoral Dissertation, M.I.T., 1970, p. 47.

BY "IT," I ASSUME YOU MEAN THE SHORTEST THING THE TALLEST PYRAMID'S SUPPORT SUPPORTS.
RED.

24. How many things are on top of green cubes?
I'M NOT SURE WHAT YOU MEAN BY "ON TOP OF" IN THE PHRASE "ON TOP OF GREEN CUBES."
DO YOU MEAN:
1—DIRECTLY ON THE SURFACE
2—ANYWHERE ON TOP OF?
2 [human's answer]
THREE OF THEM.

25. Had you touched any pyramid before you put the green one on the little cube?
YES, THE GREEN ONE.

26. When did you pick it up?
WHILE I WAS STACKING UP THE RED CUBE, A LARGE RED BLOCK AND A LARGE GREEN CUBE.

27. Why?
TO GET RID OF IT.

28. Why did you do that?
TO CLEAR OFF THE RED CUBE.

29. Why did you clear off that cube?
     TO PUT IT ON A LARGE GREEN CUBE.
30. Why did you do that?
     TO STACK UP THE RED CUBE, A LARGE RED BLOCK AND A LARGE
     GREEN CUBE.
31. Why did you do that?
     BECAUSE YOU ASKED ME TO.   (Winograd, 1970, pp. 35–51)

To understand how SHRDLU was able to respond to requests as it
did, we must understand:

1. How it determined the meaning of requests presented to it in En-
    glish, and
2. How it carried out the requests once it knew what they meant.

We will start deep down inside SHRDLU by examining its knowledge of the world of blocks. First, SHRDLU differentiates itself, the
robot, from its friend, the person who types the requests. SHRDLU
knows about a world of objects—blocks, boxes, pyramids—which can
be grasped, resting on a table, which can not be grasped. The objects
have properties such as color, length, width, height, and location.
SHRDLU knows various relations among the objects. For example, it
knows if one object supports another or if the top of an object is clear of
other objects. Further, it knows if an object is larger or smaller, in front
of or behind, and above or below another object.
     SHRDLU uses these properties and relations in carrying out its three
basic functions: moving to a location, grasping, and ungrasping. For
example, it will not move an object to a place that is already occupied
by another object nor will it ungrasp an object unless it is supported.
These basic actions may be combined to form more complex actions
such as "stack-up"—that is, pile up in order of size, and "get-rid-of"—
that is, find an available space and put this object in it.
     Carrying out an action may prove to be more complex than it first
appears. Suppose that SHRDLU is asked to pick up Object A. If it is
already grasping Object B, it executes a program called "get-rid-of."
Get-rid-of searches for an empty place on the table large enough for B,
moves B to that place, and releases it. Next SHRDLU determines
whether the top of A is clear or not. If there are objects on A, the
"get-rid-of" program is used to move them to other locations. When the
top of A is finally clear, SHRDLU will grasp A and pick it up.
     SHRDLU's procedures for determining what a request means are
quite complex. Among other things they involve a dictionary, a
grammar, and semantic analysers. We might at first think that a dictionary would be enough. SHRDLU could look up each word of the request in the dictionary, plug the definitions into the right places in the

sentence—and *voila!*—it would have the meaning of the request. Alas, it is almost never that simple. Consider a sentence such as:

"Grasp the red block and put it on the green block."

When we look up the content words of this sentence in Webster's *New International Dictionary*, we find that no word has less than seven distinct definitions and one has as many as 22. The numbers of definitions categorized by grammatical class are shown in Table 9–1. Now, if an interpretation of the sentence is a choice of one meaning for each of the content words, then there are nearly three million (8 × 7 × 22 × 10 × 11 × 22) possible interpretations of this sentence. Some of these interpretations do make sense, for example, "Understand the communist obstruction [red block] and blame it on the immature coalition [green block]," but clearly, putting our sole reliance on the dictionary is not the way to get from words to the desired meaning.

In this same example, let us consider the advantages we can gain by making use of grammatical analysis. This analysis indicates that in the sentence above, *grasp* is used as a transitive verb, *red* as an adjective, *block* as a noun, and so on. Identifying the grammatical classes allows us to reduce the number of possible meanings for each content word. The reduced numbers are indicated by the circled numbers in Table 9–1. With grammatical analysis, the number of possible interpretations

Table 9–1. Number of definitions categorized by grammatical class

Word	Part of speech				Σ
	Transitive verb	Intransitive verb	Noun	Adjective	
Grasp	③	1	4	—	8
Red	—	—	4	③	7
Block	7	1	⑭	—	22
Put	⑥	1	2	1	10
Green	—	—	3	⑧	11

Source: Data from Webster's New Third International Dictionary (Springfield, Mass.: G & C Merriam, 1971).

of the sentence is reduced to fewer than 113,000. This is still a large number, but it is more than 25 times smaller than it was without grammatical analysis.

The problem of ambiguity is not as severe for SHRDLU as it is for people. SHRDLU is not sophisticated enough to know that *red* could mean a communist and *grasp* could mean to understand. There are still ambiguities which SHRDLU has to deal with, however; so grammatical analysis is an essential part of its language interpreting.

Clearly, grammatical analysis will not do the whole job of reducing ambiguity to an acceptable level. We also need semantic analysis—that is, analysis based on knowledge of the world. Consider the meaning of the word *take* in each of the three imperatives below:

Take a lion to the zoo.

Take a taxi to the zoo.

Take your children to the zoo.

In each case, the action indicated by the verb *take* is very different. For example, to take a lion might involve a truck and a very strong crate, but to take one's children usually would not. Similarly, taking a taxi involves getting inside it—something you should avoid when taking a lion.

We are able to deal with the ambiguities of *take* because our knowledge of lions and taxis allows us to determine which sense of the verb is required. This is knowledge about how the world works, not about how the language works. It is semantic knowledge.

SHRDLU also uses its knowledge of the world (the blocks world) in interpreting language. It knows that moving something to a definite place requires one procedure, while moving something to an indefinite place requires a different procedure. Thus, the verb *move* for SHRDLU is ambiguous in the same sense that the verb *take* is for people. SHRDLU is able to respond appropriately to the directions, "Move a block into the box," and, "Move a block anywhere," by:

1. Examining the rest of the sentence to determine whether the situation described involves a definite or an indefinite location, and
2. Using its knowledge of which action (which meaning of *move*) is appropriate to the situation, to resolve the ambiguity.

SHRDLU is a very impressive achievement, even more impressive than we have been able to indicate in this short description. We should not jump to the conclusion, though, that the problem of computer understanding of language is now solved. The blocks world is a very small world compared to the world people deal with. If SHRDLU's knowledge were greatly increased, it is not clear that its grammatical and semantic routines would be adequate to handle the increased linguistic ambiguity that would necessarily result.

UNDERSTANDING LARGER LANGUAGE UNITS

The work discussed earlier in this chapter focused on the interpretation of individual sentences. Recently cognitive psychologists have turned their attention to the processes involved in understanding larger units of language—paragraphs, stories, problem descriptions, scripts, and even whole belief systems. A number of researchers have developed story grammars, that is, sets of rules which describe the structure of simple stories such as folk tales and fables (Colby, 1973; Rumelhart, 1975; Kintch and Van Dijk, unpublished; Stein and Glenn, in press). Hayes and Simon (1974) have studied the processes by which people achieve understanding of a one or two paragraph problem description. Schank (1975), Abelson (1975), and their coworkers (Schank et al., 1975) have been carrying out extremely interesting work on the importance of familiar scripts (a sequence of actions expected in a situation) in the understanding of stories. Abelson, a social psychologist, has long been interested in the processes underlying belief systems— systems which may influence one's understanding of language and events very broadly. He has attempted to simulate the belief system of a "true believer" of the political right who sees Communist plots in many places.

We will not discuss the recent research on larger language units in great depth. We have too much ground to cover for that. Instead we will try to convey the nature of the problems which are currently being investigated.

Story grammars

The purpose of a story grammar is to describe the structure that makes a story different from a random string of sentences. Take the two examples below (quoted from Rumelhart, 1975, pp. 211–212):

1. Margie was holding tightly to the string of her beautiful new balloon. Suddenly, a gust of wind caught it. The wind carried it into a tree. The balloon hit a branch and burst. Margie cried and cried.
2. Margie cried and cried. The balloon hit a branch and burst. The wind carried it into a tree. Suddenly a gust of wind caught it. Margie was holding tightly to the string of her beautiful new balloon.

The first is a coherent story, but the second, while it consists of exactly the same sentences, is not. Rumelhart has attempted to develop a story grammar to describe the structure which is required to make a string of sentences into a story. A story grammar is similar to a phrase structure grammar (described above), but its elements are such things as episodes and events rather than noun phrases and adjectives. Further, a story grammar is applied to a string of sentences to decide if they constitute a legal story, while a phrase structure grammar is applied to a string of words to determine if it is a coherent sentence.

Rumelhart's story grammar consists of the six rules shown in Table 9–2. Table 9–3 shows the seven elements of the Margie story, and Fig-

Table 9–2. Rumelhart's story grammar

Rule 1 (story)	→ setting + episode
Rule 2 (setting)	→ state and state and. . . .
Rule 3 (episode)	→ event + reaction
Rule 4 (event)	→ episode or change of state or action or event + event
Rule 5 (reaction)	→ internal response + overt response
Rule 6 (internal response)	→ emotion or desire

Source: Adapted from D. E. Rumelhart, "Notes on a Schema for Stories," *Representation and Understanding*, eds. D. G. Bobrow and A. Collins, New York: Academic Press, 1975, pp. 213–216.

Table 9–3. The units of Margie's story

1. Margie was holding tightly to the string of her beautiful new balloon.
2. Suddenly, a gust of wind caught it and
3. carried it into a tree.
4. It hit a branch and
5. burst.
6. [sadness]
7. Margie cried and cried.

Source: D. E. Rumelhart, "Notes on a Schema for Stories," *Representation and Understanding*, eds. D. G. Bobrow and A. Collins, New York: Academic Press, 1975, p. 216.

ure 9–11 shows the structure generated by the six grammar rules to incorporate these elements. In Figure 9–11, Rule 1 following *story* indicates that Rule 1 was applied to *story* to yield *setting* and *episode* at the next level. Similarly, Rule 3 was applied to *episode* to yield *event* and *reaction*.

The grammar could not generate a structure to incorporate the string of sentences starting, "Margie cried and cried." All coherent structures have to start with a setting, and there is no sense in which "Margie cried and cried" can be viewed as a reasonable setting for sentences which follow it. Therefore, this string is not a coherent story.

There are two sorts of difficulties with Rumelhart's story grammar as it currently stands, both of which can very likely be remedied. The first is that it is not sufficiently complex to handle really involved stories. When Dickens opened *A Tale of Two Cities* with the words, "It was the best of times, it was the worst of times . . ." he was doing just what Rumelhart would expect. He was providing a general setting for the

Figure 9–11. Rumelhart's story grammar applied to the Margie story

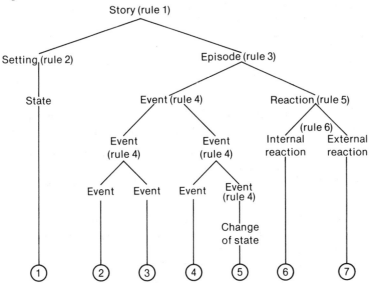

Source: Modified from D. Rumelhart, "Notes on a Schema for Stories," *Representation and Understanding*, eds. D. G. Bobrow and A. Collins, New York: Academic Press, 1975, Figure 1b, p. 217.

story to follow. When Melville opened *Moby Dick* with, "Call me Ishmael," however, and waited chapters before mentioning the white whale, it is much less clear that he did what Rumelhart's grammar requires. Before story grammars can be applied to such complex cases we will need much more elaborate rules for deciding what constitutes a setting, a reaction, and so forth. Despite such shortcomings, the idea behind story grammars appears quite sensible. Developing them further seems scientifically promising.

The other difficulty with Rumelhart's grammar is that element 6 [sadness], which is required by the grammar, really is not present in the story at all. It must be inferred from element 7. There is nothing in Rumelhart's grammar which would tell us how to make such inferences.

There is another line of research, however, which may help to fill this gap. In his analysis of belief systems, Abelson (1975, p. 291) describes the complex relations between attitudes and values and the actions which express them. He has attempted to simulate a "cold warrior"— that is, an individual who holds a right-wing political ideology—with a computer program which incorporates the following beliefs:

The Communists want to dominate the world and are continually using Communist schemes . . . to bring this about; these schemes when successful bring Communist victories . . . which will eventually fulfill their ultimate purpose; if on the other hand the Free World really uses its power . . . , then Communist schemes will surely fail . . . , and thus their ultimate purpose will be thwarted. However, the misguided policies of liberal dupes . . . result in inhibition of full use of Free World power . . . ; therefore it is necessary to enlighten all good Americans with the facts so that they may expose and overturn these misguided liberal policies.

When the "cold warrior" was asked to comment on the assertion, "The Kennedy administration was soft toward the Berlin Wall," it replied:

> Yes, I would not hesitate to say that recent administrations not make trouble for Communist schemes. Liberals want East-West agreements and administration theorists influenced the Kennedy administration (Abelson, 1975, p. 290).

Not perfect English certainly, but the attitude is appropriate.

While in general the responses of the "cold warrior" follow in the expected right-wing spirit, Abelson notes that sometimes the program makes serious mistakes. For example, the program reasoned that Fidel Castro would throw eggs at Taiwan since South American radical students had thrown eggs at Nixon. The problem was that while the program knew that Castro was likely to be hostile to Taiwan, it was innocent enough to believe that throwing eggs from Cuba to Taiwan was a reasonable way to express that hostility. Abelson concluded that if it is to behave sensibly, the program must have not only an ideology but also some practical knowledge of the everyday world. It must have knowledge of such things as what is involved in throwing objects, going to restaurants, taking trips, etc.

Schank (1975) suggests that knowledge of a familiar activity such as going to a restaurant is stored as a *script*. A script is a suggested sequence of actions which defines a situation. For example, when we go to a restaurant, we expect to be seated, to receive a menu, to eat, to pay a bill, and so forth. When we, as reader or listener, recognize that a script has been entered, objects and events that are part of the script may be referred to as if they had been mentioned before. Consider the following narrative:

> Taking Aunt Edna to the movies was always something of a trauma. She insisted on bringing her own popcorn, offering loud advice to the hero, and laughing sarcastically during tender love scenes.

The narrative is intelligible because our movie-going script includes the knowledge that movie theaters typically sell popcorn, that films are shown involving heroes and love scenes, and that there is an audience which might be upset by loud comments and laughter at inappropriate times.

Schank and his co-workers (1975) have designed a question-answering system called SAM. Central to SAM is a store of knowledge encoded as a number of scripts. In answering questions about the following story (reported in Lehnert, 1977), SAM used three scripts: a bus trip script, a pickpocket script, and a restaurant script. Remember, the questions are typed by people, but the answers are by the computer (Schank and the Yale AI Project, 1975, pp. 15–19).

> John went to New York by bus. On the bus he talked to an old lady. When he left the bus, he thanked the driver. He took the subway to Leone's. On the subway his pocket was picked. He got off the train and entered Leone's. He had some lasagna. When the check came, he discovered he couldn't pay. The management told him he would have to wash dishes. When he left, he caught a bus to New Haven.

(Q1) Why did John go to New York?

(A1) BECAUSE JOHN WANTED TO GO TO LEONE'S.

(Q2) How did John get to Leone's?

(A2) JOHN WENT TO NEW YORK BY BUS AND THEN HE WENT TO LEONE'S BY SUBWAY.

(Q3) Did anything unusual happen on the bus?

(A3) I DON'T REMEMBER ANYTHING.

(Q4) Did anything unusual happen on the subway?

(A4) A THIEF PICKED JOHN'S POCKET.

(Q5) What did John order?

(A5) JOHN ORDERED LASAGNA.

(Q6) Did anything unusual happen at the restaurant?

(A6) JOHN DISCOVERED THAT HE COULDN'T PAY THE CHECK AND SO HE HAD TO WASH DISHES.

(Q7) Why couldn't John pay the check?

(A7) BECAUSE JOHN DID NOT HAVE ANY MONEY.

(Q8) Why didn't John have any money?

(A8) BECAUSE A THIEF PICKED JOHN'S POCKET.

(Q9) How did John get back to New Haven?

(A9) JOHN WENT TO NEW HAVEN BY BUS.

(Q10) How was John able to take the bus to New Haven?

(A10) PROBABLY JOHN HAD A TICKET.

SUMMARY

The computer has become an increasingly important tool in recent language research. Earlier models could be tested relatively easily using just pencil and paper. More recent models tend to be very complex and are therefore more easily tested using a computer. This is true in large part because of the developments which we have reviewed in this chapter:

1. Modern grammars such as phrase structure and transformational grammars are both highly complex and highly computable.
2. Artificial intelligence studies such as that of Winograd emphasize the importance of the processes of accessing world knowledge and of making inferences from that knowledge. These processes, when they are at all complex or involve a large amount of knowledge, are best modeled with a computer.
3. The emphasis on larger language units such as stories, problems, and paragraphs which reference many scripts requires models which process many sentences and make many memory based inferences. Again, the more complex the model, the more important it is to test it with a computer.

We can expect that future studies of language will depend even more heavily on computers than they do at present.

FURTHER READING

In this brief review, we have been able to give the reader only the sketchiest account of modern grammar and of the developments in psycholinguistics related to it. For a comprehensive treatment of psycholinguistics, we recommend from References following Clark and Clark's book, *Psychology and Language*. For the reader who desires more detailed background information we recommend Chomsky's *Syntactic Structures* (1957), the first two very readable chapters of his *Aspects of the Theory of Syntax* (1965), and such review articles as that of Miller (1962) and that of Fodor and Garrett (1966).

Research on information-processing models of language is described in a number of volumes containing articles by workers active in the field. Among these are M. Minsky's *Semantic Information Processing* (1968), H. Simon and L. Siklossy's *Representation and Meaning* (1972), R. Schank and K. Colby's *Computer Models of Thought and Language* (1973), and D. Bobrow and A. Collins' *Representation and Understanding* (1975). Many articles in this area are published in the journals *Cognitive Science* and *Cognitive Psychology*.

REFERENCES

ABELSON, R. P. "Concepts for representing mundane reality in plans," *Representation and understanding*, eds. D. G. Bobrow and A. M. Collins. New York: Academic Press, 1975.

BEVER, T. G.; FODOR, J. A.; GARRETT, M.; and MEHLER, J. "Transformational operations and stimulus complexity," Unpublished manuscript, M.I.T., 1966.

BOBROW, D. G., and COLLINS, A. M., eds. *Representation and understanding.* New York: Academic Press, 1975.

BROWN, R. *Social psychology.* New York: Free Press, 1965.

CHOMSKY, N. *Syntactic structures.* The Hague: Mouton, 1957.

CHOMSKY, N. *Aspects of the theory of syntax.* Cambridge: M.I.T. Press, 1965.

CLARK, H. H., and CLARK, E. V. *Psychology and language.* New York: Harcourt, Brace, Jovanovich, 1977.

COLBY, B.N. "A partial grammar of Eskimo folk tales," *American Anthropologist, 75* (1973), pp. 645–662.

FODOR, J. A., and GARRETT, M. "Some reflections on competence and performance," *Psycholinguistic papers: The proceedings of the 1966 Edinburgh Conference,* eds. J. Lyons and R. J. Wales. Edinburgh: Edinburgh University Press, 1966.

FODOR, J. A.; JENKINS, J.; and SAPORTA, S. "Some tests on implications from transformational grammar," Unpublished manuscript, Center for Advanced Study, Palo Alto, California.

HAYES, J. R., ed. *Cognition and the development of language.* New York: John Wiley & Sons, Inc., 1970. Reprinted by permission of John Wiley & Sons, Inc.

HAYES, J. R., and SIMON, H. A. "Understanding written problem instructions," *Knowledge and cognition,* ed. L. Gregg. Hillsdale, N.J.: Lawrence Erlbaum, 1974.

KINTSCH, W., and VAN DIJK, T. A. "Recalling and summarizing stories," Unpublished manuscript, University of Colorado.

LEHNERT, W. "Human and computational question answering," *Cognitive Science, 1* (1977), pp. 47–73.

MEHLER, J. "Some effects of grammatical transformations on the recall of English sentences," *Journal of Verbal Learning and Verbal Behavior, 2* (1963), pp. 346–351.

MILLER, G. A. "Some psychological studies of grammar," *American Psychologist, 17* (1962), pp. 748–762.

MILLER, G. A., and MCKEAN, K. "A chronometric study of some relations between sentences," *Quarterly Journal of Experimental Psychology, 16* (1964), pp. 297–308.

MILLER, G. A.; MCKEAN, K.; and SLOBIN, D. "The exploration of transformations by sentence matching," in G. A. Miller, "Some psychological studies of grammar," *American Psychologist, 17* (1962), pp. 748–762.

MINSKY, M., ed. *Semantic information processing.* Cambridge, Mass.: M.I.T. Press, 1968.

RUMELHART, D. E. "Notes on a schema for stories," *Representation and understanding: Studies in cognitive science,* eds. D. Bobrow and A. M. Collins. New York: Academic Press, 1975.

SAVIN, H., and PERCHONOCK, E. "Grammatical structure and the immediate recall of English sentences," *Journal of Verbal Learning and Verbal Behavior*, 4 (1965), pp. 348–353.

SCHANK, R. C. "The structure of episodes in memory," *Representation and understanding: Studies in cognitive science*, eds. D. G. Bobrow and A. M. Collins. New York: Academic Press, 1975.

SCHANK, R. C., and COLBY, K. M., eds. *Computer models of thought and language*. San Francisco: Freeman, 1973.

SCHANK, R. C., and THE YALE AI PROJECT. "SAM—A story understander," Department of Computer Science Research Report 43, Yale University, New Haven, Connecticut, 1975.

SIMON, H. A., and SIKLOSSY, L., eds. *Representation and meaning: Experiments with information-processing systems*. Englewood Cliffs, N.J.: Prentice-Hall, 1972.

STEIN, N. L., and GLENN, C. G. "An analysis of story comprehension in elementary school children," *Multidisciplinary approaches to discourse comprehension*, ed. R. Freedle. Hillsdale, N.J.: Ablex, Inc., in press.

WEIZENBAUM, J. "ELIZA—A computer program for the study of natural language communication between man and machine," *Communications of the Association for Computing Machinery*, 9 (January 1966), pp. 36–43.

WINOGRAD, T. "Procedures as a representation for data in a computer program for understanding natural language," Doctoral dissertation, M.I.T., 1970.

Chapter 10

Problem solving I:
Searching for solutions

What is a problem?

If you want to do something but do not know how, then you have a problem. The problem is the gap which separates where you are from where you want to be. We can view problem solving as consisting of two major problem-solving processes:

1. *The understanding process:* the procedures we use to comprehend the gap which separates us from our goal; and
2. *The solving process:* the procedures we use to bridge the gap.

Understanding and representation

Problems are presented to us by the outside world. This outside problem environment defines the gaps we try to bridge when we solve problems. But to solve a problem, we must first construct an adequate internal representation of the problem—that is, we must understand it. Sometimes, because of our perspective, our egocentrism, it is hard for us to distinguish between our representation of the problem and the problem as it exists in the outside world, but it is important to do so.

A problem may be represented in many different ways. In some representations, the problem may be very easy to solve while in others it may be extremely difficult. Our choice of representations, then, can make a considerable difference in our problem-solving success.

Before proceeding, try to solve the problem shown in Figure 10–1. Now, what the mathematician claimed is, in fact, true. If it does not seem obvious to you, it is probably because of the way you are representing the problem to yourself. The problem is written so that you will think of the monk going up the mountain one day and coming down

177

Figure 10–1. The Old Monk problem

> Once there was a monk who lived in a monastery at the foot of a mountain. Every year the monk made a pilgrimage to the top of the mountain to fast and to pray. He would start out on the mountain path at 6 A.M., climbing and resting as the spirit struck him, but making sure that he reached the shrine at exactly 6 P.M. that evening. He then prayed and fasted all night. At exactly 6 A.M. the next morning, he began to descend the mountain path, resting here and there along the way, but making sure that he reached his monastery again by 6 P.M. of that day.
>
> That evening as he was hastening to a much needed dinner, he was stopped by the monastery's visiting mathematician, who said to him, "Do you know, I suddenly realized a very curious thing. Every time you make your pilgrimage there is always some point on the mountain path, perhaps different on each trip, that you pass at the same time when you are climbing up as when you are climbing down." "What!" snorted the monk, annoyed. "Why, that's ridiculous! I walk at all manner of different paces up and down the path. It would be a great coincidence if I should pass any spot at the same time of day going up as coming down. The idea that such a coincidence might happen time after time surpasses belief!" The mathematician, who had a touch of fiendishness in his soul, smiled sweetly and said, "Bless you, Brother, not only should you believe it, but if you will just think about it in the right way, it's obvious." He then locked himself in his cell, confident that he had spoiled the monk's dinner and probably his night's sleep as well.

again the next. But suppose you change that representation. Imagine instead of one monk who ascends the mountain on one day and descends on the next, that there are two monks, one of them ascending the mountain on the same day that the other is descending. At some point on the mountain path, the two monks meet, and must therefore be at the same place at the same time.

Figure 10–2 shows another way to represent the Old Monk problem which some find easier to understand than the one just given. In this figure the monk's altitude on the mountain (shown vertically) is graphed against the time of day (shown as increasing from left to right). The monk's progress up the mountain on the first day is shown by the line which moves from the lower left corner to the upper right corner. His progress down the mountain on the next day is shown on the same graph by the line which moves from the upper left corner to the lower right corner. Clearly, these two lines must cross somewhere. (Convince yourself of this by drawing other possible ways to ascend and descend the mountain on the graph, but remember, do not draw any trips which make time run backward.) The point where the lines cross shows the altitude which the monk reached at the same time on his two trips.

Figure 10-2. Alternate representation of the Old Monk problem

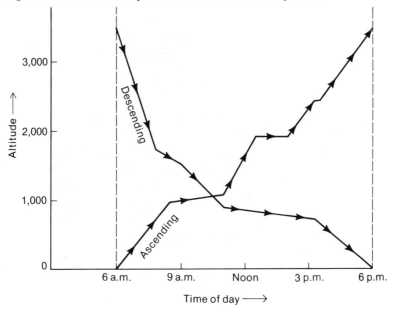

Time of day ⟶

Another illustration of the importance of representations is provided by comparing the Mutilated Checkerboard problem and the Matchmaker problem.

The Mutilated Checkerboard—A hard problem

Imagine an ordinary checkerboard with 64 squares and a set of 32 rectangular dominoes, each of which covers exactly 2 checkerboard squares. Clearly, the 32 dominoes can be arranged to cover the board completely—for example, by placing them in four parallel rows of eight dominoes each. Now suppose that two black squares were cut from opposite corners of the board as shown in Figure 10-3. Can the remaining 62 squares of the checkerboard be covered using exactly 31 dominoes?

Since no one we know has solved this problem in a reasonable amount of time, we think that it is only fair to indicate that the answer is "No" and to pose instead an easier task. Before reading the solution given below, try to prove that the mutilated checkerboard can not be covered with 31 dominoes.

A solution. Since each domino covers 1 white square and 1 black square, 31 dominoes cover 31 white squares and 31 black squares. Since the two corners we have removed are both black, the mutilated checkerboard has 32 white squares and 30 black ones. It follows that the mutilated board can not be covered by 31 dominoes.

Figure 10–3. The Mutilated Checkerboard problem

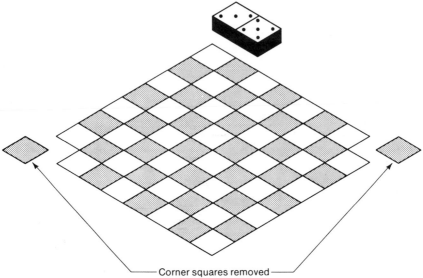

Corner squares removed

Now consider another very easy problem which is really the Mutilated Checkerboard problem disguised in other words.

The Matchmaker: A trivial problem or the Mutilated Checkerboard revisited

In a small but very proper Russian village, there were 32 bachelors and 32 unmarried women. Through tireless efforts, the village matchmaker succeeded in arranging 32 highly satisfactory marriages. The village was proud and happy. Then one drunken Saturday night, two bachelors, in a test of strength, stuffed each other with pirogies and died. Can the matchmaker, through some quick arrangements, come up with 31 satisfactory marriages among the 62 survivors?

Why is this second problem so much easier than the first? Presumably because the importance of matching males to females in the Matchmaker problem is much more obvious than the importance of matching black and white squares in the Mutilated Checkerboard problem.

For most people, the Old Monk problem is very difficult in the first representation, but relatively easy in either of the other two representations. The Mutilated Checkerboard problem is difficult or impossible for most people while the Matchmaker problem is trivial. Clearly, the way we represent a problem makes a big difference in our ability to solve it. When we are faced with a difficult problem, considering alternative ways to represent it may make the problem very much easier to solve.

The essential aspects of a representation

If you have a problem, then there is a gap between where you are now—the initial situation—and where you want to be—the goal. If the problem can be solved, then there are procedures for getting from the initial situation to the goal. These procedures are called moves or operators. Operators act to change one state of the world into another, for example, one checker position into another. In many cases, the operators have restrictions, that is, they can be applied only under certain conditions. An adequate representation of the problem, then, must include the relevant information about four aspects of the problem:

1. The initial situation.
2. The goal.
3. The operators.
4. The restrictions on the operators.

Consider the River Crossing problem shown in Figure 10–4. In this problem, the initial position is that all three possessions are on the first

Figure 10–4. A River Crossing problem

A farmer has a dog, a goose, and a sack of grain, all of which he wants to take across a river. Unfortunately his boat does not have enough room to allow him to row more than one of his possessions across the river at a time. Furthermore, he knows that if he leaves the goose alone with the dog, the goose will not survive, and that if he leaves the goose with the grain, neither will survive. How does he get his possessions safely across the river?

side of the river. The goal is to get the possessions to the other side of the river. The operator is rowing a possession across the river and the restrictions are:

1. Only one possession may be rowed at a time.
2. The dog must not be left with the goose.
3. The goose must not be left with the grain.

Examine the Railroad Shunting puzzle shown in Figure 10–5 and identify the initial state, goal, operators, and restrictions in this problem.

Figure 10–5.   A Railroad Shunting puzzle

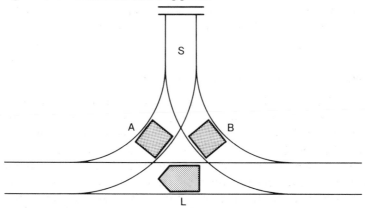

A and B are boxcars on a railroad siding and L is a locomotive. You want
to interchange the positions of A and B and to return L to its present position.
The locomotive can push or pull the cars either separately or attached together. The spur, S, however, can hold only one of the boxcars or the locomotive. What sequence of moves will solve the problem?

Source: From W. W. Rouse Ball (revised by H. S. M. Coxeter), *Mathematical Recreations & Essays.* New York: The Macmillan Company, 1962, p. 114.

In problems such as those in Figures 10–3 to 10–5, the four parts of
the representation are easy to identify. There are problems, however,
such as that shown in Figure 10–6, where identification of the four parts
is trickier. This problem is an example of a type we will call completion

Figure 10–6. Three characters in search of an author

Three people, Smith, Jones, and Robinson, have the jobs, Poet, Podiatrist,
and Prothonotary.
Smith is not the Poet or Podiatrist.
Jones is not the Podiatrist.
What job does each person have?

problems. Here we are given some facts about a situation and are asked
to deduce others. In these problems, the initial state is the set of given
facts and the goal is the set of facts to be deduced. The operators and
their restrictions are usually not mentioned explicitly in this type of
problem. The problem solver has to infer them from the subject matter
of the problem.

The problem solver's representation of the problem determines the
sequence of moves which the solver regards as legal. These sequences
form paths forward from the initial state or backward from the goal.

One or more of these paths connect the initial state to the goal and solve the problem. These are called *solution paths*. The total set of moves which the problem solver regards as possible in the problem is called the *problem space*. Remember that the problem space depends on the problem solver. The problem space is not the space of legal moves in the problem. It is the space of moves which the problem solver *regards* as legal. This space may be larger than the space of legal moves if the problem solver fails to recognize some of the restrictions on the operators. Again, the problem space may be smaller than the space of legal moves, if, as often happens, the problem solver forgets that backward as well as forward moves are legal.

Problem solving as search

We can think of problem solving as a process in which the problem solver searches through the problem space to find a solution path. If there are many blind alleys for each solution path, then we would expect the problem to be harder than if there were just a few blind alleys. Searching for the one needle hidden in a big haystack should be harder than searching for the needle in a small haystack. The size of the space through which the problem solver must search, however, is not nearly so important as the method by which the search is conducted.

To emphasize the importance of the search process, we should point out that some relatively simple problems may have surprisingly large search spaces. Consider the problem of finding the correct combination for a four-dial combination lock with ten positions on each dial. To open the lock, we confront a space of $10 \times 10 \times 10 \times 10 = 10,000$ paths in which to search for the correct combination. If we work systematically, we will try an average of half of these, or 5,000 combinations, before we open the lock. If we take ten seconds per trial, we should be able to solve the problem in about 14 hours. If the lock has ten dials, then the search space has $10^{10} = 10,000,000,000$ (10 billion) paths. If we were still able to try a combination every ten seconds, it would take us an average of 16,000 years to open this lock—an observation which may give us some confidence in a ten-dial combination lock.

The enormous difference between the search spaces for the four-dial and ten-dial locks illustrates the phenomenon called the combinatorial explosion. This phenomenon plagues us whenever we must pile choice on choice, as in mazes, games, and complex actions. A one-dial combination lock has a search space of ten paths. A two-dial lock has a search space of 100 paths, not 20. Each new choice multiplies the size of the space rather than simply adding to it. Newell and Simon (1972) estimate that the search space for a 40-move chess game is about 10^{120} paths. To say that this is a large number seems a bit understated. The estimated number of atoms in the universe is only 10^{80}. A complete search of the search space for chess is, of course, impossible.

Methods of search

In this section, we will discuss the search methods listed in Table 10–1. The most important distinction among these methods is the dis-

Table 10–1. Search procedures used in problem solving

I. Random search
II. Heuristic search
   A. Proximity methods
      1. Hot and Cold
      2. The Hill Climber
      3. Means-ends analysis
   B. Pattern matching
   C. Planning by
      1. Modeling
      2. Analogy
      3. Abstraction

tinction between *random search* and *heuristic search*. In heuristic search, the problem solver uses information about the problem to help choose the right (or more probably right) paths in looking for a solution. In random search, on the other hand, paths are chosen without any special knowledge to guide the search for a solution.

If we want to find our cat, we can look at random all over the house or we can perform a heuristic search by applying our knowledge of its habits. For example, we could look first in front of a favorite heating vent, or we could track to their source the sounds of a piece of paper being tortured to death.

Random search. Random search is the most primitive search process. It is carried out without any knowledge which would suggest more promising paths to try or blind alleys to avoid. It is blind trial and error. The only efficiency we can introduce in random search is to be systematic in order to avoid searching the same path twice. Systematic random search will find the combination of the four-dial lock on the average in 5,000 trials. Unsystematic random search, in which no record is kept of the path already tried, would take on the average 6,930 trials. Systematic random search then is about 40 percent more efficient than unsystematic search. When we are dealing with really large search spaces, such as those for the ten-dial lock or for chess, these differences in efficiency are far too small to be important. Random search cannot handle problems with very large search spaces. To solve such problems, we have to turn to heuristic search.

Heuristic search. Heuristic search is defined broadly as search in which the problem solver uses knowledge to identify promising paths in looking for a solution. There are, of course, a great many ways in which knowledge can be used to identify promising paths, and, therefore, many varieties of heuristic search. We will discuss three quite general varieties of heuristic search: proximity methods, pattern matching, and planning.

Proximity methods. The most important feature of proximity methods is contained in the familiar child's game, "Hot and Cold." In this game, one person hides an object and the other, the one who is "it," searches for the object. As he or she searches, though, the hider is required to give hints by saying "warmer" when the searcher is moving closer to the goal and "colder" when he or she is moving farther away. Through these hints the searcher is able to use some of the hider's knowledge of the problem to guide the search for the hidden object. Such hints supplied throughout the search can have a very powerful guiding effect. Each time the searcher hears "warmer" he or she knows that the path is in the best half of the paths available (the best 180 out of 360 degrees). When he or she hears "colder," he or she can get on a warmer path simply by turning around and going the opposite way. (I am not suggesting that children actually play the game this way. It is just that if they really are tense about winning, they should.) The hints then can cut the searcher's alternatives at any choice point in half. To see what effect this "trimming of the search tree" can have on the search space, consider the four-dial lock. We can give hints to the person who is trying to open the lock which will cut the alternatives in half at each choice point just as was done for the player of Hot and Cold. For example, we may tell the person that the correct combination contains only even numbers. In this case, the search space consists of just $5 \times 5 \times 5 \times 5 = 625$ alternative combinations of even numbers. This is just one-sixteenth of the total number of combinations. Clearly, such hints may help a great deal in searching for the solution.

Many of us have employed a proximity method when searching for a person in a large house. For example, we enter the house and shout, "Are you home?" and hear the faint reply, "Yes, I'm in the mumble room." "Where?" we shout, moving rapidly to another room, but the reply, "I'm mumble mumble" is even fainter. Wrong direction! We retrace our steps and strike out on a new path shouting, "You're where?" This time the reply is louder indicating that we are on the right path. Just a few more repetitions of the method will typically allow us to track down the person we are looking for.

Hill climbing. Another example of a proximity method is hill climbing which is like the Hot and Cold game except that it is played with altitude. The goal in hill climbing is to find the way to the top of a hill. The hints of warmer and colder are replaced by indications that the hill climber is moving up or down. Hill climbing is a very simple procedure. It involves picking a direction at random and then trying a step. If the step increases the hill climber's altitude, then the step is accepted; if not, a different direction is chosen. While the hill climber may appear to wander rather aimlessly it actually always makes progress toward the goal. Whenever the hill climber is located on the side of a hill, it can find a step which increases its altitude. When it is at the top of a hill, however, all steps lead down. Since it can find no step which increases its altitude, it stops, resting comfortably on a peak.

The hill climber does not necessarily climb to the highest point in its region. It climbs to the top of the first hill it finds without asking if that is the tallest hill around (see Figure 10–7). Thus, if we solve a problem

Figure 10–7. A hill climber finds the top of a hill but not necessarily the top of the highest hill in the region

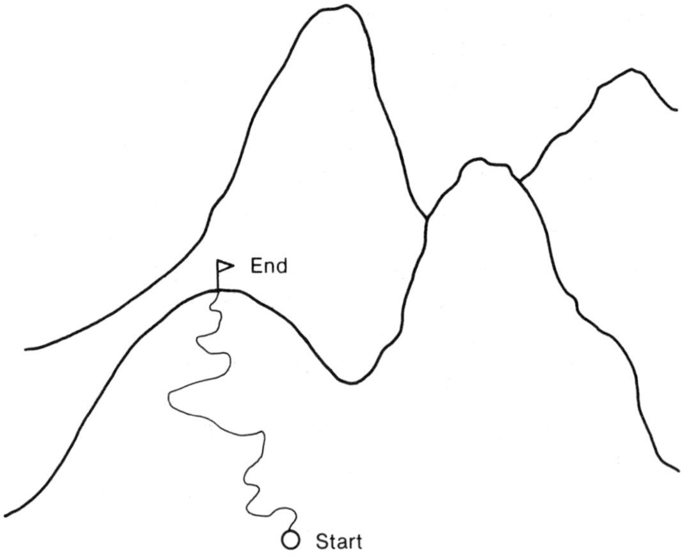

by a hill-climbing method, we should get a good solution, but we may not get the best possible solution.

As a practical example of hill climbing, suppose that we are running a school for hyperactive children. We want to conduct the school so that the children learn as much as possible, but finding out what is best for them is a very complicated problem. Some people claim that discipline is best; others recommend freedom. Some want to emphasize physical activity; others, the skills of sitting quietly. Some favor Skinnerian schedules of reinforcement; others, warmth and affection; and so on. Since our school is a small one, we cannot launch a massive research program, but we can approach the problem with a hill-climbing method. In our problem, altitude corresponds to the children's academic performance. Better grades are "up." We can take a single step by varying one factor at a time, say, by emphasizing physical activity while keeping other aspects of the school program constant. If academic performance improves, we accept this step and try a new step by varying, say, the amount of discipline. Operating in this way, we can continue to improve the school by taking the steps that help and rejecting those that do not until we run out of things to change. At this point we have reached the top of a hill. As was true in Figure 10–7, we may not have climbed the highest hill in our neighborhood. There may be another design for a school which is better than the one we have arrived at. Nonetheless, we will have improved our school.

Means-ends analysis. In the Hot and Cold game and in hill climbing, there was just one way to get closer to the goal—it happened to be walking in these two cases, but it could have been driving, pogosticking, or any other single means of moving in the space of interest. Means-ends analysis differs from these methods in that it involves choice among different *means* of approaching the goal.

We will illustrate the workings of *means-ends analysis* through Simulated Ape, a banana-mad means-ends analyzer. Imagine a large ape exercise cage similar to those used by Köhler. A banana is tied high up off the ground in the center of the cage. Off to one side, stage right, there is a long stick. On the other side of the cage stands Simulated Ape, glowering at the banana and waiting to be switched on. *But first,* let's have a quick peek at Simulated Ape's internal mechanisms.

Aside from eating bananas, Simulated Ape can do three things. He can grasp, he can walk, and he can hit things with a stick to knock them down. He applies these three activities in ways appropriate to the situation by consulting a means-ends table like that shown in Figure 10–8,

Figure 10–8.   A means-ends table

	Short distance	Long horizontal distance	Long vertical distance
Grasp	X		
Walk		X	
Hit			X

built into his simulated brain. The table is his source of knowledge that grasping is appropriate when the goal is near; walking, when it is a long horizontal distance off; and hitting, when it is high out of reach.

For a mechanical device, Simulated Ape has a rather complicated structure of goals involving three goal-types and a goal-stack. The first goal-type is a goal to get an object, for example, a stick or a banana. If the object cannot immediately be grasped, the difficulty is noted, for example, that the object is a large horizontal distance away. In addition, a subgoal is established to reduce the difficulty. The second goal-type, called a reduce goal, is a goal to reduce a difficulty. The effect of these goals is to identify an operator which is appropriate to reduce the difficulty and then to set up a subgoal to apply the operator. The final goal-type—the apply goal—is a goal to apply an operator. If a difficulty is encountered in applying the operator, a subgoal is established to reduce the difficulty. These goal-types are diagrammed in Figure 10–9.

The profusion of goals and subgoals requires some sort of goal-handling system. For this purpose, Simulated Ape has a goal-stack. The goal-stack is rather like the spring activated devices used in cafeterias to hold stacks of plates (see Figure 10–10). Plates put on top of the stack

Figure 10–9. Flow diagram of General Problem Solver methods

Goal: Transform object A into object B

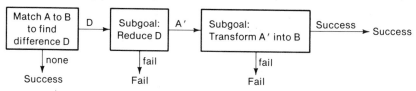

Goal: Reduce difference D between object A and object B

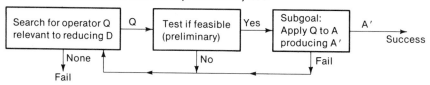

Goal: Apply operator Q to object A

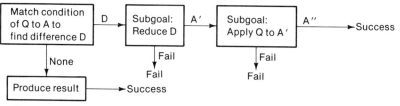

Source: A Newell and H. A. Simon, *Human Problem Solving*, Englewood Cliffs, N.J.: Prentice-Hall, 1972, p. 417.

Figure 10–10. Goal-stack

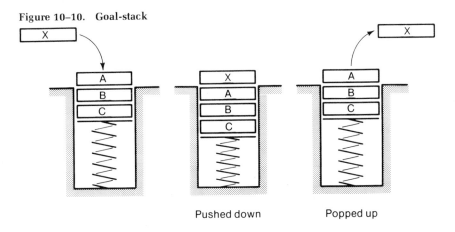

Pushed down   Popped up

push down the plates which were already on the stack. If a plate is taken from the top of the stack, the plates below it pop up. The goal-stack in Simulated Ape also has this push-down, pop-up feature. To start, there is just one goal in the goal-stack—the current goal. Difficulty in achieving the goal may cause a subgoal to be established. The subgoal is added to the stack pushing down the original goal and replacing it as the current goal. If the subgoal is achieved, it is removed from the stack and the original goal pops back up. Difficulties in achieving the subgoal, however, may cause a sequence of other subgoals to be established and dealt with before the original goal can be achieved.

Now back to Simulated Ape, who, like the rest of us, has been waiting patiently to be turned on. S.A.'s first goal is to obtain the banana which he sees hanging from the roof of the cage. He cannot grasp it, however, because of the large horizontal and vertical distances. Therefore, he sets up a subgoal to reduce the distance (if there are two distances to reduce, it always starts with the horizontal one). The sequence of events which finally leads to the acquisition of the banana is diagrammed in Figure 10–11.

The most impressive thing about Simulated Ape's performance is its ability to establish sequences of subgoals in order to overcome difficulties encountered in a direct approach to solution. At Step 7, for example, four subgoals have been placed in the goal-stack. At Step 5, Simulated Ape established a subgoal to reduce the vertical distance of the banana; at Step 6, to knock the banana down; at Step 7, to get a stick; and at Step 8, to walk to the stick. Simulated Ape finally achieved its primary goal, getting the banana, by working through this complex sequence of subgoals. Sultan, Köhler's smartest ape, need not have been ashamed of this performance. By the use of its goal-stack, Simulated

Figure 10–11. Performance of Simulated Ape

Step		Goal:		
1	G1	Get banana	Difficulty:	large horizontal distance
				large vertical distance
2	G2	Reduce horizontal distance of banana	Succeed:	operator walk
3	G3	Apply walk	Succeed:	horizontal distance small
4	G1	(reinstated)	Difficulty:	large vertical distance
5	G4	Reduce vertical distance of banana	Succeed:	operator hit
6	G5	Apply hit	Difficulty:	no stick
7	G6	Get stick	Difficulty:	large horizontal distance
8	G7	Reduce horizontal distance of stick	Succeed:	operator walk
9	G8	Apply walk	Succeed:	horizontal distance small
10	G6	(reinstated)	Succeed:	stick grasped
11	G5	(reinstated)	Difficulty:	large horizontal distance
12	G9	Reduce horizontal distance	Succeed:	operator walk
13	G10	Apply walk	Succeed:	horizontal distance small
14	G5	(reinstated)	Succeed:	banana knocked down
15	G1	(reinstated)	Difficulty:	small distance
16	G11	Reduce small distance	Operator:	grasp
17	G12	Apply grasp	Success:	banana crushed

Ape is able to display a modicum of intelligence in its problem-solving activities.

Means-ends analysis, which Simulated Ape illustrates in crude fashion, has been embodied by Newell, Shaw, and Simon (1960) in a computer program which has considerable problem-solving power and generality. The program, called General Problem Solver (GPS), has solved a wide variety of problems including logic proofs, trigonometric identities, formal integration, series extrapolation, and sentence parsing. Means-ends analysis has been explored in far greater depth than we have been able to do here by Newell and Simon (1972) and by Ernst and Newell (1967). The interested reader should find these sources quite rewarding.

In summary, a problem solver using means-ends analysis continually tries to reduce the distance between itself and its goal. It does this by determining the character of the remaining distance and using its means-ends table to find a means appropriate to reduce that distance.

Pattern matching. Another important heuristic search method quite different from the proximity methods is pattern matching. Pattern matching is the process of recognizing that two patterns are the same. The patterns may both be in the outside world. ("By George, they are wearing the same hat!") or one may be in the outside world and the other in memory ("I'd remember your face anywhere, you swindler!").

An especially clear illustration of the function of pattern matching in searching for problem solutions is provided in the game of chess. It was commonly believed that chess masters played good chess because they were able to see farther ahead in the game and to examine more alternative moves than less skillful players. The Dutch psychologist de Groot (1965) showed to nearly everyone's surprise that these beliefs were false. Chess masters search about as deeply as weak players, and if anything consider fewer moves than weak players do before choosing a move. In a difficult chess position, masters will typically search 2 to 3 moves deep and consider between 30 and 50 moves. Rarely will they search more than 5 moves deep or consider more than 100 moves. The same can be said of weak players as well. While masters seem to go about choosing moves in much the same way as weaker players do, the masters characteristically choose better moves. The question is, "How do they do it?"

In the course of his investigations, de Groot also noticed that chess masters have an unusual ability to remember chess positions. For example, he noted that chess masters could recall (with great accuracy) a board position which they had been able to examine for only a few seconds. Less experienced players were unable to match this performance. Further, the ability of masters to remember positions applies only to real chess positions. Chess masters are no better than novices at remembering random arrangements of pieces on the chessboard. This ability of chess masters then is not just a general aptitude for remembering perceptual patterns. Rather it has something specifically to do with chess masters' knowledge of chess. Simon and his co-workers (Simon and Chase, 1973; Simon and Gilmartin, 1973) believe that the difference between the master and the novice is that the master has stored many chess patterns in memory while the novice has not. They estimate that a chess master typically spends between 10,000 and 20,000 hours studying chess boards and chess magazines. This is sufficient time to store lots of chess patterns in memory. Simon and Gilmartin estimate that the chess master has stored somewhere between 10,000 and 100,000 chess patterns. These patterns allow the master to recognize that the situation on the board is similar or identical to one seen before and therefore to recognize that the move that was best in the earlier situation is also best now. The superior ability of the chess master, then, depends on a large number of chess patterns stored in memory which allow the master to look at a position and "see" which move would be best with far more ease than a novice who does not have the relevant chess patterns stored.

Planning. A third class of heuristic search methods distinct from the proximity methods and pattern matching is the group of planning procedures. Problem solvers have plans if they decide beforehand how they are going to solve a problem. The plan itself is often a rough description of the proposed solution. The description may list some subgoals; for example, "I'm going to eat worms (subgoal) so that everyone around will turn an interesting shade of green (goal)." The description may specify a procedure; for example, "I'll solve by completing the square"; or it may employ analogy; for example, "I'll solve it *as if it were* a river-crossing problem." By whatever method the plan is formed (we will discuss three methods below), it serves to guide the problem solver's search through the problem space. Plans can be immensely powerful aids in problem solving. The observation that even very weak plans can be useful is entombed in the folk wisdom of Minsky's Maxim: "Some plan is better than no plan."

The hill climber does no planning since it never looks beyond its next step. GPS, which is a much more powerful problem solver than the hill climber, owes at least part of that power to the plans which it holds as a sequence of subgoals in its goal-stack.

Planning methods

Planning by modeling. In many practical situations, the solution of a problem involves taking actions which may require considerable cost or effort and may have irreversible effects. Carpentry, for example, involves operations of joining and cutting which are expensive in effort and materials and which have irreversible effects on the materials used.

Errors and false starts using the real materials may leave the carpenter with large quantities of expensive but odd-shaped and useless bits of wood. In such situations, it is sensible to build a model of the real-world situation from inexpensive and easy to manipulate materials, for example, balsa wood, pencil sketches, chalk on blackboard. The problem may then be solved by manipulating the model and translating the model solution into a real-world solution. This procedure reduces greatly the cost of making errors and of exploring promising leads which turn out to be blind alleys.

The usefulness of modeling is obvious in such dramatic applications as building skyscrapers or designing ship hulls. We sometimes fail to realize that exactly the same procedure is used very widely in everyday reasoning. For example, suppose you are playing a game of checkers, and you are considering what move to make next. You want to look ahead a few moves but you do not want to make the moves on the board. Instead you imagine moves and store the results of each in memory. If the final result is satisfactory, the sequence of moves becomes your game plan. You take the first move of the plan and wait for your opponent to fall into your trap so that you can execute the rest. The problem you solve using your mental model of the checker game is exactly as complex as the problem on the board. The moves in the mental game, however, are reversible. You can take back mental moves, but your opponent will not let you take back moves you make on the board. This sort of mental planning, while it is by no means all of our thinking, is certainly very common.

Planning by analogy.   Plans are formed by analogy when the solution of one problem is used to suggest the steps which should be used to solve another problem. An experiment by Köhler (1940) provides an interesting example of solution by analogy in algebra. Köhler asked people to solve the equation 21 $(19/7 + 6) + 14 = X$. For most people, this involved multiplying 21×19 in the usual way. When the subjects reached their solution, Köhler pointed out, apparently as an aside, that 21×19 is the same as $(20 + 1)(20 - 1)$ and that this in turn is the same as $400 - 1$, or 399. Later in the experiment, Köhler asked the subjects to solve

$$(15 + 64 - 47)\,28 + (-20 + 34) = X$$

This problem involves the multiplication of 32×28, which could be solved by analogy to the first problem as

$$(30 + 2)(30 - 2) = 900 - 4$$

Köhler was able to show that under some conditions, most of the subjects (73 percent) used the analogy to solve the problem. In another condition, the subjects solved many other algebra problems in the interval between the trial problems. Here relatively few subjects (26 percent) used the analogy to solve the problem. The subjects had not forgotten the trick they were shown. When asked, they all remembered it. They just had not spontaneously thought to apply it. A similar failure by problem solvers to make use of available analogies has been observed by Greeno (1974), Reed, Ernst, and Banerjii (1974), and by Hayes and Simon (1976). The failure to make use of available analogies should be taken seriously since it means that the problem solver's effective intelligence is less than it might otherwise be. The problem solver has a plan available which would have solved the problem but he fails to make use of it. We will discuss techniques for facilitating the use of analogy in problem solving in the chapter on creativity (Chapter 12).

Planning by abstraction. People form plans by abstraction when they simplify the original problem to obtain what they hope is a related but easier problem. If the simpler problem can be solved, its solution can be used by analogy as a plan for solving the original more complex problem.

Several years ago, I was involved in the teaching of elementary calculus to a group of college students who rated themselves poor in mathematical ability. Some of these students had a peculiar sort of difficulty in solving algebra problems. The task was "to express X in terms of Y" given a set of four or five relations, such as the following:

$$R = Z^2$$
$$X = R + 3$$
$$2M = 3L + 6$$
$$Y = M + 1$$
$$R = 3L$$

In this situation, students appeared to combine relations and draw inferences without apparent pattern and of course rarely solved the problems. Student performance improved considerably when I taught them to plan their approach to the problem by abstraction as follows:

1. First they were to reduce all equations to simple connections as shown:

$$R ---- Z$$
$$X ---- R$$
$$M ---- L$$
$$Y ---- M$$
$$R ---- L$$

2. Since the problem was to express X in terms of Y, next they were to find a path through the relations connecting X and Y. This path is shown below:

$$X ---- R ---- L ---- M ---- Y$$

Forming this path is the solution of the simpler abstracted problem, which will now be used as a plan for the solution of the more complex problem.

3. Write the equation for the first link:

$$X = R + 3$$

4. Using this equation and the equation for the second link,

$$R = 3L$$

derive an equation which connects X and L:

$$X = 3L + 3$$

5. Using the equation above and the equation for the next link, derive a new equation until the equation relating X and Y is found:

$$X = 2Y - 5$$

In this case, the abstraction has been carried fairly far. The chaining problem does not bear much resemblance to the original algebra problem because it has been simplified in several ways. Often the abstracted problem will be closer to the original than this. A common way to use abstraction is simply to reduce the number of things to be considered in a problem. To solve a 6-disc Tower of Hanoi puzzle, we may start with three discs. To solve a 12-coin weighing problem, we may want first to solve a 3-coin problem. In each case, the strong family resemblance between the original and the simplified problems is obvious.

Planning by modeling and planning by abstraction are similar in that both involve the solution of an auxiliary problem. In planning by abstraction the auxiliary problem is chosen to be simpler than the original problem. In planning by modeling, however, the auxiliary problem is not necessarily simpler. The important thing is that the problem materials are easier or cheaper to manipulate than in the original problem.

SUMMARY

Problem solving consists of two processes:

1. An understanding process which constructs a representation of the problem.
2. A solving process which finds a path from the initial state of the problem to the goal.

The representation which the problem solver chooses may make a big difference in the ease with which the problem is solved.

The solution process may be viewed as a process of search through a space of alternative moves (the problem space). For many problems the problem space is so large that it cannot be solved by systematic search or by random search. For such problems, heuristic search is necessary. Three varieties of heuristic search—proximity methods, pattern matching, and planning—were described.

FURTHER READING

As described in References following, Newell and Simon's 1972 book, *Human Problem Solving*, is the best single source of further information on the topics of this chapter. Those who find its 920 pages too informative should read just Chapter 14 and the historical appendix.

Miller, Galanter, and Pribram's 1960 book, *Plans and the Structure of Behavior*, is an important early contribution. It is also very readable.

REFERENCES

DE GROOT, A. D.   *Thought and choice in chess*. The Hague: Mouton, 1965.

ERNST, G. W., and NEWELL, A.   *GPS: A case study in generality and problem solving*. New York: Academic Press, 1969.

GREENO, J. C.   "Hobbits and Orcs: Acquisition of a sequential concept," *Cognitive Psychology*, 6 (1974), pp. 270–292.

HAYES, J. R., and SIMON, H. A.   "Psychological differences among problem isomorphs," *Cognitive theory*, Vol. II eds. N. Castellon, Jr.; D. Pisoni; and G. Potts. Potomac, Maryland: Lawrence Erlbaum, 1976.

KÖHLER, W.   *Dynamics in psychology*. New York: Liveright, 1940.

MILLER, G. A.; GALANTER, E.; and PRIBRAM, K. H.   *Plans and the structure of behavior*. New York: Henry Holt & Co., 1960.

NEWELL, A.; SHAW, J. C.; and SIMON, H. A.   "Report on a general problem-solving program for a computer," *Information processing: Proceedings of the International Conference on Information Processing*. Paris: UNESCO, 1960. Pp. 256–264.

NEWELL, A., and SIMON, H. A.   *Human problem solving*. Englewood Cliffs, N.J.: Prentice-Hall, 1972.

REED, S. K.; ERNST, G. W.; and BANERJII, R.   "The role of analogy in transfer between similar problem states," *Cognitive Psychology*, 6 (1974), pp. 436–450.

ROUSE BALL, W. W.   *Mathematical recreations & essays* (revised by H. S. M. Coxeter). New York: The Macmillan Company, 1962.

SIMON, H. A., and CHASE, W. G.   "Skill in chess," *American Scientist*, 61 (1973), pp. 394–403.

SIMON, H. A., and GILMARTIN, K.   "A simulation of memory for chess positions," *Cognitive Psychology*, 5 (1973), pp. 29–46.

THOMAS, J. C., JR.   "An analysis of behavior in the Hobbits-Orcs problem," *Cognitive Psychology*, 6 (1974), pp. 257–269.

Chapter 11

Problem Solving II: Representations, plans, and ill-defined problems

In this chapter, we will (1) discuss the nature of the processes by which people form representations of problems; (2) introduce the idea of an ill-defined problem and illustrate it through an example of an architect at work; and (3) characterize ill-defined problems by the special way in which the processes of representation and planning must be carried out in these problems.

Constructing problem representations

A person must have an internal representation of a problem to solve it. We have seen that the particular way in which people represent a problem will influence the way they solve it. But representations do not just happen. They are constructed by people facing a problem in the real world and trying to understand its important aspects. Two general principles about the construction processes may be specified. In constructing representations:

1. People attend selectively to the data presented to them.
2. People make use of several types of prior knowledge:
   a. Syntactic knowledge: knowledge of the language,
   b. Semantic knowledge: knowledge of the world, and
   c. Knowledge about specific problem types.

Selective attention in the construction of representations

If we listen carefully to a person who is solving a problem, we can often observe processes of selective attention in action. Here, for example, is what one subject says while solving a monster problem aloud (Simon & Hayes, 1976). The subject reads: "Three five-handed extraterrestrial monsters were holding three crystal globes." Pause. The subject comments: "OK." The subject continues reading: "Because of the quantum-mechanical peculiarities of their neighborhood . . ." The subject, referring to what he has just read, says: "Forget that garbage!"

Despite the fact that the subject was only halfway through the second sentence and surely could not have understood very much of the problem (no more than you at this point), he was confidently making judgments as to what was important and what was not. This subject is by no means unique. People are quite capable of making judgments of the importance of problem information on first reading and they can do so reasonably accurately. Hayes, Waterman, and Robinson (1977) asked subjects to make importance judgments about the Allsports problem shown in Figure 11–1. On first reading the subjects identified 81 per-

Figure 11–1. The Allsports problem

I went to tea yesterday with an old friend, Mrs. Allsports.

She has three daughters; Amelia, Bella, and Celia.

On the doorstep I met another friend, who remarked that her own daughter was spending a yachting holiday at Sandville with one of Mrs. Allsport's girls.

Over the teacups it turned out that all three of the daughters are on holiday.

Their interests are diversified.

One is at Mudville; one is at Rockville; one is at Sandville.

To make the thing more confusing, one is playing tennis, one is yachting, and one is playing golf.

It further transpired that Amelia is not at Sandville, Celia is not at Mudville, and the girl who plays golf is not at Rockville.

I tried to discover who the yachting enthusiast is but could only find out that she is not Celia.

Who is playing golf and where?

Source: H. Phillips, *My Best Puzzles in Logic and Reasoning*. New York: Dover Publications, Inc., 1961, pp. 20–21.

cent of the information necessary for solution as important but only 21 percent of the information not necessary for solution as important. The practical value of these judgments is that they allow the problem solver to attend selectively to what is important in the problem while still attempting to understand the problem, that is, while building a problem representation. In the case of the Allsports problem, these judgments allow the problem solver to ignore more than 40 percent of the original problem text and still solve the problem.

Making use of prior knowledge

A. Syntactic knowledge. When humans attack a problem presented in words, they characteristically attack it using both syntactic and semantic knowledge. It is difficult to find a sensible example in which people use just syntactic knowledge. There is, however, a computer program which operates with syntactic knowledge alone which we can use to illustrate what can be done in this way.

Bobrow's program, STUDENT (1964), was designed to solve algebra word problems. STUDENT attacks most problems through a direct translation using only syntactic knowledge. It translates successive sentences of the problem text into equations and then tries to solve the equations. Consider the following simple problem:

> The number of applicants is twice the number of jobs.
> The number of jobs is 5.
> What is the number of applicants?

To solve this problem, STUDENT would translate these sentences into the following equations and then solve them:

> (The number of applicants) = 2 $*$ (The number of jobs)
> (The number of jobs) = 5
> X = (The number of applicants)

Initially, STUDENT makes no use of the meaning of the words in the problem. A phrase such as "the number of applicants" is treated as a meaningless symbol, such as X or Y. STUDENT has no processes for understanding the words *number* or *applicant*. But if the direct translation process fails to yield a solution, STUDENT will then search its memory for relevant semantic knowledge. For example, if solution has failed and the problem contains a key word such as *distance* or *miles*, STUDENT will retrieve the equation: distance = rate X time from its memory, add it to the list of equations produced by direct translation, and try again.

B. Semantic knowledge. Paige and Simon (1966) have provided evidence that the direct-translation process can serve as a good first approximation in describing some human behavior in solving algebra word-problems. They have also shown through their observations on contradictory problems that direct translation, as it is implemented in STUDENT, cannot account for human solution processes which rely on semantic knowledge. An example of a contradictory problem is:

The number of quarters a man has is seven times the number of dimes he has. The value of the dimes exceeds the value of the quarters by $2.50. How many has he of each coin?

Some subjects who solve the problem by the direct translation process come up with a negative number of dimes and are perfectly happy. Others, making use of their semantic knowledge, for example, that a negative number of dimes is an unacceptable solution to a practical problem, recognize this problem as contradictory. Some subjects, then, seem to solve such algebra problems by the direct translation process using largely syntactic information. Other subjects clearly make use of semantic information in formulating the same problems. To account for the behavior of humans, then, we must assume that they make use of both syntactic and semantic knowledge.

Surrealistic algebra problems. The importance of semantic information in the formulation of problems may be illustrated dramatically by taking standard algebra word-problems and tinkering with their meanings while leaving their grammatical structure unchanged. For the problems shown in Figure 11–2, the semantic changes yield new

Figure 11–2.   Original and changed problems

1. *Changed*   In a medical exam, a man weighs 150 pounds on a scale which goes from 0 to 300 pounds. What would he weigh on a scale which goes from 0 to 240 pounds?

   Original   In a psychology test, a man scored 150 points on a scale which goes from 0 to 300. What would he score on a scale which goes from 0 to 240?

2. *Changed*   Jerry looks one block east along a vacant lot and then looks two blocks north to a friend's house. Standing at the same point, Phil looks diagonally across the vacant lot at Jerry's friend's house. If Jerry looked 217 feet east and 400 feet north, how far did Phil look?

   Original   Jerry walks one block east along a vacant lot and then two blocks north to a friend's house. Phil starts at the same point and walks diagonally through the vacant lot coming out at the same point as Jerry. If Jerry walked 217 feet east and 400 feet north, how far did Phil walk?

problems which are intelligible but quite different from the original problems. To understand the difference between the original and the changed problems, one has to have knowledge about the world. One must know that the properties of psychological scales are different from the properties of weight scales, and that walking has effects different from looking.

Figure 11–3.   Original and changed surrealistic problems

1. *Changed*   A box containing 5,000 cubic feet is constructed by cutting from each corner of the town square a five foot square and then turning up the sides. Find the area of the original town square.

   Original   A box containing 180 cubic inches is constructed by cutting from each corner of a cardboard square a small square with side 5 inches, and then turning up the sides. Find the area of the original piece of cardboard.

2. *Changed*   If Jones had two more ideas than he has now, he would be a half-wit. If he had two less ideas than he has now, he would be a sixth-wit. How much of a wit is he now?

   Original   If 2 is added to the numerator of a fraction, the value of the fraction becomes $1/2$. If 2 is subtracted from the numerator of the original fraction, the value of the fraction becomes $1/6$. Find the original fraction.

3. *Changed*   A certain wine takes seven years to mature properly from the time the grapes are harvested but only four years for the return trip. How fast would the wine mature in still time?

   Original   A boat takes 2 hours to steam 20 miles up a river but only 1 and $1/3$ hours for the return trip. Find the rate of the boat in still water.

4. *Changed*   By singing 2 decibels per hour louder than usual, Mr. Calhoun saved half an hour in singing a 110 decibel song. Find his usual loudness.

   Original   By travelling an average of 5 miles per hour more than usual, Mr. Calhoun saved half an hour on a 275-mile trip. Find his usual speed.

5. *Changed*   At the end of each month, a credit union charges interest equal to 1 percent of the unlived balance of a life. A man has 50 years to live and lives 5 years of it at the end of each month for ten months. What is the total amount of interest he is charged?

   Original   At the end of each month a credit union charges interest equal to 1 percent of the unpaid balance of a loan. A man borrows $100 from the credit union and pays back $10 at the end of each month for ten months. If his first payment is made one month after the date of the loan, what is the total amount of interest charged?

For the problems shown in Figure 11–3, the semantic changes yield results which range from simply odd to bizarre, or surrealistic. They require us to imagine impossible or at least very surprising worlds in which time may travel forward or backward, or stand still, and singing loud is equivalent to singing fast. In these imaginary worlds, some of our knowledge of the real world which we might use in formulating the problem is either useless or misleading.

C. Knowledge of specific problem types. People learn to recognize a number of different problem types, for example, crossword puzzles, mystery stories, and riddles. Puzzle enthusiasts, of course, may distinguish many more. They may distinguish among such oddities as shunting puzzles, cryptarithmetic problems, parity problems, palindromes, and Smith-Jones-Robinson problems. Science students acquire a surprising ability to distinguish types of algebra word-problems. Hinsley, Hayes, and Simon (1977) have shown that college students can distinguish no fewer than 18 different types of algebra problems. These are listed in Figure 11–4.

Figure 11–4. Representative problems from each of the 18 clusters

1.   Triangle

Jerry walks one block east along a vacant lot and then two blocks north to a friend's house. Phil starts at the same point and walks diagonally through the vacant lot coming out at the same point as Jerry. If Jerry walked 217 feet east and 400 feet north, how far did Phil walk?

2.   Distance-Rate-Time (DRT)

In a sports car race, a Panther starts the course at 9:00 A.M. and averages 75 miles per hour. A Mallotti starts four minutes later and averages 85 miles per hour. If a lap is 15 miles, on which lap will the Panther be overtaken?

3.   Averages

Flying east between two cities, a plane's speed is 380 miles per hour. On the return trip, it flies 420 miles per hour. Find the average speed for the round trip.

4. Scale Conversion

Two temperature scales are established, one, the R scale where water under fixed conditions freezes at 15 and boils at 405, and the other, the S scale where water freezes at 5 and boils at 70. If the R and S scales are linearly related, find an expression for any temperature R in terms of a temperature S.

5.   Ratio

If canned tomatoes come in two sizes, with radius of one $2/3$ the radius of the other, find the ratios of the capacities of the two cans.

6.   Interest

A certain savings bank pays 3 percent interest compounded semiannually. How much will $2,500 amount to if left on deposit for 20 years?

7.   Area

A box containing 180 cubic inches is constructed by cutting from each corner of a cardboard square a small square with side 5 inches, and then turning up the sides. Find the area of the original piece of cardboard.

8.   Maximum-Minimum (Max-Min)

A real-estate operator estimates that the monthly profit p in dollars from a building s stories high is given by $p = -2s^2 + 88s$. What height building would he consider most profitable?

Figure 11–4. *(continued)*

9. Mixture

One vegetable oil contains 6 percent saturated fats and a second contains 26 percent saturated fats. In making a salad dressing how many ounces of the second may be added to ten ounces of the first if the percent of saturated fats is not to exceed 16 percent?

10. River Current

A river steamer travels 36 miles downstream in the same time that it travels 24 miles upstream. The steamer's engines drive in still water at a rate which is 12 miles an hour more than the rate of current. Find the rate of the current.

11. Probability

In an extrasensory-perception (ESP) experiment, a blindfolded subject has two rows of blocks before him. Each row has blocks numbered 1 to 10 arranged in random order. The subject is to place one hand on a block in the first row and then try to place his other hand on the block having the same numeral in the second row. If the subject has no ESP, what is the probability of his making a match on the first try?

12. Number

The units digit is one more than three times the tens digit. The number represented when the digits are interchanged is eight times the sum of the digits.

13. Work

Mr. Russo takes three minutes less than Mr. Lloyd to pack a case when each works alone. One day, after Mr. Russo spent six minutes in packing a case, the boss called him away, and Mr. Lloyd finished packing in four more minutes. How many minutes would it take Mr. Russo alone to pack a case?

14. Navigation

A pilot leaves an aircraft carrier and flies south at 360 miles per hour, while the carrier proceeds north and 30 degrees west (N30W) at 30 miles per hour. If the pilot has enough fuel to fly four hours, how far south can he fly before returning to his ship?

15. Progressions

From two towns 363 miles apart, Jack and Jill set out to meet each other. If Jill travels 1 mile the first day, 3 the second, 5 the third, and so on, and Jack travels 2 miles the first day, 6 the second, 10 the third, and so on, when will they meet?

16. Progressions (2)

Find the sum of the first 25 odd positive integers.

17. Physics

The speed of a body falling freely from rest is directly proportional to the length of time that it falls. If a body was falling at 144 ft. per second 4.5 seconds after beginning its fall, how fast was it falling 3.75 seconds later?

18. Exponentials

The diameter of each successive layer of a wedding cake is two thirds the previous layer. If the diameter of the first layer of a five-layer cake is 15 inches, find the sum of the circumferences of all the layers.

Source: M. P. Dolciani, S. L. Berman, and W. Wooton, *Modern Algebra and Trigonometry: Structure and Method.* Boston: Houghton Mifflin, 1973.

The importance of these problem types is that people not only recognize them, but that by recognizing them they may also make use of information about the type which helps to formulate them for solution. When the subjects recognize that a problem is of a familiar type, they may know what to pay attention to, they may be able to retrieve relevant equations from memory, and they may have a good idea about what the question will be. To determine what useful information becomes available to people when they recognized a problem type, Hinsley, Hayes, and Simon read problems in small fragments to their subjects. The subjects were asked to tell what they knew about the problems after each fragment. In some cases, subjects failed to retrieve any useful knowledge. In other cases, though, they retrieved a great deal of information after hearing only a few words of the problem.

For example, after hearing the three words, "A river steamer . . ." from a problem, one subject said: "It's going to be one of those river things with upstream, downstream, and still water. You are going to compare times upstream and downstream—or if the time is constant, it will be the distance." Another subject said, "It is going to be a linear algebra problem of the current type—like it takes four hours to go upstream and two hours to go downstream. What is the current—or else it's a trig problem—the boat may go across the current and get swept downstream." After hearing the words, "Jerry walks one block east . . ." a subject said, "This may be something about 'How far is he from his goal' using the Pythagorean theorem."

A dramatic illustration of the importance of identifying the problem type is provided in another experiment reported by Hinsley, Hayes, and Simon (1977). Subjects solved the Smalltown problem shown in Figure 11–5 which contains conflicting clues about its type. For some sub-

Figure 11–5. The Smalltown problem

Because of their quiet ways, the inhabitants of Smalltown were especially upset by the terrible New Year's Eve auto accident which claimed the life of one Smalltown resident. The facts were these. Both Smith and Jones were New Year's Eve babies and each had planned a surprise visit to the other on their mutual birthday. Jones had started out for Smith's house travelling due east on Route 210 just two minutes after Smith had left for Jones' house. Smith was travelling directly south on Route 140. Jones was travelling 30 miles per hour faster than Smith even though their houses were only five miles apart as the crow flies. Their cars crashed at the right angle intersection of the two highways. Officer Franklin, who observed the crash, determined that Jones was travelling half again as fast as Smith at the time of the crash. The crash occurred nearer to the house of the dead man than to the house of the survivor. What was the name of the dead man?

jects, the problem appears initially to be a triangle problem. Others classify it initially (and correctly) as a distance-rate-time problem. All of the subjects who treat the problem as a triangle problem draw a triangle and interpret the five mile distance between the houses as the hypotenuse of the triangle. Further, several of these subjects apply or attempt to apply the Pythagorean theorem. None of the subjects who treat the problem as a distance-rate-time problem do these things. Instead these subjects form an initial representation of the problem in which the drivers are travelling east and west rather than east and south. Further, several of these subjects asserted that the five mile difference between the houses is not important.

The way subjects categorize the problem, then, determines what they regard as important in the problem, what information they will retrieve from memory, and even what errors they are likely to make in interpreting the problem. Clearly, making the correct categorization will aid problem formulation.

There is another rather surprising observation in the Hinsley, Hayes, and Simon study of how people use familiar problem types to help them formulate problems. Subjects were asked to solve the nonsense problem shown in Figure 11–6. This problem was constructed by replacing content words by nonsense words in a typical mixture problem.

Figure 11–6. Nonsense problem

> According to ferbent, the optimally fuselt grix of voipe umolts five stens of voipe thrump 95 bines per sten. In order to embler some wuss voipe, each grix will umolt one sten at 70 bines per sten. If the grix is to be optimally fuselt, what should the bines per sten of the rest of the voipe be?

Subjects were understandably taken aback when they first read the problem. After they recovered, however, they dealt with the problem of interpreting it as a known problem type and then formulating it for solution. One subject said:

> There is some sort of machine, let's call it the grix. Which receives some sort of input, or let's say fuel, called a sten. And it produces, let's say work, out of that sten, usually whips out 90 bines per unit of sten. Now for some obscure reason one of those input units will be converted at 70 . . . OK, I'm assuming that they want something which can be expressed in the following equations. . . .

A second subject, commenting on his own solution process, said:

> What I was trying to do all the time was to try to fit it [the problem] into some normal schema. . . . As soon as I could pop it into a frame where I could deal with things normally, it was much easier to deal with.

These subjects clearly used familiar problem types to help them in solving these problems. (They did actually solve them correctly.)

The experimental results, then, indicate that people do recognize many problem types, and that they use their knowledge of these types in formulating not only standard problems but nonsense problems as well.

Ill-defined problems

Such problems as the mutilated checkerboard and the river crossing problem are presented in a way that leaves little to one's imagination. They state the essential conditions of the problem and just what it is one is expected to find out. Such problems are *well-defined*. Their solutions are the same for all problem solvers. Many school problems, such as those in algebra, geometry, and chemistry, are well-defined.

Many problems, however, are *not* well-defined. When an architect is given a commission to design a building, the client will typically specify some requirements such as cost and general function. Most aspects of the design, though, will be left to the architect. The solution arrived at will be in a very important sense the architect's solution. Other architects would have achieved other solutions. The problem is *ill-defined* because, to solve it, the problem solver takes an active role in specifying what the problem is. In the same way, the computer consultant who is asked to design an accounting system for a bank and, more obviously, the composer who is commissioned to write a symphony, are faced with ill-defined problems since in each case, the problem solver must contribute a great deal to the problem before it can be solved.

Here is an example which illustrates some of the methods people use to solve ill-defined problems. We will examine the behavior of an architect solving the shop design problem, as presented by Baer (1975).

Initial statement of the shop design problem

1. Mr. H. owns a shop which specializes in contemporary furniture.
2. He also deals in such household items as imported appliances (coffee machines, toasters, humidifiers), handcrafted fabrics, and various kinds of lighting.
3. Although the shop has recently been plagued with shoplifting and furniture has been damaged by unobserved strolling customers, his sales are rapidly growing since it is the only shop of its kind in town.
4. H. generally stores all items in the same areas of the shop since he orders risky items in small numbers.
5. H. plans to move his shop to a new location which would allow him to show a number of complete interior design arrangements.

6. He likes his customers to have a free access to the merchandise, allowing them to see the quality of his products.

7. Although H. makes most of his sales on items priced between $20 and $50, he would like to get customers more interested in his furniture.

The architect first read the above statement which outlined the problem. He was told that he could obtain further information about the problem by asking questions of the experimenter and by requesting various sketches of the location, (site plan, elevation, and so on).

The architect's solution is divided into distinct segments. In each of the segments the problem solver's attention is confined fairly strictly to a single aspect of the problem to the exclusion of others.

Segment 1. After reading the problem statement, the architect asked a sequence of questions concerning the environment of the new shop. These proceeded from more general questions to more specific ones.

"In what city is it?"
". . . is it downtown or . . . ?"

Next the subject asked for the site plan shown in Figure 11–7. This plan shows the streets, shops, and a park neighboring the new shop. He then asked about the nature of the business of neighboring shops and about the occupancy of the other floors of the building.

Segment 2. The subject reread the first three sentences of the initial statement and said, ". . . shoplifting . . . aha—why is he moving to this place? Is this place safer than what he has?" This question introduced a sequence of questions on safety. The answers to these questions led him to conclude that safety was not a problem in the new location.

Segment 3. Pointing to Sentence 5 in the introductory statement, the subject indicated that space requirements were a serious consideration in the problem. He requested a floor plan and elevation and measured the length, width, and height of the shop.

Segment 4. In this segment, two design ideas—levels and transparency—appeared quite suddenly. As he was measuring the height of the shop from an elevation, he said,

and—the height is—my God—this is good—because you can have levels in here—six and a half (marks)—I had that in mind—actually—eh—when I thought of a space to—(pause)—one meter and five and one half meters—that I could put some split levels in here—I think it would make it look neat too—some sort of a transparency—some sort of transparency here would be nice because—(pause)—you have the park on one side— and you have the street on the other side—and—if—like if one person could see through here (left-right on 1.3)—whereas he may not be able to see through these (other shops in site sketch) I think it would make it

Figure 11-7. Site plan of shop-design problem

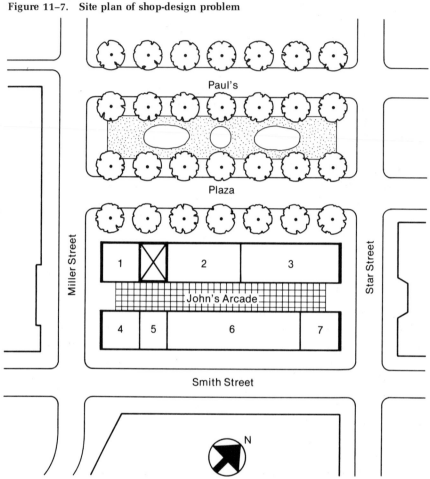

Source: A. Baer unpublished manuscript, Carnegie-Mellon University, Pittsburgh 1975, p. 23.

more appealing—do you have elevation or layout of these (shops)—all right, give me these adjacent shops here—

The subject then determined that the neighboring shops were not transparent and said: "They are not transparent—ok—that's nice." Next he considered whether the structure of the building might not be appropriate for transparency. He said:

—now—that transparency business is a little shaky here because of this bulky elevation—it's light—but I had something in mind like—eh—more—eh—slim sections in your elevation and sort of more transparency—but still—

Segment 5. In this segment, the architect returned to the issue of space. He said, "All right—I want to know what kind of space constraints this guy has—I mean down to the square footage . . ." He then asked a sequence of questions about the amounts of furniture, household goods, and fabrics which were to be displayed in the shop.

Segment 6. The designer abruptly returned to consideration of the "levels" idea, the way it related to the movement of customers in the store, and to the efficient use of space.

> all right, let's see now—when you think of two levels, what are you going to put up there—now who the hell is going to go up there in a small shop like this, take the trouble to climb up there to look at stuff—so it shouldn't be just a very distinct split level but you should have maybe a couple of levels (starts drawing level scheme) building up to it—if you have that situation then what the hell are you going to do with what the space left under here (draws shade in level scheme).

Here the designer was concerned with the area under the lowest level.

> so you gonna lose space in here (points to shaded area in level scheme) if you do that—(pause)—ah (points to bottom end of copy of floor plan)— so—that's precious space, you can't do that—well (points to shaded area in level scheme) but consider the fact that you can't put something up above it—because people just won't take—to bother to climb up there (points to space above levels) to look at this dinky little lamp—if they have to climb 50 stairs—so—it may not be after all a loss—some of those levels could be used underneath too—ha—this looks nice—all right— (points to space underneath middle level)—like—underneath here you can put all these appliances and stuff like that because people do not need too much grandeur to look at those things—so they could be under some low ceiling somewhere—this is more cozy—more scaled to the artifact.

Later segments were concerned with such remaining aspects of the preliminary plan as the design of entrances and display spaces. The final version of the preliminary plan included the ideas of levels and transparency.

There are three very important things to notice about this problem-solving session. First, the formulation of the problem involved decisions on the part of the problem solver. Two important decisions were (a) the shoplifting problem could be ignored, and (b) a transparent design would be attractive. Another architect who solved the same problem made very different decisions. He decided that the primary design goal was to prevent shoplifting. The designs which resulted from these two sets of decisions were, of course, very different.

Second, decisions have effects which spread and influence later efforts to solve the problem. The decision to design for transparency led the problem solver to consider the transparency of adjacent shops, and to explore the suitability of the building's structure for a transparent design. Neither activity would have been undertaken without the prior decision to consider transparency. In the same way, the problem of using the space under the middle level could not have arisen until the decision was made to have a middle level.

The third important thing to notice is that the problem solver dealt with a single issue at a time, devoting separate problem-solving segments to environment, security, space, transparency, levels, etc.

What makes a problem ill-defined?

Ill-defined problems, such as the shop design problem, are both common and important. They constitute the bulk of the hard problems which architects, engineers, lawyers, legislators, and other professional problem solvers face everyday.

What is it that makes an ill-defined problem different from a well-defined one? We believe that the important difference is that ill-defined problems require problem solvers to contribute to the problem definition. They must take an active role in specifying the problem beyond the processes normally involved in understanding a well-defined problem. There are two sorts of activities which an ill-defined problem may demand of problem solvers: (1) They may be required to make decisions which fill gaps in the problem definition. (2) They may be required to "jump into" the problem—that is, they may need to attempt a solution to the problem before they can fully understand it.

Decisions which fill gaps in the problem definition. Reitman (1964) posed the example of a specialist in a company whose boss asks him to design an inventory-control system which eliminates stockouts—that is, which will insure that none of the company's products will be out of stock when a customer wants to buy them. The specialist knows that he cannot interpret the word *eliminate* to mean that stockouts *never* occur. To do so would require huge (or infinite) stockpiles which the company cannot afford. Therefore, he must interpret the problem to mean that the system should reduce the frequency of stockouts to some acceptable level. To solve the problem, he must then decide, by himself or with help, on an acceptable level.

This problem is ill-defined because it requires the problem solver to make a decision which fills in a gap in the problem definition. Similarly, the shop design problem contained gaps which demanded decisions of the architect concerning the shop's structure and appearance. The architect's levels and transparency decisions filled these gaps.

Jumping into the problem. Often it is necessary for problem solvers to "get their feet wet" in the problem before they can fully understand what it is about. By working into the problem, they can get information about how bothersome the problem constraints are, how the "moves" work, or how various parts of the problem influence each other—information which they could not or did not foresee before trying seriously to solve the problem. There are a number of problem-solving situations in which "jumping in" is helpful. One is the situation in which the problem solver has formed an incorrect initial representation. This is illustrated in the problem presented in Figure 11–8. Attempt to solve the problem before proceeding further.

Figure 11–8.   An oddity problem

Which figure doesn't fit with the others?_____

Many people at first formulate this problem as one in which they are required to find one odd element concealed among a number of regular ones, as in Figure 11–9. With this view of the problem, people who spot the triangle in Figure 11–8 as obviously different from the other figures and who do not check further may choose 3 as the answer. People who

Figure 11–9.   One item is odd

do check further, however, and find, say, that item 2 is also an odd one, may well become confused. They may wonder whether or not the problem has a unique solution. To arrive at the correct answer, 5, the problem solver must reformulate the problem and recognize that the task is really to find the one regular item concealed in a group of odd ones, as shown in Figure 11–10. In this problem, if jumping in is to be helpful, the problem solver must jump way in. That is, he must not only propose a solution, such as "3 is odd," but must also check to see that the solution is unique—that is, that there are not better solutions.

Some subjects formulated the Smalltown problem (Figure 11–5) as if it were a triangle problem. Unsuccessful problem solving attempts,

Figure 11–10.   One item is not odd

such as efforts to apply the Pythagorean theorem, convinced the subjects that a different formulation was necessary. For these subjects, the
Smalltown problem was ill-defined, since they did not formulate it correctly until their first attempts to solve it failed.

Other situations in which jumping in is useful are ones in which the
problem solver is unable to foresee the relations among the parts of the
problem. This may happen either because the problem is too big to view
all at once (Simon [1973] has discussed this situation in detail) or as in
chess, because problem solvers cannot always look far enough ahead to
predict the consequences of their problem-solving efforts.

When faced with a problem that is too large, the problem solver may
have to break it into smaller, more easily handled parts and attempt to
find solutions for the part-problems separately. The architect solving
the Shop Design Problem appeared to do just this, dealing in quite
separate problem-solving segments with the issues of environment, security, space, transparency, and levels.

Combining the solutions of the part-problems may yield an adequate
solution of the total problem, but it may not. The strategy of dealing
with the problem a part at a time ignores possible incompatibilities
among the part solutions. With this strategy, problem solvers will discover such incompatibilities (and the necessity for reformulating the
problem) only after they have attempted a solution.

This sort of problem reformulation in which problem solvers change
their problem representation as a result of their experience in trying to
solve the problem is not at all unusual. In fact, it is a rather common
occurrence in design problems. For example, architects may be asked to
design a low-cost housing unit of specified size and cost. In attempting
to solve the problem, they may discover that they cannot provide the
required space within the project budget unless they change their initial assumptions about materials or about the appropriate structure for a
dwelling. Thus, what started out as a fairly routine problem of arranging rectangular rooms into an acceptable house design may turn into a
problem of adapting materials to new uses or of exploring new styles of

family living. In the same way, aeronautical engineers in their attempt to solve a wing-design problem may discover that weight and strength requirements conflict to such an extent that they must change their initial assumptions about the wing's structure.

We will call problems of this sort discovery problems. A discovery problem is the sort of ill-defined problem in which the problem solver's attempts to solve the problem reveal that the initial formulation of the problem was inadequate. Discovery problems are important because they remind us that there is another source of information which people use in constructing their problem representations. In addition to using prior knowledge of syntax and semantics and of familiar problem types as we discussed earlier, they may also construct a representation of a problem using information gained while trying to solve that problem.

SUMMARY

When people approach an unfamiliar problem, they must first understand it, that is, they must construct an internal representation of the important parts of the problem. The process of constructing the representation involves:

1. Selective attention to relevant parts of the problem description.
2. The use of prior knowledge.
    a. About language.
    b. About the world in general.
    c. About specific problem types.
3. Information gained while solving the problem.

An ill-defined problem is one in which the problem solver must take an active role in specifying the problem. This can be done by making *gap-filling decisions,* that is, by making necessary choices which were not specified in the problem description, and by *jumping into the problem,* that is, by making tentative problem solving attempts designed to reveal what the problem really is.

FURTHER READING

The topics discussed in this chapter are relatively new and have not as yet been widely reviewed for a general audience. The interested reader should consult the articles listed in References following for further information:

On constructing representations: Hayes and Simon (1974); Hayes, Waterman, and Robinson (1977); Simon and Hayes (1976).

On algebra problems: Bobrow (1968); Paige and Simon (1966); Hinsley, Hayes, and Simon (1977).

On ill-defined problems: Reitman (1964); Simon (1973).

REFERENCES

BAER, A.   Unpublished manuscript. Carnegie-Mellon University, Pittsburgh, 1975.

BOBROW, D.   "Natural language input for a computer problem-solving system," *Semantic information processing*, ed. M. Minsky. Cambridge, Mass.: M.I.T. Press, 1968.

DOLCIANI, M. P.; BERMAN, S. L.; and WOOTON, W.   *Modern algebra and trigonometry: Structure and method.* Boston: Houghton Mifflin, 1973.

HAYES, J. R., and SIMON, H. A.   "Understanding written problem instructions," *Knowledge and cognition,* ed. Lee W. Gregg. Potomac, Md.: Lawrence Erlbaum Associates, 1974.

HAYES, J. R.; WATERMAN, D. A.; and ROBINSON, C. S.   "Identifying relevant aspects of a problem text," *Cognitive Science* (1977), pp. 297–313.

HINSLEY, D.; HAYES, J. R.; and SIMON, H. A.   "From words to equations," *Cognitive processes in comprehension,* eds. P. Carpenter and M. Just. Hillsdale, N.J.: Lawrence Erlbaum, 1977.

PAIGE, J. M., and SIMON, H. A.   "Cognitive processes in solving algebra word problems," *Problem solving: Research, method, and theory,* ed. B. Kleinmuntz. New York: Wiley, 1966.

PHILLIPS, H.   *My best puzzles in logic and reasoning.* New York: Dover Publications, Inc., 1961.

REITMAN, W. R.   "Heuristic decision procedures, open constraints, and the structure of ill-defined problems," *Human judgments and optimality,* eds. M. W. Shelley and G. L. Bryan. New York: Wiley, 1964. Pp. 282–315.

SIMON, H. A.   "The structure of ill-structured problems," *Artificial Intelligence, 4* (1973), pp. 181–201.

SIMON, H. A., and HAYES, J. R.   "The understanding process: Problem isomorphs," *Cognitive Psychology, 8* (1976), pp. 165–190.

Chapter 12

Creativity

Somehow, creativity seems a more exalted topic than problem solving. When we think of creativity, we think of such events as Van Gogh painting *Sun Flowers* or Darwin conceiving the theory of evolution. When we think of problem solving, we think of much more mundane events, such as our mechanic figuring out what is the matter with our car or a high school student doing algebra. In this chapter, we will treat Van Gogh's act of artistic creation and our mechanic's automotive troubleshooting in the same framework so that we can evaluate the differences and perhaps, more importantly, the similarities of creativity and problem solving. We will view creativity as a special form of problem solving which emphasizes certain of the problem-solving processes.

The chapter has two major sections. In the first section, the characteristics of creative individuals will be explored. We will discuss such questions as, "Are people the only creative animals?" "Is creativity inherited?" and "How is creativity related to intelligence quotient (IQ)?" In the second section, we will describe, as best we can, the nature of the creative process.

PART 1

An informal definition of creativity

A creative act must:

1. *Have some valuable consequence,* that is, the act should have an effect which is interesting or useful in some way; and
2. *Be novel or surprising.* The harder it is for us to understand the origins of an act, the more creative we are likely to judge it. Often

215

our response to a creative act is, "How did that person ever think of
that!"

Armed with this definition, we will now explore the characteristics
of creative individuals.

Are people the only creative animals?

Köhler (1925), whose work we discussed extensively in Chapter 4,
observed a colony of 12 chimpanzees both in experimental situations
and in their normal daily activities. From these observations, he identified a number of behaviors which are very hard to interpret except as
creative acts of invention.

Köhler observed three ape inventions: pole-jumping, chicken-
teasing, and stick-lengthening. Pole-jumping was the invention of
Sultan, the most intelligent of Köhler's apes. It started as Sultan's personal game and was soon copied by the other apes in the colony. The
trick was to set a long pole on end and then climb madly to the top and
jump off before the pole fell. (This game is not recommended for
humans.)

After inventing pole-jumping, Sultan had an opportunity to put it to
practical use in an experiment. A basket of fruit was tied overhead out
of Sultan's reach but very much on his mind. First, he tried to reach it
with mighty freestanding jumps. Discouraged with jumping, he picked
up a pole and attempted to knock the basket down with it. Failing at
this, he placed the pole on the ground and used it for jumping to the
basket. This was the first time he had used pole-jumping as a means to
get something he wanted rather than just for fun.

Is Sultan's invention of pole-jumping really a creative act according
to our definition of creativity? It appears to be. As a game, it was clearly
interesting to chimpanzees and probably would be to humans, too, if
they had the agility to play it. Sultan showed that it could be useful as
well as fun when he used it to solve the problem of the fruit basket.
Further, the invention was novel. None of the other apes did pole-
jumping until Sultan led the way.

Unfortunately, the creator of the game of chicken-teasing is un-
known. No monument comparable to that of Abner Doubleday, the
inventor of baseball, can be built to his memory by grateful apes.
Chicken-teasing is a lunchtime game played in two forms—with and
without violence to the chickens. In its first form, the ape holds out a
piece of bread to the chickens who feed just outside the apes' large
exercise cage. When a chicken approaches and trustingly pecks at the
bread, the ape whisks it away, leaving the chicken with a healthy bite of
air. Since the chickens never achieve a full appreciation of their role in

this game, it can be repeated as many as 50 times in the course of a jolly ape lunchtime.

In the rough form of the game, the ape holds the bread in one hand and a stick in the other. When the chicken approaches to eat, he gets a sharp poke in the feathers. While one might question the cosmic utility of chicken-teasing, there is little question of its interest value to the apes in the colony or of its novelty.

The third invention, stick-lengthening, was created by Sultan in an experimental session. Sultan was given two bamboo rods, one of which could be jammed into the end of the other to form a longer rod. A banana lay beyond the bars of the cage just far enough away so that it could not be reached with either of the rods separately. Sultan tried hard to reach the banana with one of the rods. It did not work. He pushed one stick toward the banana with the other stick. Again, it did not work. The experimenter tried to help by putting his own finger in the open end of the rod, but Sultan did not take the hint. After a few more attempts to reach the banana, Sultan appeared to give up. He lounged on top of a box. He got up, picked up the sticks and played with them. He held them so that they lay in a straight line. Suddenly, he pushed the small one into the large one, jumped up and was on the run for the bars where he began to draw in the banana. While many other apes in the colony were exposed to this same situation, only Sultan invented stick-lengthening.

With this invention, as with the previous two, there can be little doubt of its utility or its novelty. All three inventions, while they involve creativity at a level below that expected of a dull human, must definitely be regarded as creative acts. While humans are undoubtedly the most creative of the animals, then, they are clearly not the only animals capable of creativity.

Is creativity inherited?

This question is the focus of Sir Francis Galton's famous book, *Hereditary Genius* (1870), a work which marked the beginning of the scientific investigation of creativity. Galton studied the family trees of more than 850 statesmen, poets, scientists, musicians, and other famous people to determine if genius runs in families. Included in the study was Galton's own famous cousin, Charles Darwin.

Among his sample of notables, Galton separated the illustrious— people whose accomplishment identifies them as one in a million or one in several million—from the eminent, those who achieve a position as does only one in 4,000. Galton found strong evidence that illustrious people have far more eminent relatives than one would expect by chance. Table 12–1 shows the proportion of eminent people among the

Table 12–1.   Proportions of eminent people among
relatives of illustrious people

Relation to the illustrious person	Relative's chance of eminence
Father	1 in 6
Brother	1 in 7
Son	1 in 4
Grandfather	1 in 25
Uncle	1 in 40
Nephew	1 in 40
Grandson	1 in 29
First cousin	1 in 100
A randomly selected person	1 in 4,000

Source: Based on data from F. Galton, *Hereditary Genius.*
New York: Appleton, 1870.

relatives of illustrious people. Thus, the son of an illustrious person is 1,000 times more likely to be eminent than a randomly chosen person; that is, his chance of being eminent is 1 in 4 rather than 1 in 4,000.

Galton concluded that genius is inherited. It is now universally conceded that Galton was too hasty in drawing this conclusion. The weakness in Galton's argument is that genes are not the only factors passed along family lines. So are money, influence, and social class. Further, an eminent relative may provide a personal model to copy—setting standards for effort, taste, and life style—which may well make eminence more likely. Since each of these can be useful in paving the way to eminence, it is not clear that heredity was the factor producing the relationships which Galton found.

To carry out Galton's study in a way that would tell us whether or not creativity is inherited, we would have to eliminate the effects of inherited wealth, influence, and social class, as well as the effects of personal contact between relatives. So far the experiment has not been done, and there is as yet no convincing evidence that creativity is inherited.

How is creativity related to IQ?

It is commonly believed that (1) creative people are generally above average in intelligence, and (2) of two creative people, the more creative one is likely also to be the more intelligent one.

As we will see below, the available evidence confirms the first belief but indicates fairly strongly (and surprisingly) that the second is false.

Catherine Cox (1926) has attempted to determine if creative people are more intelligent than others by estimating the IQs of great geniuses. Her sample of geniuses was drawn from Cattell's list of the 1,000 most eminent people in history. (Actually, Cattell's list is restricted to the western world.) By eliminating members of the hereditary nobility and those born before 1450, Cox identified 300 scientists, writers, politicians, artists, and others whose fame appears to be related to their own activities rather than to an accident of birth.

To get estimates of IQ, Cox had four judges, each a highly qualified expert in intelligence testing, examine some 8,500 pages of biographical material about her sample. The task of the judges was to search for evidence of "brightness" in each individual and to arrive at two IQ estimates. The first estimate was to include data up to the age of 17 and the second one, all of the data from birth to age 26. The judges were cautioned not to overrate the IQs.

The biographies which the judges read included evidence of progress in school, age at which reading and writing were learned, inventions and poems produced, and so on. The material on J. S. Mill, for example, included the facts that he began to learn Greek at three, read Plato at seven, and studied algebra and geometry at eight. He wrote a history of Rome at six-and-a-half—not a masterpiece but considered very good indeed for a six-and-a-half-year-old. Faraday's biographical materials, on the other hand, indicate that he showed no early talent for school work and as a result was apprenticed to a bookbinder at the age of 14. IQ estimates for some of Cox's eminent people are shown in Table 12–2. For the group as a whole, these estimates range from 100 to 200, with a mean of 135 for the estimate based on the first 17 years and 145 for the estimate based on the first 26 years.

Table 12–2. IQ estimates (taken from Cox, 1926)

Eminent person	First 17 years	First 26 years
Bach	125	140
Beethoven	135	140
Copernicus	105	130
Darwin	135	140
Descartes	150	160
Faraday	105	150
Franklin	145	145
Galileo	145	160
Goethe	185	200
Lavoisier	120	150
Michelangelo	145	160
J. S. Mill	190	170
Milton	145	170
Mozart	150	155
Napoleon	135	140
Newton	130	170
Rembrandt	110	135
Voltaire	170	180

Source: Based on data from C. M. Cox, *Genetic Studies of Genius: II. The Early Mental Traits of 300 Geniuses.* Stanford, Calif.: Stanford University Press, 1926.

These IQ estimates are subject to a number of errors and biases which, while by no means negating the value of Cox's study, should make us cautious in interpreting the results. The estimates could be biased upward since the early accomplishments of people who later became famous may be better reported than similar accomplishments of people who do not. If the local mortician wrote poetry at the age of 2, very few people would know it. If Jimmy Carter wrote poetry at the age of 2, the whole country would know it.

The estimates could also be biased downward because of missing data. Evidence of exceptional performance which was never recorded might make an outstanding intellect appear more ordinary than it ought. It is quite possible, for example, that the first IQ estimate for Copernicus (see Table 12–2) is biased downward because biographical data concerning his youth are very scarce. In her book, Cox introduced a correction factor for the bias due to missing data which has the effect of increasing some of the estimates by as much as 30 points. We have not included the correction here, believing that the justification for its use is not solid enough. Despite the faults of these IQ estimates, their very high average suggests strongly that the eminent are superior in intelligence to the general public.

Anne Roe (1953) studied characteristics of a group of 64 American physicists, biologists, and social scientists selected for the importance of their scientific contributions to their fields. The verbal IQs of this group ranged from 121 to 177 with a median of 166. Gough (1960), who studied writers, mathematicians, and architects selected for outstanding creativity, also found that his subjects overall scored very high on intelligence tests.

As a group, then, creative people are also very intelligent people. We should notice, however, that many creative people have IQs which are surprisingly ordinary when we consider their unusual creative accomplishments. For nearly two-thirds of the geniuses in Cox's sample, the IQ estimates for the first 16 years are 140 or less. Among those with IQs of 140 or less are Bach, Beethoven, Copernicus, Darwin, and Rembrandt. Roe noted also that a number of the scientists in her sample had IQs of 140 or less. Now 140 is a very respectable IQ in most circles. Only one person in about 250 scores higher than 140—a distinction comparable, say, to being chosen valedictorian of a high school class. But having an IQ of 140 is definitely not as singular a distinction as being included in Roe's sample of eminent scientists (I estimate that only one person in 10,000 is eminent enough for this distinction) or in Cox's list of 300 geniuses. These facts suggest what the reader must already suspect—that there is more to creativity than high IQ.

We have seen that creative people in a wide variety of professions are clearly superior to the general public in IQ. It might seem a simple extension of this finding that the more creative people in a profession are the more intelligent ones. In fact, this is not the case.

Several studies have explored the relation between creativity and IQ within professional groups. Harmon (1963) measured creativity, intelligence, and academic performance in a sample of 504 physical and biological scientists, most with Ph.D.s. The creativity of each subject was judged independently by three knowledgeable scientists who examined the subjects' lists of publications, patents, and other information related to research productivity. Harmon found no relation between creativity and either IQ or school grades.

Bloom (1963) studied two samples of chemists and mathematicians. One sample consisted of individuals who had been judged outstandingly productive by fellow scientists. The second sample consisted of scientists who were matched in age, education, and experience to the first sample, but who had not been judged as outstandingly productive. While the creative group produced nearly eight times as many publications per year as the unselected group, Bloom found no evidence that the groups differed in IQ.

In a similar study, McKinnon (1968) compared research scientists, mathematicians, and architects who had made distinguished contributions to their fields with matched groups of professionals who had not made distinguished contributions. McKinnon found no difference in IQ between the more creative and the less creative people. All groups ranged in IQ from 120 to 140 with a mean of 130. McKinnon also found that the person's school grades were unrelated to later creativity.

How can it be that creative people are more intelligent than the general public and yet there is no correlation between creativity and IQ among professionals? At least two alternatives seem plausible. First, it might be that a person's IQ must be above some minimum level (perhaps in the neighborhood of 120) if that person is to be creative. Above this level, however, higher IQs do not lead to greater creativity. The reason one finds no correlation between IQ and creativity among professionals is that individuals with low IQs are weeded out by the educational process. Thus, among professionals, one sees only people above the minimum IQ—the range in which there is no relation between IQ and creativity. Consistent with this point of view is the observation that the average IQ for people who struggle through to get a bachelor's degree is 120 and for people who earn Ph.D.s, about 140. People with degrees are a highly selected population with respect to IQ.

A second possibility is that IQ and creativity are not directly related but that a person needs certification in the form of one or more academic degrees if he or she is to be given the opportunity, the encouragement, and perhaps access to the information necessary for creativity. In other words, society may require academic certification if it is to allow a person the opportunity to be creative. If this hypothesis is correct, we would expect that creative people would be above average in IQ to the extent that high IQ is needed to obtain the degrees required for certification in their fields. We would expect the IQs of creative people to be similar to the IQs of other professionals in their field who hold the same degrees.

These two hypotheses are importantly different. According to the minimum IQ hypothesis, there is an intrinsic relation between IQ and creativity. According to the social certification hypothesis, the relation between IQ and creativity is not intrinsic. Rather, it is socially created and could perhaps be changed by changing the way our educational system works and the way we select people for employment in creative fields. Responding to the absence of a demonstrated relation between IQ and creativity, Wing and Wallach (1971) have proposed using measures of creativity in selecting students for admission to college in addition to the standard measures of academic ability such as grades and IQ.

At present, the available data are consistent with both of the hypotheses about the relation of IQ and creativity. It is not yet possible to decide whether the observed relations between creativity and IQ are intrinsic or a result of the way we treat creative people.

Identifying creative individuals

A fair amount of effort has been expended in attempts to identify creative individuals through the use of standardized tests. No fewer than 21 different creativity tests are currently in print (Buros, 1974). We will discuss two approaches to identifying creative individuals which seem to capture the most interesting ideas in this field. These are (1) the remote associates approach, and (2) the divergent thinking approach.

The Remote Associates Test (RAT). The Remote Associates Test (Mednick and Mednick, 1967) is the only standardized creativity test which is tied very directly to a psychological theory of creativity. The Mednicks defined creative thinking as the process of forming new combinations of ideas that meet some need. They consider combining remote ideas as more creative than combining ideas that are more closely related.

The RAT is designed to measure a person's ability to find a common relation among diverse ideas. The test consists of triplets of words such as those shown below:

RIVER   NOTE   BLOOD

The test-taker is asked to find one word which will fit with each of the three to provide a common associate of these diverse ideas. The answer in this case is the word BANK since it combines with the members of the triplet to form RIVER BANK, BANK NOTE, and BLOOD BANK. Table 12–3 contains a set of test items similar to those used in the RAT. The answers, if you are forced to give up, are provided at bottom of page 224.

Table 12–3. Test items similar to those on the Remote Associates Test (RAT)

OUTER	SHIP	CRAWL
CAT	SLEEP	BOARD
TOOL	WILL	WATER
CUP	BIRTHDAY	WALK
BALL	STORM	MAN
FAMILY	APPLE	HOUSE
TIDE	SKI	BED
WORM	SCOTCH	RED
WATER	PICK	SKATE

In their test manual, the Mednicks cite some encouraging results suggesting that high scores on the RAT are associated with superior creative performance in real-life situations. They report, for example, that Gordon (1966) found a significant relation between RAT scores and job success among scientists in a chemical firm and that Mednick and Halpern (1962) found a significant correlation between RAT scores and teachers' ratings of architecture students for creativity. Studies conducted since the publication of the RAT, however, have found essentially no evidence of a relation between RAT scores and creativity in real-life situations. Datta (1964), Pelz and Andrews (1966), and Goodman, Furcon, and Rose (1969) found no relation between the RAT and ratings of creativity in samples of research scientists and engineers. Karlins et al. (1969) found no relation between the RAT and ratings of creativity of graduating architecture students. Pelz and Andrews (1966) found almost no relation between the RAT and the number of papers, patents, or reports generated by a sample of scientists and engineers.

Further, the RAT appears to be highly correlated with IQ. Indeed, one reviewer (Baird, 1972) concluded that much of what it measures is actually academic or verbal intelligence. We have to conclude, then, that while the RAT was a "neat idea," it apparently does not measure creativity.

The divergent thinking approach. A different and much more ambitious approach to the measurement of creativity has been undertaken by Guilford and his co-workers. Guilford (1967) holds that the human intellect draws on a large number of independent mental abilities—at least 120 of them. An example of an independent ability is the ability to remember symbols. People who are good at remembering lists of numbers are high in this ability. Other abilities among the 82 which Guilford has identified are evaluating meaningful implications and recognizing symbolic classes. Tasks used for measuring these abilities are shown in Table 12–4.

Table 12–4. Test items to evaluate mental abilities

A. Types of test items used to measure ability to evaluate meaningful implications
   1. Selecting conclusions
      Given statement: In the mid-Pacific, on Buna-Buna, the game of ticky-ticky is played out of doors.
      Alternate conclusions:
      A. People in Buna-Buna like to play games.
      B. Ticky-ticky is a difficult game to play.
      C. There is an island called Buna-Buna.
      Answer: C
   2. Word meanings
      A radio program always involves
      A. An announcer
      B. A sponsor
      C. Sound
      D. A commercial
      Answer: C

B. Types of test items used to measure ability to recognize symbolic classes
   1. Number classification
      Which one of the five numbers, A to E, fits into each of the classes?

I	44	55	33	A.	421
II	10	45	70	B.	53
III	23	83	31	C.	219
IV	89	49	109	D.	22
				E.	25

      Answer: I, D; II, E; III, B; IV, C
   2. Which number pair does not belong with the others?
      A. 1–5
      B. 2–6
      C. 5–8
      D. 3–7
      Answer: C

Source: J. P. Guilford, *The Nature of Human Intelligence*, New York: McGraw-Hill, 1967, A1 + 2, p. 201; B1 + 2, p. 81.

Guilford believes that about one-fifth of our mental abilities are creative abilities or, as he calls them, divergent production abilities. A divergent production ability is one which a person needs to do a task in which many different responses to the same situation must be gener-

---

Answers to items in Table 12–3: SPACE; WALK; POWER; CAKE; SNOW; TREE; WATER; TAPE; ICE.

ated. The following is a typical divergent production task: Name all the words you can think of which start with R and end with M.

A convergent production task, in contrast, is one in which the person is expected to generate a single correct answer. Typical convergent production tasks are naming opposites, finding a hidden figure, and solving simple algebra problems.

Other divergent production tasks are shown in Table 12–5. Guilford notes that tasks of this sort are typically not found in IQ tests.

Table 12–5. Types of test items used to measure divergent production abilities

1. Classify the following names in as many ways as possible.
    a. Gertrude
    b. Bill
    c. Alex
    d. Carrie
    e. Belle
    f. Don, etc.
    Answers: a, c, d (two syllables)
              b, d, e (double consonants)
              a, d. e (begins with consonant, ends with vowel),
              etc.
2. Given the numbers 1, 2, 3, 4, and 5, combine them in several different ways to achieve a total of 7, using each number only once in each answer.
    Answers: 2 + 5 = 7; 3 + 4 = 7; 1 + 2 + 4 = 7, etc.
3. Fill in the missing word in as many ways as you can.
    "His smile was as wide as a(n) _____."
4. Suggest two different and unusual methods for dealing with the following problems:
    a. Boredom of employees
    b. Walking the dog

Source: J. P. Guilford, *The Nature of Human Intelligence*, New York: McGraw-Hill, 1967, 1, p. 145; 2, 3, p. 147; 4, p. 146.

Divergent production (DP) tests have met with both success and failure in predicting creativity in real-life situations. In a study of research scientists, Taylor, Smith, and Ghiselin (1963) found very little relation between creativity and DP test scores. Elliott, however, (1964) found a strong relation. He compared the 14 people in a copywriting department rated most creative with the 14 rated least creative. Twelve of the people in the creative group scored well on five DP tests but only one of the people in the noncreative group obtained comparably high scores.

We should not be too discouraged by these mixed results. As Guilford points out, predicting who will be creative in real-life situations is a very complex matter. There are a great many divergent production abilities—Guilford suggests 24—and it may be difficult to know which of them will be required for any particular creative act. Further, Guilford recognizes that a creative act may involve much more than just divergent production abilities.

The divergent thinking approach is far from providing us with a complete understanding of the creative process. It does, however, show promise of helping us to predict who the creators will be.

PART 2
THE NATURE OF THE CREATIVE PROCESS

A traditional view

Graham Wallas (1926) articulated the traditional view of the creative process as four ordered stages:

1. Preparation
2. Incubation
3. Illumination
4. Verification

Preparation is a stage of often intensive work in which the person gathers information and investigates the problem in a variety of ways. It is the period in which the mind is prepared for the creative act to follow. While there is a romantic notion that creative ideas spring without effort to the minds of the truly creative, the weight of evidence and opinion suggests that this very rarely happens. Pasteur said, ". . . chance favors only the prepared mind." Creativity typically requires lots of hard work—work spent in learning fundamental skills and knowledge and in exploring countless blind alleys.

Incubation is a stage following preparation in which the person is not consciously thinking about the problem but during which there is nevertheless some progress toward solution. It is as if ideas which were first encountered during preparation are maturing.

Illumination is the stage in which a plan or idea for solving the problem is discovered. What one gets as the result of illumination is not a completely solved problem or a set of calculations completely carried out. Rather, as the French mathematician Raymond Poincaré (1924) says, "All one may hope from these inspirations . . . is a point of departure for such calculations."

Verification is the final stage of the creative process in which the plan discovered during illumination is tested and carried out.

Poincaré (1924, pp. 383–94) has provided some dramatic examples which illustrate these stages in the creative process. The incident he describes below occurred when he had already made some important progress in solving a problem. Poincaré had been working hard for more than two weeks on the properties of Fuchsian functions.

> Just at this time I left Caen, where I was then living, to go on a geological excursion under the auspices of the school of mines. The changes of travel made me forget my mathematical work. Having reached Coutances, we entered an omnibus to go some place or other. At the moment when I put my foot on the step the idea came to me, without anything in my former thoughts seeming to have paved the way for it, that the transformations I had used to define the Fuchsian functions were identical with those of nonEuclidian geometry. I did not verify the idea; I should not have had the time, as, upon taking my seat in the omnibus, I went on with a conversation already commenced, but I felt a perfect certainty. On my return to Caen, for conscience sake I verified the result at my leisure.

Thus, after two weeks of intensive preparation, the excursion forced a period of incubation. The stage of illumination which followed was very brief—not more than the time it takes to climb on a bus. In this instance, the separation of the illumination and verification stages was very clearly marked by intervening activities which had nothing to do with solving the problem.

The next incident occurred when Poincaré had been working hard on a problem but without much apparent success.

> Disgusted with my failure, I went to spend a few days at the seaside, and thought of something else. One morning, walking on the bluff, the idea came to me, with just the same characteristics of brevity, suddenness and immediate certainty, that the arithmetic transformations of indeterminate ternary quadratic forms were identical with those of nonEuclidean geometry.
>
> Returned to Caen, I meditated on this result and deduced the consequences.

Here again, the four stages are quite apparent.

The third incident occurred when Poincaré was working on a group of related problems.

> I made a systematic attack on them and carried all the outworks, one after another. There was one, however, that still held out, whose fall would involve that of the whole place. But all my efforts only served at first the better to show me the difficulty, which indeed was something. All this work was perfectly conscious.
>
> Thereupon I left for Mont-Valerien, where I was to go through my military service; so I was very differently occupied. One day, going along the street, the solution of the difficulty which had stopped me suddenly

appeared to me. I did not try to go deep into it immediately, and only after my service did I again take up the question. I had all the elements and had only to arrange them and put them together. So I wrote out my final memoir at a single stroke and without difficulty.

Incidents of this sort have been reported by many creative people—artists, writers, musicians, and scientists, as well as mathematicians. A large number of such incidents are reviewed by Hadamard (1945) and by Koestler (1964).

A critique of the traditional view

The stages of incubation and illumination are the two most interesting aspects of the traditional description of the creative process. While the occurrence of illumination, that is, the sudden appearance of a problem solution, is generally accepted, some psychologists have voiced doubts about the reality of incubation. These doubts are based on the weakness of the positive evidence supporting incubation—psychologists tend to be very wary of using anecdotes as evidence, even anecdotes told by famous people—and the failure of a number of attempts to demonstrate incubation in the laboratory (Cook, 1934, 1937; Erickson, 1942). In relatively recent years, however, the psychological laboratories have produced several clear demonstrations of incubation observed under well-controlled conditions.

In one of these studies, carried out by Fulgosi and Guilford (1968), the subjects performed a divergent production task such as stating as many consequences as possible which would follow if people no longer needed to eat or could no longer read. Some subjects worked on the task continuously. Others were interrupted by a distracting task for either 10 or 20 minutes. While the 10-minute break yielded little gain over uninterrupted problem solving, the 20-minute break yielded a significant improvement.

In another study, conducted by Silveira (1971), the subjects solved a rather difficult detour problem. Silveira compared uninterrupted problem solving with solving interrupted either early or late in the process. The break was either short (a half hour) or long (four hours). When interruption followed the longer period of work on the problem, both the short and the long delay produced a marked increase in the subjects' chances of solving the problem.

Murray and Denny (1969) found that a period of incubation helped the poorer problem solvers among their subjects but not the better ones.

Given that incubation really happens, how are we to understand it? Does the human brain house two separate problem solvers—one of them conscious and the other unconscious—which may operate simultaneously? Certainly the facts do not require us to believe any such thing. Remember that what one gets as the result of incubation and illumination is not a completed problem solution. Rather, it is simply a plan or an idea for a solution. What we must account for is not how a problem may be completely solved unconsciously but only how unconscious processes can promote the discovery of a plan for a solution.

Selective forgetting is the best candidate for the unconscious process underlying incubation. A possible role for selective forgetting in incubation has been discussed by Woodworth (1938), Hadamard (1945), Posner (1973) and others. The most complete theoretical account of the processes by which forgetting leads to incubation is that given by Simon (1966). Briefly, his position is the following:

1. In the early stages of problem solving, problem solvers form a solution plan to direct their problem solving effort. Simon noted that people seem to get lost easily in executing their solution plans. They are frequently heard to ask questions such as, "Why did I want to do that again?" and "Where am I?" On these grounds, he postulated that solution plans are stored in a relatively short-term working memory rather than in some more permanent form.

2. In the course of attempting to execute the plan, problem solvers learn a great deal about the problem and they may discover the nature of constraints not suspected at the beginning of the solution process. They may form information groupings or "chunks" which they did not have before. They may put together individual problem steps into subroutines. Information of this sort may be stored in relatively long-term memory.

3. During a delay, the initial solution plan is forgotten or at least suffers more forgetting than the newly acquired information about the nature of the problem.

4. When problem-solving attempts are reinitiated after the delay, the old plan is gone, and so a new one must be formed.

The new plan is formed with better information about the true nature of the problem than was available when the initial plan was formed. Hence, it is likely to be a better plan than the one in operation before the break. The break, then, should have the effect of increasing the probability of solution. This, of course, is just what is observed in the incubation phenomenon. If this analysis is correct, incubation should be characteristic of problems in which the subject learns about the nature of the problem while solving it. This is the defining characteristic of discovery problems as discussed in the previous chapter.

While incubation and illumination are real phenomena, we must ask if they are truly characteristic of the creative process. Are they always present in the creative act, or is there a lot of creative activity in which incubation and illumination play no part? The fact that psychologists had difficulty demonstrating incubation and the fact that it appears only under some conditions strongly suggests that it is a "sometimes" phenomenon, playing a role in some creative acts but not in others.

What about illumination? Is it always present in the creative act? Do creative acts always involve a sudden flash of insight? Re-examining the incidents which we presented to illustrate the traditional stages of creativity, we find that they actually contain more examples of gradual solutions than sudden ones. In the first incident, Poincaré had already made other important discoveries about his problem before the one involving an illumination occurred. In the third incident, there was a whole set of problems solved without illumination and just one solved with it. Illumination, then, is not part of every creative act.

Perhaps, though, it does characterize the more creative or revolutionary discoveries. The one solution in which Poincaré experienced illumination may have been scientifically more interesting or more trendsetting than the others. There is reason to believe, however, that the most creative discoveries do not proceed from sudden illuminations. The historian of science, Thomas Kuhn (1970), makes a powerful argument that truly revolutionary discoveries are never sudden. Kuhn describes two kinds of science—normal science and revolutionary science. In the course of normal science, which is most science, the scientific community operates with a generally accepted set of ideas about how some part of nature works. For example, there may be a dominant theory about magnetic phenomena or about the nature of the earth's crust. The researcher in normal science interprets data in terms of the accepted theory. New discoveries are simply new applications of the accepted theory. Typically observations which do not fit the accepted theory create no problem. They are either ignored, or if the lack of fit is recognized, scientists wait patiently, expecting that soon the anomaly will be resolved in favor of the accepted theory.

Sometimes an observation so obviously violates the accepted theory that it creates a crisis. In revolutionary science, a relatively rare occurrence, the scientist proposes a new theory to incorporate the facts covered by the old theory together with the new anomalous facts. Kuhn claims that the discoveries of revolutionary science are never sudden and that it is precisely their revolutionary character that makes it impossible for us to discover them suddenly. A revolutionary discovery requires not just new observations but also the assimilation of those observations into a new understanding of the workings of nature. The new view of nature and the understanding of the phenomena grow simultaneously. As an example, Kuhn points out that the discovery of oxygen was not a momentary event but rather a process which was spread out at least over the three years from 1774 to 1777. Lavoisier, in his work on oxygen, performed many experiments with the new gas during this time and gradually refined his understanding of the phenomena he was observing over this whole period. There was no precise moment in time when oxygen was discovered. Rather, there was a growing understanding, a gradually evolving new view of how the world worked chemically. Kuhn believes that sudden discoveries can occur only when the theory for understanding them is prepared beforehand, that is, when a pattern discovered in the data matches a theoretical pattern already available in memory. This can happen in normal science, but in revolutionary science, there is no such preestablished pattern which matches the data. Therefore there can be no sudden revolutionary discoveries.

In summary, then, the traditional view of creativity provides valuable insights about the creative process. It emphasizes the importance of the preparatory stage for creative work and identifies the phenomena of incubation and illumination. On the negative side, however, the traditional view overemphasizes the importance of incubation and fails to provide very much detail in the description of creative processes.

What is the nature of a creative act?

Judging creativity is important in our culture, and we do it a lot. Sometimes we agree quite well in our judgments. Most will agree that Picasso was a creative painter and that Yeats was a more creative poet than, say, Rod McKuen. Agreement in such judgments is by no means perfect, however, and sometimes it is terrible. What delights one audience may horrify another. Beethoven and Stravinsky were called madmen by early critics. Important scientific discoveries may at first be received with open hostility, for example, X-rays (see Kuhn, 1970). Our judgments of creativity are subject to errors and uncertainties, and the boundaries that separate the creative from the noncreative are fuzzy and may shift. How do we make judgments of creativity?

One possibility is that we can look for special processes which are found in creative acts, but not in noncreative ones. The evidence, however, does not support such a position. We saw earlier that the processes of incubation and illumination are not reliable clues to creativity. Research on creativity specifically aimed at finding out what is special about creative acts has failed to reveal any process unique to them. Patrick (1937) asked 50 artists and 50 nonartists to describe their mental processes as they each produced a drawing. Although the artists produced far better drawings, both groups appeared to go about the task of drawing in much the same way. Both groups showed evidence of Wallas' four stages of thought: preparation, incubation, illumination, and verification. Both groups required an average of about 20 minutes to produce a drawing and they distributed their time in much the same way between unorganized thought, organized thought, and revision. In a similar study of poetry writing, Patrick (1935) found that while poets produced better poems than nonpoets, they did not use processes obviously different from nonpoets.

The research on chess, which we reviewed in the previous chapter, revealed an important difference in chess knowledge between chess masters and nonmasters which influenced the way masters represent chess problems. For example, the master may recognize a game situation as a variant of one studied before, while the novice does not. The reasoning processes which masters apply to their representations, however, appear to be identical to those used by less expert players.

In their studies of musical composition, Reitman (1965) and Simon and Sumner (1968) emphasize the importance of planning and inference processes which are familiar in everyday reasoning. In none of these studies of creative activities is there evidence of special thinking processes which appear only in creative acts.

Newell, Shaw, and Simon (1962) have suggested that people use multiple criteria for judging creativity:

> Problem solving is called creative to the extent that one or more of the following conditions are satisfied:
>   1. The product of the thinking has novelty and value (either for the thinker or for his culture).
>   2. The thinking is unconventional, in the sense that it requires modification or rejection of previously accepted ideas.
>   3. The thinking requires high motivation and persistence, taking place either over a considerable span of time (continuously or intermittently), or at high intensity.
>   4. The problem as initially posed was vague and ill-defined, so that part of the task was to formulate the problem itself.

I believe that the Newell, Shaw, and Simon approach of identifying multiple criteria for judgments of creativity is the right one. I will propose, however, a different scheme which, while in the same spirit as theirs, is, I believe, more consistent and complete.

A theory of creativity judgments

People will call a problem-solving act creative if they believe two things about it:

1. that it provides a good solution to the problem solver's problem.
2. that most people could not or would not have arrived at the same solution.

I do not propose to say very much about how an observer judges whether a solution is a good one or not. I assume that the judgment involves estimating the extent to which the goal is achieved, minimizing costs, and adhering to constraints. Much more interesting for our purposes are the conditions which lead the observer to judge that most people would not or could not have arrived at the same solution. I believe that there are five conditions which lead to such judgments. As we will see, many of these conditions have the effect of hiding the nature of the solution process from the person making the judgment of creativity. The judge therefore may be unable to answer the question, "How did he ever think of that!!"

Condition 1.   Situations in which the solution depends on knowledge which the problem solver has but the observers do not. There are a number of situations which fulfill this condition.

A.   Problem solvers who come from a professional field different from the observer, may, in solving problems, draw on analogies to processes or phenomena in their own field. To the observer, who cannot make these same analogies, the solution may appear surprising and hence creative. Gordon (1961) makes specific use of this situation as a means of promoting creativity. He recommends that a problem-solving team should include people from very diverse fields. When asked to assemble a group to work on improving paint, he included not just paint chemists but also an artist, a biologist, an engineer, and a zoologist as well. As a result, the group proposed an organic paint. The idea was that the spores of mosses and lichens could be canned in an adhesive nutrient solution. When the paint is applied to a wall, rather than just sitting there like most paint and passively decaying, it will grow and renew itself.

B.   Knowledge of an individual fact may allow the problem solver to complete a chain of inference which the observer cannot complete. Dr. Watson, as observer, was continually amazed when Sherlock Holmes pulled this sort of stunt.

C.   Sometimes the problem solver makes use of a broad range of knowledge in solving a problem. The use of broad knowledge seems to characterize creative acts involving the organization and arrangement of diverse elements where knowledge is the raw material that the creative act transforms. Examples of such acts are the classification of the universe of living things by Linneaus into phyla, classes, families, etc., and Darwin's development of the theory of evolution over the course of nearly 30 years of scholarship. Coleridge's poetry is another instance of creativity of this sort since, as we will see, it involved the transformation of extensive knowledge which he had stored in memory.

In all of these instances, and particularly where broad knowledge is involved, the observers will tend to judge the problem solver's performance as more creative than if they had shared the problem solver's knowledge.

Condition 2. Situations in which the solution depends on perceptual or judgmental skills which the problem solver has acquired but the observer has not. To illustrate what we mean by perceptual skills, we may imagine that the problem solver and the observer are confronted with a complex circuit and are required to determine its properties. Because of skills in identifying familiar circuit patterns, the problem solver is able to see the complex circuit as a combination of several simpler circuits whose properties are already known. Thus, the expert is able to solve a problem which appears very complex to the observer, who operates without these perceptual skills.

By judgmental skills, we have in mind abilities which enable the artist to decide how much detail a drawing should have, and the ability skilled teachers acquire which enables them to decide how much material students are ready to absorb at the moment.

Perceptual and judgmental skills are typically acquired slowly through extensive practice. Further, they are often difficult to talk about or even to think about. If we ask artists how it is that they are able to draw faces so well, they may have a very difficult time telling us anything at all about how they perceive appropriate proportions or decide on revisions in performing this skilled act. A difference in these skills may appear large to the observer, and may in fact represent a big difference in problem-solving ability between the observer and the problem solver. Thus, when the solution of a problem depends on a perceptual or judgmental skill which the observer does not have, the observer is likely to judge the solution as very creative.

Condition 3. Situations in which it is difficult for the observer to predict or reconstruct the problem solver's solution path.

A. In discovery problems, which we discussed in detail in the last chapter, the problem solvers learn something essential for solving the problem in the course of problem-solving attempts. For example, after some work on the problem, they may discover that the problem is of an entirely different type from what they had assumed after first reading the statement of the problem. They may say, for example, "Oh, this isn't a triangle problem at all!" The observer, who has not had the experience of working into the problem, may be surprised at the problem solvers' approach and therefore judge it creative.

In design problems, it often is not obvious how two problem requirements will interact with each other until one tries them out. A strength requirement may be compatible with a weight requirement or it may not. In a math problem, what seems the obvious approach may run into an intractable snag when one tries to carry it out. New knowledge about the problem, derived from the failure of our initial attempts to solve it, may lead to solution procedures which will not occur to the observer, who lacks similar experience.

B. In some problems, the observer may inadvertently be misled about the nature of the solution path. It is not uncommon, for example, for a mathematician to discover the solution to a problem by working backward and then to publish the steps of the solution in the forward direction. This is a perfectly valid thing to do mathematically, but it may produce a proof that is very hard to understand. The observer may find that the motivation of the proof—that is, the reason for the steps—is hard to discover. For example, the observer is completely baffled as to how the problem solver ever thought to make the step from C to D. In fact, the problem solver actually went from D to C, a step which may be much easier for the observer to understand.

There is a trick which makes intentional use of such reversal of steps to score smartness points. It works this way: The aspiring impressor walks down the street with the selected impressee. He says, apparently casually, "Oh, that's interesting! That licence plate number, 1311, is divisible by 437." If the impressee believes that his companion routinely notices numbers that are divisible by 437 and Lord knows what else, the impressor has gained his objective. What the impressor actually does is covertly look for a number divisible by 3. When he finds one, he pretends that the quotient, in this case 437, was actually the divisor and thereby collects a great deal of unearned credit for arithmetic prowess.

Whether the problem solver intends to deceive or not, the observer may give undue credit for creativity if the problem solver presents the steps of the solution in an order which is different from the order in which they were discovered.

C. Since an observer typically has a harder time following a solution plan which has many steps than one which has few steps, problem solutions which involve many steps should be judged more creative than ones which involve few steps. This principle may be viewed as an alternative to Newell, Shaw, and Simon's (1962) principle that problems requiring persistence or intense effort tend to be judged as creative.

Condition 4. Situations in which the different backgrounds of the problem solver and the observer lead to different patterns of set and functional fixity (See Chapter 4, pp. 70–72). Observers will tend to judge a solution as creative if because of set or functional fixity they would not have thought of it themselves.

People have a great deal of training and experience in dealing with other people. We all know that it is not polite to violate another's personal space. We learn for one reason or another not to reach for the butter directly through our neighbor's forkful of lasagne or even to stare too intently at his wart. Therefore, to a human observer, it came as a surprise when an ape used his keeper as a stepladder to get a banana (see Chapter 4). From the human point of view, and because of a very strong functional fixity which people have about the uses of people, such a solution appears creative.

In some cases, particularly in artistic fields, it is difficult to evaluate over the short run what will have lasting value and what will not. In such cases, judgments of creativity may depend to an inappropriate degree on the oddity or bizarreness of what is produced. We are all familiar with the stereotype of the artistic fraud who attempts to exploit this difficulty of judgment by substituting bizarreness of output for hard work in the solution of aesthetic problems.

Condition 5. Situations in which the problem solver introduces a new goal which the observer accepts as a valuable one.

When the goal of Impressionism, an important school of painting at the time, was the objective, almost scientific analysis of the light received by the eye, Van Gogh introduced a new goal in his own painting—personal expression rather than objective reporting. While today Van Gogh's goal is accepted as a valuable one without question, this was not always the case. In his lifetime, his work received only one favorable review, and he was able to sell only one painting. Both Beethoven and Stravinsky were called madmen early in their careers, presumably by critics who did not feel that the musical goals they were trying to accomplish were good ones.

Acceptance of a new goal may take considerable time. A composer of my acquaintance told me that he does not expect public acceptance of his work because the taste of both the public and the performing musicians is rooted, naturally, in an earlier tradition. He feels that the important thing for a composer is to have an esthetic position—one's own musical goal—and to pursue it without expecting it to be understood in one's own lifetime.

Public acceptance may come relatively quickly for those who introduce new means for achieving old goals—such people as Edison and Watt for example. On the other hand, those who introduce new goals—who identify new directions for exploring the worlds of beauty and knowledge—will probably wait much longer to be understood and accepted by their culture and may meet severe criticism on the way, as did Galileo and Darwin.

How is it that the innovator is able to conceive a new goal different from the dominant goals of the field? Even though this question has not been studied sufficiently well, we need not view the process of creating new goals as a mysterious one. There are several factors we can identify as potential sources of such new goals. The current goals in a field tend to age and they do so in two ways. First, as time passes, more and more of the possibilities of the current goals are explored, and more and more frequently the limitations imposed by current goals are reached. Experiencing these limitations may serve to suggest the advantages that new goals could bring. Cezanne worked intensively in the Impressionist tradition before moving on into the post-Impressionist movement. Lavoisier's work in the older phlogiston chemistry, and the failure of that chemistry to account for his data, led him to initiate the new chemistry.

Second, when goals have been accepted for a number of years, they tend to lose their ability to excite. The more revolutionary members of a field may search consciously for new goals to renew the excitement and to distinguish themselves from the older members of their field.

In some cases, new goals may be borrowed from other fields and other cultures. In designing the first primitive computer (see Chapter 8), Charles Babbage was inspired by the punched-card controls of the Jacquard loom (Cardwell, 1972). In his revolutionary analysis of heat engines, Carnot made extensive use of analogy to the then familiar water engines. Van Gogh and Whistler borrowed Japanese ideas in the visual arts, and the American composer Lou Harrison makes use of ideas from Polynesian and Javanese music.

New goals, then, may arise (1) from experiencing the limitations of the old goals, and (2) by borrowing elements from other fields and cultures. Whether or not these two sources, together with happy accident, are sufficient to account for the introduction of new goals into our culture is a question well worth studying.

Can an individual become more creative?

Of course, there is no procedure which will guarantee that a person will invent something important or initiate a new artistic movement. At least three kinds of things that we can do, however, seem likely to increase our chances of being creative. One requires lots of work, and the other two are relatively easy. We will start with the one that is lots of work.

1. Developing a knowledge base. In this chapter, we have referred repeatedly to the importance of knowledge in the creative act. Knowledge may be helpful in many different phases of the problem-solving process. It can make it possible for us to complete a chain of inference. It may be the body of knowledge which the creative act transforms. It may provide us with an analogy which helps us form a solution plan. In the form of a value, it may help us to make a critical decision. In all of these ways, knowledge aids the creative process.

There are some creative acts, however, which appear to have little to do with organized knowledge. Coleridge's poem "Kubla Khan" and its manner of composition suggest far more a process of building from nothing—from pure imagination—than a use of deep scholarship and knowledge. The poem was conceived in an opium dream and transcribed immediately after. It puts together elements which seem to have absolutely no factual or logical connection—the Asian Khan, an Abyssinian maid, a dangerous man "with flashing eyes and floating hair," fountains spewing rocks, a mysterious river Alph, etc.

Despite the poem's appearance of providing us with a capricious blend of arbitrary images, the literary scholar, Lowes (1927), has been able to trace the basis in knowledge from which the poem proceeded. Coleridge had kept a notebook of his voluminous reading for the three years before the writing of "Kubla Khan," jotting down comments on and quotations from what he had read. With the aid of this notebook, Lowes was able to locate exactly what Coleridge had been reading, and by matching wording and imagery in the poem to that in the books, he was able to identify the sources of the poem with considerable certainty. For example, the river Alph was the Alpheus, a mythological river which Coleridge identified with the Nile; the fountains spewing rock were identified with the mythological source of the Nile in the underworld which sprang from the ground in Abyssinia—hence, the Abyssinian maid, and so on.

Our point is not that knowledge explains the process of poetic composition—it doesn't. Others with the same knowledge would have been very unlikely to generate a memorable poem. What we want to illustrate is that the poet does draw on his knowledge in an important way in the process of creating a poem. He makes use of images and ideas stored in memory as material from which he fashions poetry. Lowes believes that what is true of Coleridge is true of other poets as well. He notes that Chaucer's knowledge of travel lore, alchemy, astrology, medicine, geomancy, and so on, all were distilled into his poetry. His poetry would certainly be less rich without this knowledge.

Van Gogh, while a revolutionary artist, had extensive knowledge and appreciation of traditional artists. Further, he spent years practicing technical skills, especially drawing, which he regarded as fundamental.

The stage of preparation must be taken very seriously if one expects to be creative. Having relevant knowledge does not guarantee creativity, but it is certainly one very important condition of creativity. Acquiring the knowledge needed for creativity may require a great deal of work. Indeed, the only trait Anne Roe found that was common to the leading artists and scientists she studied was the willingness to work extremely hard (Roe, 1946, 1953). Those who plan to relax until their creative inspiration seizes them are likely to have a long, uninterrupted rest.

2. Create the right atmosphere for creativity. For many people, an effective method for increasing the flow of ideas is the "brainstorming" technique designed by Alex Osborn (1948). It is a technique used when we want to get a large number of suggestions for solving a problem. For example, in a marketing problem we might want to get a large number of ideas for possible uses of a new product.

The essential principle of the brainstorming technique is that the processes of idea generation and idea criticism must be kept completely separate. First the brainstorming group generates as many ideas as possible without any criticism or evaluation. Only after the group has exhausted its supply of ideas is criticism allowed to start. Imagine a group gathered around a table in a typical idea-generating session. The first person says, "I have an idea—Let's. . . ." Instantly, a second person says, "Oh, that won't work because. . . ." In brainstorming, it is just this sort of critical comment that is ruled out during the idea-generating phase. All ideas, no matter how silly, are welcomed. Humor is accepted, and members are encouraged to build on earlier ideas. An idea which is proposed as a joke may not be useful in itself as a solution of the problem, and yet it may aid the solution by suggesting a new dimension of the problem, or by opening a new line of inquiry. In a recent brainstorming session on campus housing, someone suggested a B.Y.O.H.—bring your own housing—university. Everyone would be required to come to college in a house trailer. While the idea was proposed as a joke, it did open up the dimension of mobility in the discussion and led to a number of more practical suggestions about the use of mobile housing units.

The atmosphere in the idea-generating phase of brainstorming is a very permissive one in which all ideas are welcomed. Only when the flow of ideas has ceased does the evaluation phase begin. Then, through discussion, the best and the most practical ideas are selected to be included on a short list as the group's problem-solving proposal.

While Osborn's original brainstorming technique is designed to be used by a group of problem solvers, the same principles can be applied by individuals in their own problem solving. To do this, the individuals must learn to control their internal editor. They must turn off the inner voice of criticism during the phase of idea generation. Flower and Hayes (1976) have applied this individual brainstorming technique as an aid in generating plans for writing essays.

3. Searching for analogies. Human problem solvers do not make optimal use of the analogies that are available to them in solving problems. A number of studies have shown that people often fail to notice that a new problem is really an old problem, a problem that they already know how to solve, disguised in different words (Köhler, 1940; Hayes and Simon, 1976; Hinsley, Hayes and Simon, 1977). Faced with a supposedly new problem, people may spend unnecessary time solving it anew, or may actually fail to solve it in its new form. This failure to recognize familiar problems constitutes an important limitation of the problem solver's effective intelligence. If we were always aware of it when a problem was identical with or similar to one we already know how to solve, our problem-solving power would clearly be increased.

Synectics is a technique designed by W. J. Gordon (1961) to help the problem solver recognize analogies between problems. The core of the technique is a set of procedures for generating four types of analogies to the problem at hand. The four types are:

1. Personal analogy
2. Direct analogy
3. Symbolic analogy
4. Fantasy analogy

Keats described his use of *personal analogy* in writing "Endymion": "I leaped headlong into the sea, and thereby have become better acquainted with the sounds, the quicksands, and the rocks, than if I had stayed upon the green shore and piped a silly pipe, and took tea and comfortable advice." In making personal analogies, the point is to imagine yourself experiencing the subject directly. If you are concerned with gear trains or dog houses, imagine yourself as a gear in the train or a dog entertaining at home.

To make a *direct analogy*, we look for something which solves essentially the same problem we are trying to solve, but in a different context. For example, Brunel invented a technique of underwater tunneling after watching a shipworm constructing a tube for itself as it moved forward.

By *symbolic analogy*, Gordon has in mind a looser class of relations than direct analogies. For example, he suggests that the Indian rope trick is a symbolic analogy to an automobile jack.

Finally, in *fantasy analogy*, anything goes. For a new means of transportation one may consider flying carpets and teleportation. For a new zipper, one may imagine trained insects linking mandibles on command.

Synectics is not the only available procedure designed to help us search for analogies. Osborn (1952) proposes a checklist of ways in which to imagine our problem changed, such as magnifying it, reversing it, and so on, so as to suggest related problems and solutions. However we do it, if we increase the probability of discovering useful analogies to our problem, we will increase our problem-solving ability and our creative power.

SUMMARY

A creative act is one which (1) has some valuable consequence, and (2) is novel or surprising. Creative acts are instances of problem solving but not all instances of problem solving are creative. The underlying psychological processes required for creative problem solving, however, appear to be the same as those required for noncreative problem solving.

In the traditional view, a creative act involves four stages: (1) preparation, (2) incubation, (3) illumination, and (4) verification.

A review of the evidence indicates that preparation is indeed essential for a creative act. The other three stages may occur but are neither essential to nor characteristic of creative acts.

A person will judge an act as creative if its execution requires knowledge which the person does not possess.

Individuals can increase their creativity by (1) increasing their knowledge, (2) creating an appropriate atmosphere, and (3) making more efficient use of knowledge through analogy and brainstorming.

FURTHER READING

Of the books in References following, Vernon's (1970) book, *Creativity*, is a good general reader on the topic, providing articles written from many points of view. Ghiselin's (1952) book, *The Creative Process*, consists of reports by creative individuals about their own creative processes. Many of them are fascinating.

Those interested in animal creativity should not miss Köhler's delightful (1925) book, *The Mentality of Apes*.

Guilford's (1967) book, *The Nature of Human Intelligence*, is the best source on divergent thinking.

REFERENCES

BAIRD, L. L. "A review of the Remote Associates Test," *The seventh mental measurements yearbook*, ed. O. K. Buros. Highland Park, N.J.: Gryphon Press, 1972.

BLOOM, B. S. "Report on creativity research by the examiner's office of the University of Chicago," *Scientific creativity: Its recognition and development*, eds. C. W. Taylor and F. Barron. New York: Wiley, 1963.

BUROS, O. K., *Tests in print: II*. Highland Park, N.J.: Gryphon Press, 1972.

CARDWELL, D. S. L. *Turning points in western technology*. New York: Science History Publications, 1972.

COOK, T. W. "Distribution of practice and size of maze pattern," *British Journal of Psychology, 27* (1937), pp. 303–312.

COOK, T. W. "Massed and distributed practice in puzzle solving," *Psychological Review, 41* (1934), pp. 330–335.

COX, C. M. *Genetic studies of genius: II. The early mental traits of 300 geniuses*. Stanford, Calif.: Stanford University Press, 1926.

DATTA, L. "A note on the Remote Associates Test, United States culture, and creativity," *Journal of Applied Psychology, 48* (1964), pp. 184–185.

ELLIOTT, J. M. "Measuring creative abilities in public relations and advertising work," *Widening horizons in creativity,* ed. C. W. Taylor. New York: Wiley, 1964. Pp. 396–400.

ERICKSEN, S. C. "Variability of attack in massed and spaced practice," *Journal of Experimental Psychology, 31* (1942), pp. 339–345.

FLOWER, L. S., and HAYES, J. R. "Problem solving and the cognitive process of writing," Unpublished manuscript, 1977.

FULGOSI, A., and GUILFORD, J. P. "Short-term incubation in divergent production," *American Journal of Psychology, 7* (1968), pp. 1016–1023.

GALTON, F. *Hereditary genius.* New York: Appleton, 1870.

GHISELIN, B., ed. *The creative process.* New York: New American Library, 1952.

GOODMAN, P.; FURCON, J.; and ROSE, J. "Examination of some measures of creative ability by the multitrait-multimethod matrix," *Journal of Applied Psychology, 53* (1969), pp. 240–243.

GORDON, G. "The identification and use of creative abilities in scientific organizations," Paper presented at the Seventh National Research Conference on Creativity, Greensboro, North Carolina, 1966.

GORDON, W. J. *Synectics.* New York: Harper & Row, 1961.

GOUGH, H. G. "Stylistic variations among professional research scientists," *Journal of Psychology, 49* (1960), pp. 87–98.

GUILFORD, J. P. *The nature of human intelligence.* New York: McGraw-Hill, 1967.

HADAMARD, J. S. *An essay on the psychology of invention in the mathematical field.* Princeton, N.J.: Princeton University Press, 1945.

HARMAN, L. R. "The development of a criterion of scientific competence," *Scientific creativity: Its recognition and development,* eds., C. W. Taylor and F. Barron. New York: Wiley, 1963. Pp. 44–52.

HAYES, J. R., and SIMON, H. A. "Psychological differences among problem isomorphs," *Cognitive theory,* Vol. II., eds. N. Castellon, Jr.; D. Pisoni; and G. Potts. Potomac, Md.: Lawrence Erlbaum, 1976.

HINSLEY, D.; HAYES, J. R.; and SIMON, H. A. "From words to equations," *Cognitive processes in comprehension,* eds. P. Carpenter and M. Just. Hillsdale, N.J.: Lawrence Erlbaum, 1977.

KARLINS, M.; SCHUERHOFF, C.; and KAPLIN, M. "Some factors related to architectural creativity in graduating architecture students," *Journal of General Psychology, 81* (1969), pp. 203–215.

KOESTLER, A. *The act of creation.* New York: Macmillan, 1967.

KÖHLER, W. *The mentality of apes.* London: Routledge and Kegan Paul, 1925.

KÖHLER, W. *Dynamics in psychology.* New York: Liveright, 1940.

KUHN, T. S. *The structure of scientific revolutions,* 2d ed. Chicago: University of Chicago Press, 1970.

LOWES, J. L. *The road to Xanadu.* Boston: Houghton Mifflin, 1927.

MCKINNON, D. W. "Selecting students with creative potential," *The creative college student: An unmet challenge,* ed. P. Heist. San Francisco: Jossey-Bass, 1968.

MEDNICK, S. A., and HALPERN, S. "Ease of concept attainment as a function of associative rank," *Journal of Experimental Psychology,* 6 (1962), pp. 628–630.

MEDNICK, S. A., and MEDNICK, M. T. *Remote Associates Test.* Boston: Houghton Mifflin, 1967.

MURRAY, H. G., and DENNY, J. P. "Interaction of ability level and interpolated activity (opportunity for incubation) in human problem solving," *Psychological Reports,* 24 (1969), pp. 271–276.

NEWELL, A.; SHAW, J. C.; and SIMON, H. A. "The process of creative thinking," *Contemporary approaches to creative thinking,* eds. H. E. Gruber; G. Terrell; and M. Wertheimer. New York: Atherton Press, 1962. Pp. 63–119.

OSBORN, A. F. *Your creative power.* New York: Charles Scribner, 1948.

PATRICK, C. "Creative thought in poets," *Archives of Psychology,* 26 (1935), pp. 1–74.

PATRICK, C. "Creative thought in artists," *Journal of Psychology,* 5 (1937), pp. 35–73.

PELZ, D. C., and ANDREWS, F. M. "Creativity," *Scientists and organizations: Productive climates for research and development,* eds., D. C. Pelz and F. M. Andrews. New York: Wiley, 1966.

POINCARÉ, H. *The foundations of science.* New York: Science Press, 1924.

POSNER, M. I. *Cognition: An introduction.* Glenview, Illinois: Scott, Foresman, 1973.

REITMAN, W. R. *Cognition and thought.* New York: Free Press, 1965.

ROE, A. "The personality of artists," *Educational Psychology Measurement,* 6 (1946), pp. 401–408.

ROE, A. *The making of a scientist.* New York: Dodd, Mead, 1953.

SILVEIRA, J. "Incubation: The effect of interruption, timing, and length on problem solution and quality of problem processing," Unpublished doctoral dissertation, University of Oregon, 1971.

SIMON, H. A. "Scientific discovery and the psychology of problem solving," *Mind and cosmos: Essays in contemporary science and philosophy,* Vol. III, ed. R. G. Colodny. Pittsburgh: University of Pittsburgh Press, 1966.

SIMON, H. A., and SUMNER, R. K. "Pattern in music," *Formal representation of human judgment,* ed. B. Kleinmuntz. New York: Macmillan, 1968. Pp. 219–250.

TAYLOR, C. W.; SMITH, W. R.; and GHISELIN, B. "The creative and other contributions of one sample of research scientists," *Scientific creativity: Its recognition and development,* eds. C. W. Taylor and F. Barron. New York: Wiley, 1963.

TORRANCE, E. P. *Rewarding creative behavior.* Englewood Cliffs, N.J.: Prentice-Hall, 1965.

VERNON, P. E., ed. *Creativity*. Middlesex, England: Penguin Books, Ltd., 1970.

WALLAS, G. *The art of thought*. New York: Harcourt Brace, 1926.

WING, C. W., and WALLACH, M. A. *College admissions and the psychology of talent*. New York: Holt, Rinehart, and Winston, 1971.

WOODWORTH, R. S. *Experimental psychology*. New York: Holt, Rinehart, and Winston, 1938.

INDEXES

Name index

247

Subject index

This book has been set in 10 and 9 point
Melior, leaded 2 points. Section numbers and
titles and chapter numbers and titles are set in
20 point Melior Bold. The size of the type page
is 27 × 45½ picas.